MAKING
CHINA
POLICY

MAKING CHINA POLICY

From Nixon to G. W. Bush

Jean A. Garrison

LYNNE
RIENNER
PUBLISHERS

BOULDER
LONDON

Published in the United States of America in 2005 by
Lynne Rienner Publishers, Inc.
1800 30th Street, Boulder, Colorado 80301
www.rienner.com

and in the United Kingdom by
Lynne Rienner Publishers, Inc.
3 Henrietta Street, Covent Garden, London WC2E 8LU

Library of Congress Cataloging-in-Publication Data
Garrison, Jean A., 1968–
    Making China policy : from Nixon to G.W. Bush / Jean A. Garrison.
        p. cm.
    Includes bibliographical references and index.
    ISBN 1-58826-360-6 (hardcover : alk. paper) — ISBN 1-58826-385-1 (pbk. :
alk. paper)
        1. United States—Foreign relations—China.   2. China—Foreign
relations—United States.   3. United States—Foreign relations—1945–1989.
4. United States—Foreign relations—1989–   I. Title.
    E183.8C5G345   2005
    327.73051'09'045—dc22

                                                            2005000411

British Cataloguing in Publication Data
A Cataloguing in Publication record for this book
is available from the British Library.

Printed and bound in the United States of America

The paper used in this publication meets the requirements
of the American National Standard for Permanence of
Paper for Printed Library Materials Z39.48-1992.

5   4   3   2   1

Contents

Tables and Figures

Tables

Figure

Preface

The origin of this book goes back to the mid-1990s, when the China threat scenario became popularized in the media and seemed on the rise in Washington policy circles. From the outside it appeared that relations with China were deteriorating and falling into a familiar Cold War pattern of inevitable conflict. I believed then (and still believe) that this rhetoric represents a dangerous political agenda rather than an inevitable future for U.S.-China relations. This does not mean that the U.S.-China relationship is not without great challenges and future bumps in the road. But I believe that if we increase our understanding of how policy toward China was made in the past and learn from this experience, we can better guarantee a future of stable, productive relations. To do this we must understand how domestic politics interact with the personalities involved to shape the U.S. China-policy agenda.

This book seeks to make practical policy and theoretical contributions by bridging the gap between policymakers and scholars of foreign policy. First, uncovering the roots of continuity and change in China policy across thirty-five years provides tools to explain the past, in order to manage the present and future volatile relationship with China more effectively. Using a comparative perspective to explain continuity and change in the policy offers a means to analyze possibilities for both positive and negative policy avenues.

Second, exploring how the individual efforts of a core set of advisers shaped the decisionmaking process regarding policy toward China, from Richard Nixon to George W. Bush, illustrates the complexity of the bureaucratic and policy interests involved. Emphasizing how foreign policy advisers strategically frame policy options provides a conceptual approach that helps us understand how advisers shape decision-making and how this affects not only U.S. foreign policy but also studies of foreign policy, the president, political psychology, and international relations more generally.

That said, this study seeks to provide a new, but complementary explanation to the volume of good work on the U.S.-China relationship and to contribute to the rich work in foreign policy analysis. This is an inside-out look that explains under what conditions individual-level factors complement domestic and systemic explanations to provide a richer understanding of U.S. relations with China. Because my expertise lies primarily in U.S. foreign policy rather than China itself, my greatest challenge has been to educate myself about that country. I was aided in this by my first teaching position, at Boston University, where I taught courses on revolution in China and U.S. policy toward China. Since returning to the University of Wyoming, I have focused my research on U.S.-China relations and taught courses on Chinese foreign policy, U.S. foreign policy, and international relations. In 2004, I benefited greatly from a short tenure in the Office of Chinese and Mongolian Affairs at the State Department's Bureau of East Asia and Pacific Affairs, as part of a Council on Foreign Relations International Affairs Fellowship.

A Note on Sources

In writing this book, I used multiple sources of evidence to reconstruct the "inside" story of how the policymaking process evolved in each presidential administration. I relied on archival material, personal interviews with those involved, memoirs, various public sources, and the experience I gained while serving on the China Desk in the State Department. Although the archival record is still sketchy, through the hard work of the National Security Archives much material has been declassified. I would especially note here that this project could not have been completed without the interviews and conversations I had with high-level and low-level officials, both on and off the record, who were centrally involved in policymaking. These officials provided invaluable insight and background information on the factors that shaped U.S. China policy. Appendix A provides a more thorough discussion of the sources and research strategy used in this book.

*　　*　　*

This book is an outgrowth of the great intellectual support I have received over the years from colleagues around the country who study foreign policy analysis, colleagues at the University of Wyoming, and family and friends. Specifically, I would like to thank Margaret Hermann for encouraging me to pursue a project on strategic framing. At the University of Wyoming, Fred Homer, Steve Ropp, and Winberg Chai listened patiently and gave important encouragement and feedback. Dan Money, Janine Jordan, and Casey Gates provided invaluable research assistance for this project. At the State Department, Joe Donovan, Bob Goldberg, Chris Marut, Ed Sagurton, and others on the China Desk took time to teach me the "ropes." During the data-gathering stage of the project, my research was aided financially by the generous support of a Basic Research Grant from the College of Arts and Sciences and funding from the Milward L. Simpson Fund in Political Science at the University of Wyoming. The generous financial support I received from the Council on Foreign Relations International Affairs Fellowship, and the particular help from Elise Carlson Lewis and others in Fellowship Affairs, provided me with a Washington experience I will never forget and the time to complete this book. Through the hard work of Marilyn Grobschmidt and the staff at Lynne Rienner Publishers, as well as those anonymous scholars who reviewed the manuscript, this has become a better book.

Finally, the whole Wyoming Garrison clan deserves an extra-special note of thanks: Ruth, Mark, Kim, Katie, and Courtney. My mother, Ruth Garrison, has taught me the most important lesson of all: I owe it to myself to do something I love and to make sure what I do is beneficial to others. Regarding this book, I know that the former is true and I hope the latter proves true as well.

—Jean A. Garrison

1

Introduction:
The China Policy Conundrum

China represents the most important future bilateral relationship for the United States, but no country seems less understood and no policy has generated more consistent controversy for presidents. The Sino-American relationship balances diverse policy interests such as security in East Asia, including the Taiwan question, trade and commercial relations, arms proliferation, and human rights. Policy formulation is fought over by various groups, including executive-branch actors such as the National Security Council (NSC), State Department, Treasury Department, Commerce Department, the White House, and the National Economic Council (NEC) on the one hand and domestic political actors such as the U.S. Congress and powerful lobbying groups on the other, each having a stake in the policymaking game. The breadth of the bureaucratic and policy interests involved provides a daunting background for effective policymaking and modern diplomacy.

More than other state-to-state interactions, U.S.-China relations have been a love-hate relationship represented in recent years by highs such as solidarity in the war on terror after the bombings of September 11, 2001, to the lows produced by the U.S. bombing of China's Belgrade embassy in 1999. Misperceptions of China abound, with overly optimistic assessments of their friendship (and what this means) on one side and inflated assessments of their hostility or threat to U.S. interests on the other. This debate is not unique to either Democrats or Republicans but instead represents a chronic problem deeply embedded in the domestic policy debate on China.

This debate gains momentum with each new presidential election cycle. During the 2004 presidential campaign, Democrats and Democratic nominee Senator John Kerry argued that President George W. Bush's policies had led to historic trade imbalances that hurt U.S. business as well as the outsourcing of tens of thousands of manufacturing jobs. In 2000 and 1996, respectively, the Republicans accused Democrats and President Bill Clinton of poor stewardship and appeasing a likely aggressor (China) while selling out a U.S. friend (Taiwan). In 1992, after Tiananmen Square, George H.W. Bush was accused by Democrats of coddling the "butchers of Beijing" for the purposes of a larger strategic alliance. What these examples show is a recurring pattern of hostility toward China—and those who advocate for engagement with China—in the domestic political context from both sides of the political spectrum. Especially since Tiananmen Square, where many U.S. illusions were shattered, and the fall of the Berlin Wall, which ended the strategic imperative for the anti-Soviet alliance, critics from multiple perspectives have aggressively attacked the U.S. engagement policy.

Explaining the Volatility in the U.S.-China Relationship

Explanations of U.S. foreign policy behavior in general, and toward China specifically, can be categorized based on the level of analysis (i.e., the system, nation-state, or individual) from which different studies begin.[1] Focusing on the system level, people assess China's future role in the world as a force for stability or instability based on different operating assumptions held by pessimists and optimists about the nature of international politics. The pessimists discuss power politics and assume states act in their self-interest to increase their power relative to others. This is a zero-sum, self-help world that requires constant vigilance to survive. In the optimistic, neoliberal world, states operate in a web of interdependence where rules and norms of behavior constrain the actions of states. Economic interdependence creates an environment in which states can seek peaceful resolution to problems for mutual gain. Thus categorizations of China as alternately enemy or friend represent very different assessments of strategic realities, each with different implications for the opportunities for cooperation or conflict in East Asia. Some call for assertive containment of the Chinese "threat," while others argue for continued engagement to promote mutual interests.[2]

These characterizations reflect two ends of a policy-choice spectrum, with most mainstream analyses somewhere in between.

Second, at the domestic or state level, regardless of which political party is in the White House, the struggle for the China agenda is usually one between members of Congress who represent competing interests (and corresponding lobbying groups) and the administration, which focuses on the general health of the bilateral relationship. As the number of interest groups has blossomed, the debate has reflected the narrow political agendas of competing groups. Early on, the pro-Taiwan lobby (the original China lobby) was the only major lobbying group represented, and historically it was the most successful in shaping the policy agenda. This group pushed forward a military alliance with Taiwan in the 1950s and shaped the Taiwan Relations Act (TRA) in 1979 that has kept a de facto military alliance in place despite normalized relations with the People's Republic of China (PRC). Through the 1970s, this group had numerous anti-Communist friends in Congress and, since the early 1990s, prodemocracy conservatives unwilling to abandon a long-term friend to threats from an authoritarian state. Other influential groups representing interests from human rights and religious freedom to nonproliferation have flourished since Tiananmen Square and placed pressure on presidents to elevate their particular issues to a more prominent place in the bilateral dialogue. On the other side of the debate, however, as the U.S.-China business relationship has flourished, a strong pro-China business lobby has developed to offset China's critics.[3]

Third, at the individual level, executive-branch policymakers come to the table with particular preferences based on their view of how to balance their own needs with strategic and domestic imperatives.[4] In complex foreign policy problems such as U.S. policy toward the PRC, which involve uncertainty, political controversy, and conflicting values, members of decision groups like the president's inner circle struggle to define the nature of the problem and build consensus for particular policy choices. Focusing on foreign policy advisers as strategic actors within a group context provides understanding about what influences discrete policy decisions. From this perspective, we assume that multiple actors have potential influence in a group but also that there are formal and informal opportunities and constraints on their influence.

This study begins by focusing on one piece of the diverse policy picture discussed above—the study of advisory groups and decision-making—to understand the inputs into presidential decisions on China. What follows is a look at how framing policy options at this level balances internal, domestic, and international imperatives in efforts to build consensus for such options.[5]

Characteristics of the Presidential Advisory Process

The classic works in the study of advisory systems by Richard Tanner Johnson and Alexander George describe an advisory structure and process based on the formal structure and patterns of interaction among advisers. They differentiate among formalistic (or hierarchical) systems, competitive systems, and collegial systems. In the hierarchical or closed advisory system, national security or other central advisers can exclude rivals from important decisions. In contrast, the more open competitive system, which pits advisers against one another, and the collegial system allow many individuals to participate and influence policy debates in a system with multiple advocates.[6]

The focus on group dynamics provides insight into potential interaction patterns in presidential advisory systems. Irving Janis's work on conformity-seeking behavior in his groupthink analysis and Graham Allison's work on infighting among advisers in the bureaucratic politics tradition present two distinct modes of thinking about how group interaction can determine policy outcomes.[7] Although Janis and Allison explain different interaction patterns in the decision context, they do share an emphasis on multiple actors contributing to the decision process and triggering different policy outcomes. Thus group interaction patterns ranging from patterns of conformity (for example, groupthink) to extreme conflict (naysaying or stalemate), with hybrids in between, shape what ideas emerge and how they are discussed.[8]

Third, presidential predispositions and preferences shape the advisory structures and interaction patterns that develop. For example, highly cognitive, complex leaders seem to prefer more-open advisory systems and are more tolerant of multiple perspectives on issues than those with lower levels of cognitive complexity.[9] While cognitively complex individuals are less likely to resort to simplified, black-and-white thinking, they are more prone to indecisiveness and deliberative decisionmaking styles. Less complex leaders are less inclined to examine multiple policy options. They foster advisory systems that downplay active involvement by advisers who present divergent policy options.[10] Additionally, some presidents are more knowledgeable, interested, and motivated than others to participate in the decisionmaking process.

When stakes are high or their interest is piqued, however, presidents and central advisers are more likely to be involved in specific decision processes.

The presidential administrations of Richard Nixon through George W. Bush offer important points of comparison based upon the factors delineated above (i.e., the degree of centralization of each advisory system, the nature of group dynamics, and the degree of presidential involvement).[11] Nixon had the greatest degree of centralization with his hierarchical and closed advisory system. Henry Kissinger, Nixon's right-hand man, handled policymaking through a series of back-channel contacts that circumvented the State Department and held policy initiatives tightly within the White House. Although George H.W. Bush's system was less formal than Nixon's, it also was centralized to the White House and a few key advisers the president trusted. Similarly, George W. Bush's system has been concentrated in the White House, with great authority given to Vice President Dick Cheney. President Jimmy Carter, by contrast, organized an open system similar to Presidents Ronald Reagan and Bill Clinton, each of whom developed decentralized systems with multiple advisers involved in the decision process. Bill Clinton went even further than previous presidents in broadening the advisory circle to form a National Economic Council whose jurisdiction overlapped the NSC on many general and China policy issues.

The level of conflict in the inner circle has varied across each administration. Both Presidents Gerald Ford and George H.W. Bush seemed to organize and maintain collegial systems that fostered consensus policies rather than conflict. In general, Secretary of State James Baker was Bush's chief action officer and major source of foreign policy advice, while the national security adviser managed the NSC and served as an honest broker presenting views objectively to the president.[12] On the surface, Nixon's hierarchical advisory organization and use of the back channel seemed to circumvent opposition and avoid confrontation. Although deep divisions developed many times, they had little effect on how the policy process proceeded because they occurred well outside the inner circle. On the other hand, Presidents Carter, Reagan, Clinton, and George W. Bush were plagued by infighting. These fights reflected deep ideological divides that had the potential to escalate over time. Carter's system, which placed him in the center of a spokes-in-the wheel advisory structure, for example, fostered competition rather than collegial relations because of the different interpretations of the Soviet threat between Secretary of State Cyrus Vance and

National Security Adviser Zbigniew Brzezinski.[13] Reagan's loose, cabinet-style system gave advisers flexibility in day-to-day policymaking but created a situation that led to high levels of infighting and turmoil among central advisers (such as Secretary of State Alexander Haig, Secretary of Defense Caspar Weinberger, and the White House staff), which created a contentious foreign policy environment.[14] Clinton's administration was open to more diverse perspectives because it welcomed new players to the inner circle, while George W. Bush's administration was served by rival factions with little inclination toward reconciliation.

The degree of presidential involvement (motivated by level of interest and expertise) has also varied across these administrations.[15] Both Nixon and George H.W. Bush had considerable experience in foreign policy and a direct interest in Sino-American relations. Nixon was heavily committed as the architect of rapprochement, and George H.W. Bush, as head of the U.S. liaison office in China under President Ford, became committed through his direct involvement in implementing the policy. Both also had compiled impressive foreign policy resumes before entering office.[16] In contrast, other presidents were much less involved or attentive for various reasons. While President Carter was very attentive and detail oriented, he had no direct interest in China and was concerned that normalization could interfere with his arms control agenda. Reagan and George W. Bush were hands-off administrators who were disengaged from daily operations of the policy process and initially were reluctant to embrace China as an important priority. For Clinton, foreign policy and consequently China were of peripheral interest; he was a novice in traditional foreign policy issues while international economic policy and domestic policy were his strengths.[17]

Taken together, these six administrations—Nixon/Ford, Carter, Reagan, George H.W. Bush, Clinton, and George W. Bush—offer an opportunity to study diverse advisory systems and how the resulting decisionmaking processes shaped presidential policy choices on China.

The China Policy Puzzle

The challenge for this study is to see how the decisionmaking focus illustrated above can explain when, why, how, and to what degree China has been an "us," a "them," or something in between in U.S. policy. The answer to these questions changes depending on who made the decision, their perceptions of China, and the context within which they operated. On the surface, there seems to be general continuity in engagement with China since Nixon, but persistent political fights and repeated controversies reveal the struggle to maintain a stable relationship.[18] I will explore the following questions to help explain how engagement policy evolved in each administration.

1. What are the patterns of continuity and change in U.S. policy toward China from Richard Nixon to the present? How have dramatic events such as the end of the Cold War and the Tiananmen Square massacre, as well as domestic political circumstances, affected policy continuity and change?
2. How do internal decisionmaking processes affect the making of China policy and the question of policy continuity and change? How and why have foreign policy decisionmakers defined the China problem and structured their policy frames to build support for their policy choices? What is the president's role in the strategic framing process?
3. To what degree can a decisionmaking perspective explain the making of U.S. policy toward China relative to other domestic political and systemic explanations?

Figure 1.1 presents a way to conceptualize the interaction between various levels of analysis that provide the context for decisions and possible policy choices available to leaders. In this model, policy decisions are shown to result from international and domestic factors filtered by a particular decisionmaking context and process that shapes how policy options are defined and presented to the president. The framing process, outlined in greater detail in Chapter 2, serves as the filtering variable to understand the interaction between those who make decisions and the context within which decisions are made. This study posits that policy decisions result from decisionmakers balancing personal, political, and policy interests against the symbolic constraints and opportunities within the domestic political context and international system.

The first step is to explore how policy problems are defined, options are framed, and choices are made. In Chapter 2, these steps are explored in more detail to provide a framework for analyzing each administration's China policy. Chapters 3–5 focus on the building of the general engagement frame through Presidents Nixon/Ford, Carter, and Reagan. Chapters 6–9 study continuity and change in that frame after the Cold War and in the post–Tiananmen Square environment with

Figure 1.1   The Context for Strategic Framing

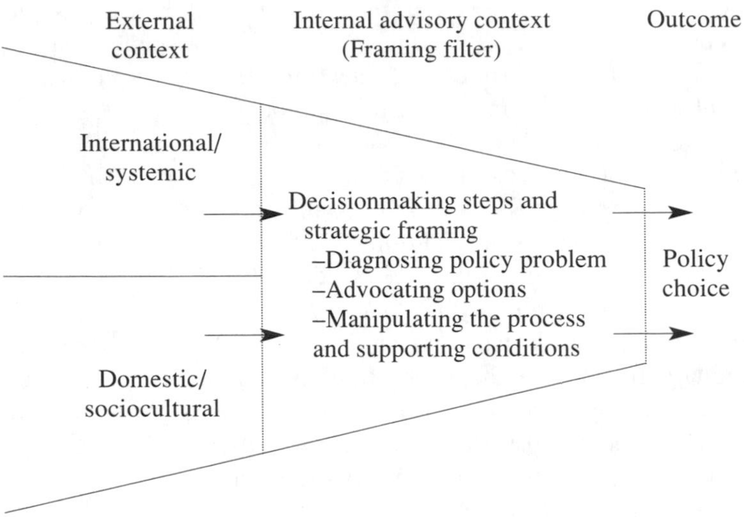

External context | Internal advisory context (Framing filter) | Outcome

International/ systemic

Decisionmaking steps and strategic framing
–Diagnosing policy problem
–Advocating options
–Manipulating the process and supporting conditions

Policy choice

Domestic/ sociocultural

Presidents George H.W. Bush, Clinton, and George W. Bush. Case studies from these six administrations provide an opportunity to explore important patterns in U.S. policy toward China.

Notes

1. The most influential framework in foreign policy is the levels-of-analysis approach that emerged from Kenneth Waltz's *Man, the State, and War,* which distinguished between three different images of war in international politics: the individual, nation-state, and the system. Later work by James Rosenau, such as his "Pre-Theories and Theories of Foreign Policy," separated the national level into separate societal and governmental levels, while others, such as Irving Janis in *Groupthink: Psychological Studies of Policy Decisions and Fiascoes* and this work, suggest a small group level as a starting point for analyzing foreign policy behavior. For a recent discussion of new research trends in foreign policy analysis, see Jean A. Garrison (ed.), "Foreign Policy Analysis in 20/20: A Symposium."

2. In the mid-1990s, various articles in *Foreign Affairs* and elsewhere articulated policy choices in these black-and-white terms. For example, see Richard Bernstein and Russ Munro, "China I: The Coming Conflict with America," and Robert Ross, "China II: Beijing as a Conservative Power."

3. For a general discussion of how domestic political factors shape for-

eign policy, see Eugene R. Wittkopf and James M. McCormick (eds.), *The Domestic Sources of American Foreign Policy*. For a discussion of domestic determinants of China policy, see Robert Sutter, *The China Quandary: Domestic Determinants of U.S. China Policy, 1972–1982*.

4. In international relations most researchers are familiar with Robert Putnam's characterization of the two-level game, where decisionmakers must balance domestic considerations with international imperatives when making policy choices. From a foreign policy analysis perspective, however, this is "old wine in a new bottle." This present study works from the perspective of central decisionmakers who must account for personal and bureaucratic factors in addition to domestic and strategic environments.

5. See Jean Garrison, *Games Advisors Play: Foreign Policy in the Nixon and Carter Administrations*, for an explanation of advisers as independent actors and the manipulation tactics at their disposal.

6. See Alexander George, *Presidential Decision Making in Foreign Policy: The Effective Use of Information and Advice*; Richard Tanner Johnson, *Managing the White House*; Cecil V. Crabb Jr. and Kevin Mulcahy, *Presidents and Foreign Policy Making: From FDR to Reagan*.

7. Graham Allison, *Essence of Decision: Explaining the Cuban Missile Crisis*; Graham Allison and Philip Zelikow, *Essence of Decision: Explaining the Cuban Missile Crisis*, 2nd ed.; Janis, *Groupthink*. In explaining policy fiascoes such as John F. Kennedy's Bay of Pigs decision, Janis concludes that group decisions can limit options and lead to suboptimal policy choices. In Janis's case studies, policymakers fail to achieve their goals because groupthink symptoms pressure members of a group into consensus-seeking behavior to the point that tolerance for dissenting viewpoints is reduced. On the other hand, the "pulling and hauling" illustrated in Graham Allison's analysis allows individuals' diverse parochial goals, beliefs, and motives to compete for influence as they work to overcome their opposition.

8. Eric K. Stern and Bengt Sundelius, "Understanding Small Group Decisions in Foreign Policy: Process Diagnosis." For a recent review of the study of small groups in foreign policy analysis, see Jean Garrison, "Foreign Policy Decisionmaking and Group Dynamics: Where We've Been and Where We're Going."

9. People who are high in cognitive complexity are more likely to be multidimensional in their thinking and more flexible in their responses to problems. They are able to analyze (i.e., differentiate) a situation into many constituent elements and then explore connections and potential relationships among various factors. Complexity theory assumes that the more an event can be differentiated and its parts considered in novel relationships, the more flexible the person can be and the more refined the response and successful the solution. For an explanation of the power of the cognitive approach see Jerel Rosati, "The Power of Human Cognition in the Study of World Politics."

10. For a comprehensive explanation of the linkage between the characteristics of the president and his advisory system, see Thomas Preston, *The President and His Inner Circle: Leadership Style and the Advisory Process in*

Foreign Affairs, and Margaret Hermann and Thomas Preston, "Presidents, Leadership Style, and the Advisory Process."

11. See John Burke and Fred Greenstein, *How Presidents Test Reality: Decisions on Vietnam in 1954 and 1965.*

12. George H.W. Bush and Brent Scowcroft, *A World Transformed*, 17–19; James A. Baker III, with Thomas M. DeFrank, *The Politics of Diplomacy: Revolution, War, and Peace, 1989–1992*, 42; Kevin Mulcahy, "The Bush Administration and National Security Policy-making: A Preliminary Assessment."

13. Garrison, *Games Advisors Play*, 11–15; Jerel Rosati, *The Carter Administration's Quest for Global Community: Beliefs and Their Impact on Behavior.*

14. Betty Glad, "Black and White Thinking: Ronald Reagan's Approach to Foreign Policy"; Ronald Reagan, *An American Life.*

15. When discussing presidential leadership styles, Thomas Preston in *The President and His Inner Circle* describes prior experience/expertise as one factor that influences presidential leadership style, along with a president's need for power and his cognitive complexity. Focusing on a president's expertise and level of interest seems one way to explain the level of effective involvement he will have in the decisionmaking process. My study does not pretend to systematically evaluate a president's need for power or cognitive complexity. Instead, this is a process-focused study that acknowledges the importance of understanding presidential characteristics to the extent that the president is an important actor within a group decision process. The literature on individual differences and leadership styles is used to compare/contrast presidents in the framing process.

16. Bush and Scowcroft, *A World Transformed*, 17–19; Baker, *The Politics of Diplomacy*, 42; Mulcahy, "The Bush Administration and National Security Policy-making."

17. Nancy Bernkopf Tucker, "The Clinton Years: The Problem of Coherence"; Donald Zagoria, "Clinton's Asia Policy."

18. Successful engagement with China has required a consistent presidential effort. As Arthur Schlesinger Jr. explains in *The Imperial Presidency,* circumstances changed drastically following the Vietnam War. After that, presidential policy agendas became more vulnerable to the blocking capabilities of other actors such as members of Congress, interest groups, and public opinion. See also Aaron Wildavsky, "The Two Presidencies Thesis."

2

Continuity and Change
in U.S. China Policy

We know that at different historical points China has been categorized both as a friend the United States believes will develop in the
U.S. image or as an enemy that rejects its lead.[1] For example, from
the time of the Open Door policy at the turn of the twentieth century,
even though the United States sought trade and profit in China, the
public retained an altruistic view of our intentions toward China that
they believed separated us from other powers interested only in carv-
ing up the country. This naïve image spawned the belief that the
United States enjoyed a special relationship with China as a kindred
spirit, reinforcing great expectations for a positive working relationship. The Chinese civil war in the late 1940s and Mao Zedong's victory in 1949 was a dramatic shock that betrayed this hope, and U.S.
policy quickly turned around and entered a period of maximum hostility.[2] The "fall" of China was dramatic evidence that monolithic
Communism was fundamentally hostile to U.S. interests and threatened our way of life; U.S. policy was shaped accordingly through
two Asian wars.

President Nixon's rapprochement with China began the process
of returning China to the "friend" category. Nixon saw China with a
different lens and defined the nature of the China policy question in
fundamentally different terms. Writing in *Foreign Affairs* in
October 1967, more than a year before his election to the presidency, Nixon argued that the United States needed to come to grips
with the opportunity China represented, rather than emphasizing its

threat, and should take the lead in reassessing China as a great and progressing nation.[3]

To redefine policy toward China, Nixon took advantage of a war-weary public and the greater salience of the Soviet threat. Two events shaped external conditions; they would be conducive to the president's argument that Communist China was not the greatest threat to U.S. interests in Asia. First, the Tet offensive in Vietnam convinced many that it was time to lessen U.S. involvement in the Vietnam War, and this primed the public for a thorough review of Southeast Asian policy and potential change. Second, the Soviet invasion of Czechoslovakia in 1968 coupled with China's border dispute with the Soviets made Chinese and U.S. assessments of the Soviet threat increasingly similar.[4] Thus both governments came to emphasize common strategic aims rather than differences. Changes in the way the strategic environment was assessed provided an opportunity for President Nixon to redirect domestic discussion on China and raised questions about status quo policies. Even here, however, Nixon's preparation of the ground was the essential component of the successful change in policy frames.

Although Richard Nixon's opening to China and the subsequent normalization of relations put China back into the friend column, and engagement has become the norm of U.S.-China relations, the relationship remained fragile and increasingly subject to controversy. Pointing to the crux of the problem, as one retired career Foreign Service officer notes, because "we oversold ourselves about the promise of the U.S.-China relationship in the period of the '70s and the '80s . . . Americans were offended by the fact that in the post-'79 period, as the '80s moved along and then climaxed by the Tiananmen massacre, the Chinese turned out not to be saints and perfect partners after all."[5] A quick look at public opinion toward China confirms a consistent volatility of attitudes toward China across the last thirty-plus years (see Appendix B for a comprehensive presentation of U.S. opinion toward China). Nixon's opening to China created a splash, but favorable public opinion toward China has never been maintained. The dramatic shift in opinion following the Tiananmen Square massacre (from 72 percent to 31 percent approval) shows that attitudes can change dramatically in response to triggering events—thus energizing the public against a strong pro-China stance. The domestic mistrust this shift represents had roots in China's human rights record since 1989 and other recurring issues such as the status of Taiwan, arms proliferation, and problems in the bilateral trade relationship.[6]

The "How" of Strategic Framing

As Nixon's efforts illustrate, leaders have an opportunity to redefine policy problems when major events refocus attention on a problem in a different way. Such events act as symbols that highlight new positive or negative themes that challenge preexisting perceptions. As John Kingdon discusses, exogenous factors like dramatic shocks or crises, a group's intense interest in a particular issue, and/or involvement of diverse sectors of society (e.g., policy entrepreneurs, Congress, media, and interest groups) create new opportunities in policy debates.[7] Nixon's new framing of the China policy problem resonated with a war-weary public and plugged in to a preexisting framework that saw the Soviets as the primary threat. Given that individuals usually follow the lead of authority figures and persons they trust in areas like foreign policy, which are remote from their everyday experiences (e.g., as network coverage follows official government policy because reporters index their coverage to government officials), it was not surprising that the country followed Nixon's lead in defining the nature of policy problems. Once the problem is defined in a particular way, certain policy choices become the logical result.[8]

Three important decisionmaking steps emerge as essential elements to understand how individuals' frames influence policy decisions: (1) understanding how advisers and their policy frames provide a new diagnosis or remedy for an existing problem; (2) understanding how advisers advocate options effectively (i.e., how framers convince the targeted audience that their diagnosis is correct); and (3) understanding the supporting conditions such as the advisory setting and manipulation of the political process that help build or undermine support for a policy prescription.

Diagnosing the Policy Problem

The central component of the decisionmaking process is the struggle over whose definition of a political phenomenon will prevail. Through the struggle over alternate realities, language is the medium that reflects, advances, and interprets alternate choices. How policy is defined or framed lends coherence to a problem, organizes the presentation of facts, and provides for alternative cognitions.[9] The best example of an overarching frame that shaped people's views is the Cold War image of an expansionist Soviet Union (equated to the fascists of Nazi Germany) that developed into the rationale for most post–World War II policy choices. U.S. hostility toward China in the 1950s and 1960s was justified as part of the defense against monolithic Communism, and the larger anti-Communist fight provided the general context for U.S. support for South Vietnam against the Communist threat. Once North Vietnamese leader Ho Chi Minh was labeled a Communist aggressor, there was little choice but to oppose Soviet plans for expansion. These images of the enemy built a strong bipartisan consensus among both the public and the policy elite that became hard to counter.[10]

The Cold War became the kind of symbol that generates a great degree of policy consensus, and it created the political environment that each administration inherited, worked within, and built upon. Cold War–threat scenarios developed and were sustained through a process of social interaction that included deliberate advocacy and augmentation by political leaders of their points of view. Policymakers used these frames to make sense of complex problems that were far removed from the direct experience of the public (and many political leaders).[11]

This focus on rhetoric emphasizes that meanings are "constructed" and that political entrepreneurs build meanings out of social and political interaction, thus making the connection between their "text" and the political context.[12] Frames are interpretive schemata that simplify the problem under discussion by selectively emphasizing and encoding situations, objects, events, experiences, and sequences of actions within a person's present or past environment. In the context of social movements, political elites who want to reshape the policy debate to favor their cause can convey their "reality" through slogans, historical analogies, stereotypes, or visual images.[13] Put simply, defining the nature of the policy problem triggers different policy analyses and prescriptions. In an advisory group setting, judgments and decisions result from an interactive process that includes individual orientations (i.e., cognitive operations, beliefs, and so on) and social interactions (i.e., how information is shared and communicated and how group members attempt to influence other members' cognitions).[14]

Communicating Themes That Resonate

After defining a policy problem, the central question shifts to how frames can change the perceptions of a targeted audience of decision-makers. It is important to remember that individuals are not always aware of their preferences, which may also change over time and be influenced by unrelated information or irrelevant options.[15] However, some preferences are consistent and resistant to change. When images like the Cold War resonate with our self-images or sense of responsibility to counter Communism, they become very resistant to change. Anti-Communism resonated across very different presidential administrations and even after the dissolution of the Soviet Union because these themes provided a political and cultural shorthand that brought together disparate, specific policies under one broad policy umbrella.[16] These labels became powerful symbols invoking a broad set of values that intensified political debates; they affected policy decisions by condensing beliefs and shaping how decisionmakers understand the policy problem.[17]

Yuen Foong Khong's study of analogical reasoning gives the example of President Lyndon Johnson accepting the analogy of Communist aggression in the Korean War as the reason to intervene militarily in Vietnam. Competing analogies and arguments, such as the one presented by Secretary of State Dean Rusk's deputy George Ball that U.S. involvement in Vietnam more closely resembled the French failure at Dien Bien Phu in 1954, were offered but largely ignored. This can be explained by noting that Johnson remained resistant to change because the initial frames resonated with his preconceived beliefs about Communist aggression, his interpretation of historical events as it related to aggression in World War II, and his desire to preserve the domestic consensus on the Great Society.[18] Discussing these three elements can help clarify what factors shape policy choices.

Personal beliefs and themes that resonate. The broader a policy is framed, the greater its appeal will be to various ideational elements in the belief system, values, cognitions, or life experience of the target(s) and the more it will resonate with them and be readily accepted. Also, those themes that are primed and readily available will be most persuasive. Conversely, if the framing effort is linked to only one core belief or value, it is more vulnerable to being discounted if that value is questioned.[19] Studies in social psychology suggest that individuals may seek cognitive consistency between deeply held beliefs and the frames that help them interpret the current policy environment. This may make them resistant to change even in the face of invalidating information.[20]

Framing studies emphasize that people attach significance to the symbols in frames that are both cognitive (one's attitude toward an object) and emotive (intensity of feeling). The affective component of the symbols creates a positive or negative feeling of attachment to them. Organized elites, by manipulating these symbols for specific ends, can arouse or placate their targeted population. This could occur through using symbols with positive sentiments such as "peace and prosperity" or labels with strong negative affect such as "Communism."[21]

Policy themes. When a policy issue has been defined as important to an accepted notion of the "national interest" and the stakes are high, leaders become committed to defend against perceived threats. In this way, strategic Cold War conceptions of the Soviet Union as an enemy deeply influenced post–Cold War foreign policy. These conceptions built a strong bipartisan consensus within the public and the elite that shaped U.S. foreign policy for years to come. Analogies such as Munich in 1938 could be used to justify appropriate policies to contain the Soviet threat.[22] When the Cold War consensus waned, it became necessary to repeatedly engage in public campaigns to reframe policies once taken for granted.

Political considerations. The Cold War placed pressure on presidents to appear tough regarding the Soviet Union and Communism; this reflects the importance of political risk analyses. As transcripts of President Kennedy's high-level meetings on the Cuban missile crisis illustrate, this concern shaped his response to the crisis. It was clear to Kennedy's inner circle that doing nothing to respond to Soviet missiles in Cuba was not a viable option and politically might lead to calls for the president's impeachment. This example points to the concept of accountability in political decisionmaking and the likelihood that presidents and their close advisers calculate cost assessments for a policy in terms of political risks. By illustrating that an option is in the best short- or long-term political interests of the target, the possibility of its selection should increase. Successful framing efforts must take the wider domestic political context into account. Politicians may be reluctant to admit that such value trade-offs exist, but a look at the volatility of public opinion with regard to China reveals how it can constrain policy.[23]

The discussion of political considerations points to the long-held assumption that domestic politics serve as a constraint on a president's ability to formulate and implement foreign policy. This has been particularly true in trade policy and other areas of "low policy" where Congress has more initiative and traditionally has taken an active role. A pattern has emerged since the end of the Cold War (especially before September 11) in which Congress has reasserted its role at the expense of presidential autonomy in foreign policy making. In China policy a corresponding rise in interest group politics has complicated the policy-making environment.

*Manipulating the Political Process,
Supporting Conditions, and Advisory System Considerations*

The advisory systems' literature discussed in Chapter 1 provides insight into the various challenges decisionmakers face when they try to define policy problems in a specific way. The closed or open nature of each system is important because those who have access to key meetings have the greatest potential influence. Similarly, those who control policy procedures have greater ability to influence how policy debates proceed.[24] In one policymaking example, Rose McDermott shows how President Carter's national security adviser Zbigniew Brzezinski emphasized the themes of national power, U.S. prestige, and the welfare of the Iranian hostages to convince the president to order the rescue mission for U.S. hostages in Iran against Secretary of State Cyrus Vance's warnings.[25] It is no coincidence that Brzezinski chaired the meetings where the rescue mission option was presented to the president or that the final decision was made while Vance was out of town and thus excluded from the decision process.

As noted earlier, multiple policymakers in the advisory group have the resources to manipulate the base of knowledge about an issue and to frame an issue advantageously in policy debates. The ability of policymakers to manipulate policy depends in part on procedural factors and also on their ability to build broad coalitions both inside and outside the administration. Table 2.1 describes how these components of strategic framing can be identified.

A number of general assertions about how attributions and policy judgments are shaped can be drawn from the previous discussion. First, leaders' interpretations of a problem should shift along predictable lines if the themes presented resonate with their preconceived beliefs, trigger the need to respond to an important policy interest, and/or when political risks become salient. Second, framing effects for leaders centrally involved in decisionmaking—who have a high level of interest or expertise—bolster, rather than shift, a target's interpretations. Conversely, framing effects for leaders who are uninvolved or uninterested provide the greatest opportunity for a change in judgment. Third, infighting and conflict provide conditions that can lead to policy stalemate and/or mixed signals. Fourth, hierarchical and closed advisory structures limit the number of options discussed, while open systems provide greater access to the decision process. Fifth, because the symbolic environment sets the parameters of debate, those who use salient symbols have the greatest opportunity to influence policy outcomes. Finally, because focusing events create conditions that can change the

Table 2.1   Components of Strategic Framing

Steps to Strategic Framing	Definition/Indicators
Diagnosing the policy problem	• Struggle over whose definition of a political phenomenon will prevail indicated best by distinct bureaucratic or ideological positions before a specific policy debate
Advocating options effectively	• Understanding how themes resonate requires understanding the cognitive and emotive means by which arguments can change the perceptions of a targeted audience
Personal themes and beliefs	• Preexisting attitudes, beliefs, cognitions, values, and life experiences that explain a target's predisposition • Themes that are primed and readily available will be most persuasive
Policy themes	• Themes important to the perceived national interest in a high-stakes game • Need to defend against perceived threats or take advantage of new opportunities
Political considerations	• Short- or long-term political calculation • Accountability in political decision-making and importance of making cost assessments in terms of political risks
Supporting conditions and manipulating the political process	• Advisory setting and level of centralization or decentralization • Supporting tactics such as controlling access, controlling information flow, and coalition building

terms of debate and provide new opportunities for influence, the greatest opportunity for change over continuity in Sino-American policymaking should have come with the end of the Cold War and the Tiananmen Square massacre.

Notes

1. John Stoessinger (ed.), *Nations in Darkness, Nations at Dawn: China, Russia, and America.*

2. Richard Ned Lebow discusses the U.S. image of China in the context of misperception and its consequences for international relations in *Between Peace and War: The Nature of International Crisis.*

3. Richard Nixon, "Asia After Vietnam."

4. Robert Garson, *The United States and China Since 1949: A Troubled Affair*, 119; Raymond Garthoff, *Détente and Confrontation: American-Soviet Relations from Nixon to Reagan.*

5. Harry E.T. Thayer, oral history interview, November 19, 1990.

6. Robert Ross, *Negotiating Cooperation: The United States and China, 1969–1989.*

7. John Kingdon, *Agendas, Alternatives, and Public Policies*, 98–112; Roger Cobb and Charles Elder, *Participation in American Politics: The Dynamics of Agenda Building*, 108–117.

8. William Gamson, *Talking Politics*, 219–224; David Snow and Robert Benford, "Ideology, Frame Resonance, and Participant Mobilization"; see also W. L. Bennett, "Toward a Theory of Press-State Relations in the United States"; John Zaller and Dennis Chiu, "Government's Little Helper: U.S. Press Coverage of Foreign Policy Crises, 1945–1991."

9. There are two types of frames delineated in the framing literature. Episodic frames respond to individual cases or situations (e.g., network coverage without contextual information provided) while thematic frames focus on broad social trends (e.g., political issues placed in a general context). Without thematic linkages there is less accountability for actions. See Gamson, *Talking Politics*; William Gamson and Andre Modigliani, "The Changing Culture of Affirmative Action"; Shanto Iyengar, *Is Anyone Responsible? How Television Frames Political Issues*; Thomas Nelson, Rosalee Clawson, and Zoe Oxley, "Media Framing of a Civil Liberties Conflict and Its Effect on Tolerance"; Nayda Terkildsen, Frauke Schnell, and Cristina Ling, "Interest Groups, the Media, and Policy Debate Formation: An Analysis of Message Structure, Rhetoric, and Source Cues."

10. Keith Shimko, "Metaphors and Foreign Policy Decision Making."

11. Leaders create common reference points to categorize information, provide for efficient communication, and establish important distinctions among groups. For example, social movements construct larger frames of meaning that resonate with a population's cultural predispositions and communicate a coherent message. See Cobb and Elder, *Participation in American Politics*, 31–32, 129–130; Sidney Tarrow, *Power in Movement*, 137.

12. Tarrow, *Power in Movement*, 119.

13. Gamson, *Talking Politics*, 219–224; Snow and Benford, "Ideology, Frame Resonance, and Participant Mobilization."

14. See Yaacov Vertzberger, *Risk Taking and Decisionmaking: Foreign Military Intervention Decisions*, 88. In his study of risk-taking decisions, Vertzberger reminds us that identifying aggregate risk assessments in a group setting is difficult because "group attitudes toward risk are not a simple average of the attitudes of all group members." For example, group preference and judgment may be shaped by a minority in the decision group and lead to a position different from the will of the majority. To understand how judgments are made, we need a closer examination of particular decision processes.

15. Daniel Kahneman and Amos Tversky, in "Prospect Theory: An Analysis of Decision Under Risk," explain prospect theory as an alternative to expected-utility theory (or the rational actor model). Prospect theory posits that people are more sensitive to changes in assets than to net asset levels. People frame choices around a reference point and give more weight to losses from that reference point than to gains (leading to loss aversion). To apply this theory to states, Jack Levy and others have developed propositions to explain stabilizing and destabilizing behavior involving risky behavior. See Jack Levy, "Political Psychology and Foreign Policy."

16. Elizabeth Hanson, "Framing the World News: The *Times of India* in Changing Times," 389–390; David Meyer, "Framing National Security: Elite Public Discourse on Nuclear Weapons During the Cold War."

17. More immediate examples of such labels demonstrate how the powerful negative symbolism associated with a term like *jihad* has shaped U.S. political attitudes toward Islam and the Middle East. Terkildsen, Schnell, and Ling, "Interest Groups, the Media, and Policy Debate Formation," 48.

18. Yuen Foong Khong, *Analogies at War*, 169–170.

19. Vertzberger, *Risk Taking and Decisionmaking,* 38; David Snow, E. B. Rochford Jr., S. Worden, and Robert Benford, "Frame Alignment Processes, Micromobilization, and Movement Participation"; Snow and Benford, "Ideology," 204–209. For the classic work in this area, see Erving Goffman, *Frame Analysis.*

20. See Leon Festinger, "Informal Social Communication"; Robert Jervis, *Perceptions and Misperceptions in International Politics.*

21. Cobb and Elder, *Participation in American Politics*, 65–70; Iyengar, *Is Anyone Responsible?*; William Jacoby, "Issue Framing and Public Opinion on Government Spending." Two other communication-effects models complement the cognitive-accessibility argument. First, the learning model posits that the presentation of new information can reshape viewer opinions (e.g., new information about violence associated with Ku Klux Klan rallies). Second, frames can influence opinion by stressing specific values or facts (or other considerations) and giving them greater relevance for the issue at hand (e.g., characterizing a Ku Klux Klan rally as free speech versus a danger to public safety). See Nelson, Clawson, and Oxley, "Media Framing," 569–574; Doris Graber, *Media Power in Politics.*

22. Shimko, "Metaphors and Foreign Policy Decision Making."

23. Vertzberger, *Risk Taking and Decisionmaking*, 139; Phil Tetlock, "An Alternative Metaphor in the Study of Judgment and Choice: People as Politicians"; Phil Tetlock, "Accountability: The Neglected Social Context of Judgment and Choice."

24. Garrison, *Games Advisors Play.*

25. Rose McDermott, "Prospect Theory in International Relations: The Iranian Hostage Rescue Mission"; Rose McDermott, *Risk-Taking in International Politics: Prospect Theory in American Foreign Policy.*

3

Challenging the Status Quo: Nixon and the Politics of Rapprochement

In the late 1960s, China was perceived to be a great threat to U.S. interests in East Asia. Writing in *Foreign Affairs* in October 1967, Richard Nixon argued that the United States should reassess the China threat and instead embrace the opportunity China represented for U.S. policy.[1] When he entered office in January 1969, his Department of Defense produced a report that supported this stance, arguing that China represented a strategic opportunity because of the seriousness of the Sino-Soviet split and the cool relationship between China and Vietnam. The report concluded that a post-Mao leadership would jettison formerly disruptive policies and work to bring Chinese policy in line with a more realistic worldview.[2]

Placing the United States on the path toward normalizing relations with China, however, would be a task the Nixon administration approached cautiously once in office. The administration proceeded carefully on China policy in large part because of anticipated resistance on the domestic front from both sides of the political divide. Many conservatives saw rapprochement as a compromise that betrayed old allies like Taiwan. The long-time U.S. recognition of the Nationalist government on Taiwan as the legitimate government of China, as well as ongoing economic and security ties with Taiwan, meant the long-established working relationship could be disrupted by Nixon's proposed changes. For their part, liberals pushed the administration to move more rapidly toward rapprochement with China because of the opportunity for peace it offered.[3] The administration's diplomatic goal to open

China would need to be reconciled with these and other competing interests.

This chapter focuses on efforts of members of the Nixon administration to strategically frame rapprochement policy both in the inner circle and in domestic and international arenas.[4] This analysis considers practical efforts to control the flow of information and both the timing and presentation of public policy initiatives. Such efforts created a policy consensus that was a mile wide but only an inch deep. In other words, while there was a general consensus behind the China opening, it represented a fledgling frame that was fragile and vulnerable to domestic political challenges. This chapter evaluates Kissinger's incremental efforts to manage the agenda through back-channel control of negotiations and to define his policy as a vehicle for peace and stability in East Asia. President Gerald Ford's failure to move normalization forward, discussed at the end of the chapter, illustrates the difficulties of taking the final step to normalize relations with China.

President Nixon's Advisory System and Controlling the Internal Debate on China Policy

In the post–World War II environment, presidents have had a greater capacity to influence the policy agenda than members of Congress or domestic actors. Once the Vietnam conflict began to shake the domestic Cold War consensus, however, presidential autonomy began to shrink. Richard Nixon became president during this time of transition. He purposefully designed an advisory structure that increased his ability to act independently in foreign policy, but he ultimately paid the cost for the outcome that led to his abuse of power. For his part, President Ford was never able to step out of Nixon's shadow.

Centralizing decisionmaking was Nixon's way to maximize control of policymaking. The formalistic advisory system created a staunch hierarchy that put Henry Kissinger in position to control the policy agenda.[5] He did this to initiate foreign policy and to shape its progress from the White House. As Kissinger articulated the policy strategy, the president made himself dependent on Kissinger for information and advice. This system worked well for several years because Nixon and Kissinger were kindred spirits who shared the same approach to politics and foreign policy. To secure his position, Kissinger reinforced the president's mistrust of the bureaucracy at every opportunity and undercut

Secretary of State William Rogers's position with the president by blaming him for policy failures.

The effort to break away from the old China policy began quietly in February 1969. The national security adviser assigned Undersecretary of State Elliot Richardson (with the undersecretary's committee) to put together a package that relaxed the blockade on China, including the rules for U.S. subsidiaries operating in China. These efforts were begun well before the president's trip to Romania and East Asia in the summer of 1969 (commonly regarded as the beginning of rapprochement) and came ten months before the Warsaw talks involving the State Department.[6]

During the first NSC meeting that specifically discussed the administration's China policy, held August 14, 1969, the president openly articulated his position for the first time. He argued that the Soviet Union was more aggressive than China and that the United States would not want to see China smashed in a war between the two Communist giants. Nixon's announcement surprised State Department officials, who were unprepared for the president's change in policy toward China. Throughout the process they had not known of White House efforts to signal the Chinese through Pakistani and Romanian back channels that Nixon was interested in normalizing relations with the PRC.[7]

Players and Positions in the China Policy Game

On China policy, the State Department adopted a "steady as you go" course reflecting careful and cautious steps toward improving relations. The State Department remained risk averse and opposed the bold moves that Kissinger soon advocated. These differences became clear once ambassadorial-level talks between Ambassador Walter J. Stoessel Jr. and his Chinese counterpart began in Warsaw in January 1970. The State Department contingency guidance for the January meeting indicated that the U.S. strategy in the talks should emphasize common interests related to avoiding war and inhibiting the Soviet Union, while setting aside the Taiwan issue in a way that preserved options for both sides. The United States was prepared to discuss any proposals that reduced tensions, including taking the middle ground on Taiwan; it would defend Taiwan but not interfere in a future peaceful settlement between Taiwan and the PRC.[8] Although the PRC accused the United States of pursuing a policy to create two Chinas, Nixon and Kissinger interpreted the nonpolemical language of the Chinese as positive indications that Beijing might be prepared to make significant policy adjustments. The United States slowly moved toward a position that improved relations with China while keeping separate the commitment to defend Taiwan.[9]

In these talks, the State Department wanted to sidestep Chinese calls for high-level talks until progress was made at the ambassadorial level. The State Department's concern centered on the attention such high-level talks would garner and the increased domestic political risks that might result; it was not yet ready to assume that Beijing was motivated by a desire for long-term improvement in relations or that its revolutionary goals had altered.[10] Furthermore, there was concern about potential repercussions from Taiwan and allies in the region and about the influence of such talks on the PRC push for a UN seat. The State Department was reluctant to agree to high-level talks before it received reassurance from China that disputes about Taiwan would be resolved peacefully through negotiations.

The national security adviser saw an advantage in high-level meetings with China in terms of bureaucratic control. These meetings could open the door for dramatic change by increasing Soviet uncertainty and potentially hurting Beijing's relationship with North Vietnam. More positively, the meetings might also encourage moderates in the Chinese government.[11] A January 23, 1970, memo to Kissinger illustrates the evolving position. In the memo, Winston Lord argued for a pragmatic approach in which the administration dealt with countries based on their actions, not their ideology.[12] This perspective was bolstered by evidence that the appeal of Communist ideology had greatly withered and that Asian nationalism, culture, religion, and regionalism were seen as barriers to Communist expansionism. Specific to China, Lord noted that its internal troubles and its military and economic limitations made it weak and not the external threat the United States once thought. This meant Chinese capabilities should not be equated with Chinese rhetoric. At the root of the policy toward Asia was the shift away from seeing China either as a threat or as part of the bipolar confrontation.[13]

In late spring 1970, Nixon signaled Kissinger's preeminence in foreign policy in two ways. First, the president's annual foreign policy report was directed from the White House rather than the State Department for the first time. Substantively, the report reflected Kissinger's geostrategic focus and stopped linking the Soviet Union and China as a single adversary. Second, and specific to China, Mao Zedong's cancellation of the May 20 Warsaw talks, in response to the Cambodian bombing campaign, gave Nixon the excuse he needed to use Kissinger's private channels to excise the State Department from all future negotiations. Vernon Walters, U.S. military attaché in Paris, became the new conduit through which contact was maintained until Kissinger's historic trip in July 1971. Calling the cancellation providential, Kissinger argued "our government was simply not ready to speak with a single voice."[14]

Consolidating Bureaucratic Control

Once Kissinger took over contacts in the back channel, the NSC became the coordinating body for great-power affairs, while the State Department provided reports to support NSC initiatives. The national security adviser successfully co-opted and used the bureaucracy by circumventing its formal structure and disregarding the regular policy inputs from State Department bureaus such as East Asia and Pacific Affairs (EAP). At times Kissinger even had three competing groups working on a problem in the NSC with none knowing about the others.[15]

China policy reports, such as National Security Study Memorandum (NSSM) 124 in May 1971, were handled by the interdepartmental group for East Asia and the Pacific and then sent to the NSC senior review group who reported to Kissinger. The overarching goal for NSSM 124 was to quickly establish governmental contacts with China without making concessions on Taiwan so as not to weaken the administration's position domestically or internationally. The study memoranda also presented specific options ranging from modest steps to those involving significant changes in U.S. policy toward Taiwan. The first group of alternatives included steps that did not require negotiation, such as reducing close-in intelligence and reconnaissance flights, while a second group involved governmental contacts with inducements for the PRC to respond; examples would be reducing U.S. forces on Taiwan in conjunction with withdrawing forces from Vietnam.

A third set of alternatives represented significant changes in the policy toward Taiwan. Possible initiatives in this third set included:

1. some form of official U.S. presence in Beijing;
2. an indication of U.S. willingness to regard Taiwan as part of China;
3. removal of U.S. forces from the Taiwan area, contingent upon, for example, an assurance that Beijing would not provoke a crisis in the Taiwan Strait area.

The report concluded that the more progressive options might strain relations with Taipei but not rupture the relationship.[16] When Kissinger made his choices from this third set of more progressive options, he clearly elevated the importance of China, vis-à-vis Taiwan and other concerns in East Asia. Kissinger's discussions during secret meetings in Beijing from July 9–11, 1971, reflected willingness to regard Taiwan as part of China, but with the caveat that reconciliation with the PRC needed to be determined peacefully. He also advocated establishing semiofficial offices with consular functions with China.[17]

This tilt toward China in relation to Taiwan specifically emerged in the internal debate over the move to seat the PRC in China's United Nations seat. Since 1949, the United States had successfully kept the Nationalist government in the UN seat. Although the State Department was authorized to coordinate U.S. strategy to preserve Taiwan's seat, the national security adviser manipulated the policy to complement his rapprochement efforts. For example, Kissinger procrastinated in making a decision on the dual-China stance (in hopes of accomplishing PRC admission to the UN without expelling Taiwan) until after he had told Zhou Enlai in July 1971. Kissinger wanted reassurance that the Chinese would not let his decision upset future progress in U.S.-China relations, and only then would the secretary of state receive authority to proceed with the dual-representation strategy in the United Nations. Kissinger notes, "I did not want to jeopardize the precarious beginnings . . . with an issue that would be provocative without being capable of resolution, and would in any event be overtaken by the evolution of our relationship with Peking."[18]

Kissinger also began to brief the Chinese on U.S.-Soviet talks. In these meetings he emphasized the Soviet threat to China and claimed that the Soviet Union's strategy was to undermine the Sino-American relationship.[19] From a December 10, 1971, memorandum of the meeting with Ambassador Huang Hua, PRC permanent representative to the United Nations, Kissinger made this point clear: "We tell you about our conversations with the Soviets; we do not tell the Soviets about our conversations with you. In fact, we don't tell our own colleagues that I see you."[20] He promised to be "meticulous" about keeping the Chinese informed on issues that pertained to them.

The secretary of state did not know of the national security adviser's July 9, 1971, trip to China and was excluded as well from most important meetings in Beijing in February 1972, including Nixon's meeting with Mao Zedong that had two NSC representatives in attendance for the drafting of the Shanghai Communiqué.[21] In Beijing, the

NSC maintained its focus on the big strategic picture while the State Department handled the detailed talks on trade, travel, consular affairs, and property rights. In the communiqué both sides recognized that "all Chinese on either side of the Taiwan Straits maintain there is but one China and Taiwan is part of China." The United States did not challenge this position and agreed in principle to gradually reduce U.S. troops on Taiwan as long a peaceful settlement was sought.[22] The president's trip solidified the tilt toward China that had begun covertly in the back channel.

The president and national security adviser sustained their policy frame through the everyday practice of controlling access and information. Because Kissinger anticipated bureaucratic resistance, he consistently worked to circumvent its authority and to control the message emerging from the administration. Domestically, he knew that opposition from left- and right-wing groups would emerge to challenge administration tenets. Kissinger's strategy was to reassure the right that the president pursued an independent policy, while simultaneously encouraging the left not to overstate the change. Kissinger also worked to keep the Chinese out of the domestic debate; in Beijing, he specifically asked them not to encourage U.S. left-wing groups to get involved.[23]

Redefining the Chinese Threat: Reconciling Perceptions of China to New International Realities

Diagnosing the Problem

Given the national security adviser's dominance of policymaking, Richard Nixon and Henry Kissinger faced no effective internal opposition in their push to elevate China over other issues. State Department concerns were soon circumvented because the White House controlled the policymaking arena and terms of debate. A bold new problem definition evolved largely without the knowledge of State Department officials who were more risk averse in regard to changing China's status. The more difficult problem would be to sell China in new terms to a skeptical public.

The administration needed to emphasize the opportunity for peace and stability that China represented if it was to dispel the lingering notion that Asian Communism was directed from Beijing and that China represented a threat to U.S. interests in Asia (specifically that Beijing was in collusion with Hanoi during the Vietnam War).[24] Some government reports at the time still recommended that Nixon contain the Chinese threat, by building missile delivery systems that targeted China separately from the Soviet Union, and avoid bold initiatives like diplomatic recognition.

Public opinion polls from the late 1960s reflected the perception that China was the greatest threat to the United States. Consistently from 1964 through 1968, when asked to look ahead to 1970 and identify which country would be the greater threat to world peace—Russia or China—those polled chose Communist China two to one over the Soviets. The greatest gap came in a March 8, 1967, poll when China was selected by 70 percent of respondents to Russia's 20 percent.[25] The polls also showed a gradual reduction in this hostile attitude in small ways. For example, in an October 1966 poll only 25 percent of the general public felt China should be admitted to the United Nations while 64 percent of a sample of leaders from *Who's Who* felt it should be.[26] By May 1971, the numbers of the general public advocating Chinese admission to the UN had increased by twenty points to 45 percent of those polled—45 percent of Republicans, 40 percent of Democrats, and 52 percent of independents.[27]

In its strategy to reframe the China problem, the Nixon administration emphasized the opportunity for peace that it represented to antiwar groups and reassured conservative Taiwan supporters that its security would not be affected. We will explore how the administration used new policy themes that resonated with a public tired of war to emphasize the opportunity for change.

Themes That Resonated for President Nixon and Shaped Public Attitudes

President Nixon's beliefs and priorities. Throughout his congressional career and as vice president, Richard Nixon had gained impeccable anti-Communist credentials. As an ardent anti-Communist, his détente efforts with the Soviet Union and rapprochement with China surprised some. As we know from many studies of Nixon's foreign policy, however, the roots of his anti-Communism reflected a pragmatic foreign policy orientation that included a belief that all states were motivated by promotion of their national interests. Politically, Nixon also was determined to avoid the Vietnam trap that Lyndon Johnson fell into.

In his approach to foreign policy Nixon saw many foreign policy problems moving in tandem and felt that each could be manipulated to strengthen the U.S. position in the world. Given his view that all states, even Communist ones, were motivated by self-interest, he felt they also would negotiate where agreements served their national interest. He argued, "Once this is understood, it is more sensible—and also safer— to communicate with the Communists than to live in icy cold-war isolation or confrontation."[28] Nixon's general outlook, which was shared by Kissinger, was "a belief in isolating and influencing the factors affecting worldwide balance of power."[29] Nixon insisted the Soviet Union was the most important factor for peace and the United States was in a disadvantageous position in the late 1960s. The Sino-Soviet split, however, could be used in the U.S. favor, and China's status should be reevaluated in these terms.

Policy themes: Defining rapprochement as part of the "structure for peace." As the national security adviser in a centralized foreign policy structure, Henry Kissinger had many bureaucratic advantages in shaping the details of the administration's message. In those early days, Kissinger asserts that the new administration "had a notion, but not yet a strategy, to move toward China."[30] He would become the architect of the evolving strategy.

At the president's behest in February 1969, Kissinger began to explore possible rapprochement with China. Because the rapprochement strategy emerged from the interagency process he directed, Kissinger controlled the evolving terms of debate. That spring, he specifically shifted the terms of debate away from a discussion of bilateral problems to the global implications of Sino-Soviet problems and the global opportunities of a triangular focus. The plans Kissinger articulated presented a blueprint, which resonated with Nixon's preexisting beliefs, to successfully change the power equation. He declared it was heavy-handed Soviet diplomacy emphasizing the Chinese threat that highlighted possible strategic gains for the United States if relations with China could be normalized. He communicated this to Nixon by arguing that China might be ready to reenter the diplomatic arena, and if so, its threat to U.S. allies in the region would diminish and Chinese pressure along the Sino-Soviet border would ease pressure on Europe.

The major stumbling block, however, was that such possibilities could not be made clear until lines of communication were opened with the Chinese. Receptive to these messages, the president agreed to step up efforts to contact the Chinese on these terms. In June 1969, certain trade controls against China were modified and Kissinger made plans for the president's trip around the world.[31] The president's strategy for

Asia, aimed at extricating the United States from Vietnam, became the rubric for changing U.S. China policy.

The president's private signals to the Chinese in back-channel contacts and the public statements he made in Asia during his August 1969 trip laid the groundwork for change. His comments in Guam, which became the basis for his "structure for peace" and the Nixon Doctrine to follow, came as a surprise to the bureaucracy and signaled a shift in the administration's thinking. Instead of a U.S. advanced military posture for Asia, Asian states would now be responsible for their own security.[32] He emphasized this in the context of change in the postwar era and the need for the United States to adjust its policy to fit current circumstances. The loosening of the bipolar order meant not only that the era of confrontation was passing but also that the era of permanent détente had not yet begun. Nixon proposed seizing the moment and shaping those changes to benefit the United States in a transition period.[33] Not surprisingly, Nixon also identified the 1970s as the coming of age for U.S. foreign policy, emphasizing a new calmness of mind, maturity of judgment, and steadiness of action. It was time to develop "an intelligent, sustainable foreign policy requiring more systematic treatment of problems, and consideration of longer-term implications of operational decisions."[34]

In his memoirs, the president pointed to his first annual foreign policy report in 1970 (of which the draft statement became a substantial part) as the first serious public indication for his China initiative.[35] The report emphasized the need to determine the causes of crises, to take the longer view, and to build international relations that created a durable peace. Repeating old themes, the Soviet Union and China were a reality that had to be dealt with pragmatically. The report also recognized the obligation of the nuclear superpowers to reduce tensions with patient and precise efforts.[36]

One year later, the second annual presidential report on foreign policy raised the stakes and expanded on the themes from the first report by identifying the developing relationship with Beijing as the challenge of the decade. Nixon made relations with China a cornerstone to creating a balanced international structure. The report also openly stated that the United States was prepared to establish a dialogue with Beijing. Interjecting a note of caution, the U.S. public was warned to be realistic about the prospects. The report stated that China must end its self-imposed exile and that the United States would seek no advantage from the hostility between the two Communist giants. Although the United States still opposed ousting Taiwan from the United Nations, China was

reassured that Taiwan would not be an obstacle to improving relations.[37] Not long after, Undersecretary of State Elliott Richardson added
that although the policy was still containment, the administration was
moving toward a more businesslike relationship in which every opportunity to reduce tensions would be approached in a hardheaded and
pragmatic way.[38]

Certain themes were used repeatedly to reassure potential critics.
Both the State of the Union address in 1972 and the third annual foreign
policy report to Congress emphasized that the United States had entered
a new era and that foreign policy must adjust to the new realities. It
restated the U.S. commitment to Taiwan and emphasized that U.S. policy was not aimed at the Soviets, while reaffirming that the United
States would not exploit Sino-Soviet tensions as it strove for better relations with both countries. Repeating the same themes from the draft
presidential statement from November 1969, the report claimed these
changes illustrated the end of the bipolar postwar world and the creation
of a new structure for peace.[39]

The theme that both China and the United States had much to gain
from an improved relationship resonated with some members of
Congress and the public. Nixon's handwritten notes before his visit to
China explain what he tried to gain. The United States hoped to get
China to help with Vietnam and to restrain Communist expansion in
Asia. China, for its part, wanted to build up its world credentials, get
the United States out of Asia, and make headway on Taiwan. Jointly, the
parties also desired to restrain the Soviets, reduce the danger of confrontation, and guarantee a more stable Asia.[40]

The administration argued that candid exchanges with Chinese officials lessened the risks of miscalculation and misunderstanding and
thereby strengthened prospects for long-term peace. The agreement
called for settling international disputes without the threat of force and
reducing tension through normalization of U.S.-China relations, and it
established the concept that neither power should seek hegemony in
Asia. In order to improve bilateral relations, contact would be maintained through various channels, trade would be more open, and cultural and scientific exchanges would increase. In conclusion, Nixon argued
that the United States made a historic beginning without abandoning its
principles or friends. The road would be long, gradual, and approached
cautiously.[41]

Domestic political considerations. Nixon realized his administration
would have to tread a delicate path down the middle to circumvent

opposition from the right and the left. The issue of China's seat in the UN illustrated the kind of pressure he faced from the right. Conservatives such as Ronald Reagan and William F. Buckley were told they should trust the president and understand that he had fought the China battle as hard as he could. Because the shift in China's UN seat had been inevitable given the tenor of the discussion in the General Assembly, the administration argued that critics should blame the United Nations and not the president. In addition, the administration told critics they must face up to the fact that the United States and the PRC did have common interests. Ultimately, the dual-representation strategy gave Nixon credit for shouldering defeat well, instead of bolstering accusations that he sold out Taiwan.[42]

When rapprochement was announced in July 1971, Nixon faced criticism from the right that the United States was letting its friends down and from the left that "tricky Dick" had not consulted Congress. Initially, the administration responded that no secret deals had been made. It used various big plays to circumvent potential domestic opposition leading up to reelection. According to H. R. Haldeman, drama was an important component of the China strategy. For example, following Kissinger's July 9–11 secret visit to the PRC, the administration closely controlled its announcement. The drama was heightened because the White House kept the trip secret until the national security adviser's return, then staged it as a presidential announcement on live television. The administration even refused to release an advance text of the president's July 15 speech announcing his upcoming trip in February 1972. Shedding his conservative tone once and for all, Nixon called the step forward with China a "major development in building lasting peace" and that in fact, all would gain from reduced tensions and no stable or enduring peace in the world could come without the PRC's participation. Kissinger's breakthrough demonstrated that Nixon could lead the party from the center.[43]

Nixon's dramatic surprise seemed to mitigate potential opposition, at least in the short term. The following day, the *New York Times* front-page headline, "Nixon Will Visit China Before Next May to Seek a 'Normalization of Relations,'" heralded his triumph. On July 16, congressional leaders unanimously expressed their hope that the president's trip would improve relations with China and help to end the Vietnam War.[44] On July 17, a story by Tad Szulc suggested that President Nixon's announcement had defused criticism of the Vietnam War and outflanked his potential presidential challengers. Most prominently, Senate Majority Leader Mike Mansfield (D-Montana) and Senator

Jacob Javits (R–New York) argued this could help end the war. Following the July announcement, Republican senators James Buckley of New York and John Tower of Texas were the lone voices concerned that the president's action would strengthen those seeking accommodation with the Communists at any price.[45] Editorials in the *New York Times* for the next several days lauded Nixon's bold decision as a new era in international politics; it was seen to mark the end of two decades of irrational intransigence on both sides. Internationally, other than Taiwan's denunciation, the response to the initiative was highly favorable.[46]

As the president's trip to China approached, and immediately after its completion, the administration emphasized selective themes that bolstered its policy position. At a February 29, 1972, cabinet meeting Nixon emphasized that the most important matter was the profound new relationship between the two countries. According to Haldeman, the president wanted to get the press to counter the claim of key Democrats that they were more for peace than the president. The point the president wanted to make was that he had better credentials than those who had gotten the United States into the war. On March 2 Kissinger described the president as a big-league operator whose personal qualities prepared him for a classic battle of wills with Mao Zedong and Zhou Enlai.[47]

The language in the Shanghai Communiqué was kept ambiguous on sticky issues such as Taiwan to placate its lobby. The president engaged in a balancing act to avoid talking about specific U.S. defense commitments to Taiwan or the claim that the PRC had renounced the use of force with respect to Taiwan. He also wanted to avoid optimistic accounts that the PRC would intervene in Vietnam negotiations or any indication that the Soviet Union was discussed in anything other than general terms. Shifting the emphasis with the Chinese, Nixon stressed that the United States was prepared to reduce its forces gradually as tensions in the area diminished. The president asserted his trip led to a better understanding of both commonalities and differences from which a future means of communication with China would be built. Following the president's meeting with the bipartisan congressional leadership after his trip, one press report declared Congress was unanimously favorable toward the president's trip and what it had accomplished.[48]

Nixon's trip also proved to be a public windfall for the president; his approval ratings rose to 56 percent. On the question "How effective do you think the trip to China will be for improving world peace?" 58 percent of those polled said very effective or fairly effective, and only

24 percent thought it would not be very effective at all. On March 12, 1972, 98 percent of those polled said they had read or heard about the presidential trip—the single highest awareness score for any event in Gallup's thirty-seven-year history. Respondents were most impressed by the opportunity it provided for improved relations and for world peace, as well as by the warm reception the Chinese gave to Nixon. In other ways, however, the record remained mixed. Of those polled in June 1972, only 23 percent rated China favorably. For the same period of time, the Soviet Union's favorable rating was 40 percent and Taiwan's was 53 percent.[49]

The February 1972 presidential visit was one of the great foreign policy triumphs of Nixon's administration. It resulted from years of effort to circumvent the bureaucracy, prime the U.S. public, and provide a broad framework for foreign policy. Richard Nixon called the China initiative "one of the most publicly prepared surprises in history."[50] One irony of Nixon's success was that while the ambiguity of the new China relationship in 1972 allowed broad support to form, it also left the most controversial decisions for later. The need to open to China had hinged on geostrategic arguments with obvious policy and political payoffs. The push for normalization, however, directly threatened the interests of the Taiwan lobby and arms control advocates.[51] Initially, the Chinese seemed unconcerned about slow progress in or the timing of reductions in Taiwan. They seemed content to leave resolution of the issue to some point in the future. As long as the goals of the Shanghai Communiqué were abided by, it seemed that normalization of relations could be attained.[52]

Supporting Conditions: Preparing the Domestic Ground Incrementally

Part of the public strategy was to adopt an approach in which layer after layer of a new policy was revealed slowly. This incremental approach was a means by which a potentially controversial policy could be adopted before opposition became galvanized. By incrementally preparing the domestic ground, the advocates (the White House) committed their targets (the bureaucracy, Congress, and public) to small acceptable steps before potential opposition recognized the extent to which the policy would change the status quo.[53]

In this vein, conservative assessments of potential progress with China began to reshape the reference point on U.S.-China relations. In the president's first news conference on January 27, 1969, he conservatively stated that "until some changes occur on their side I see no immediate prospect of any change in our policy," including continued opposition to the admission of Communist China into the United Nations.[54] While Secretary Rogers and others explained that the United States sought a dialogue, they added that the United States had only a limited ability to influence the rate of improvement in relations.[55] In vague terms, the administration's stated goal was to establish a more normal relationship, including instituting trade relations and other exchanges.

Evidence for the gradual shift can be seen particularly in trade policy. In a series of unilateral moves, primarily the easing of trade and travel restrictions, the administration reexamined its long-standing embargo against China. Beginning with NSDM 17 in June 1969, the administration removed some restraints on foreign subsidiaries of U.S. firms involved in nonstrategic transactions with China. This initiative relaxed passport restrictions, allowed U.S. citizens traveling abroad to purchase Chinese goods in limited number, permitted licenses for exports of agricultural goods and equipment, and modified import and export controls to permit a gradual development of balanced trade.[56] It also emphasized that change would occur eventually anyway because both Chinas were facts of life. Those on the political left who believed chances for peace would brighten if the United States withdrew from Vietnam and moved more quickly on the China issue were warned not to get their hopes too high. Richard Nixon attacked those who criticized the United States and its military position as obstacles to peace, arguing that the country could not make deep cuts to reach a peace because that would lead to a disastrous result.[57]

These seemingly routine policy alterations gradually committed the administration and the nation to rapprochement. Such efforts established the groundwork to change the perception of China as a threat in Vietnam to China as a force for stability in East Asia. In a presidential address in October 1969, the president argued the United States should move from an era of confrontation to one of negotiation with Communist powers like China as soon as they stopped their self-imposed isolation.[58] In an internal paper, the policy planning staff acknowledged that the series of public signals indicated the administration was willing to deal with Beijing on a progressively more normal basis.[59]

The slow change in the administration's position succeeded in keeping potential critics off balance. Building a lasting basis for policy change, however, required a more comprehensive effort to justify the change within a broader framework. This coordinated framing effort (discussed in the previous section) began in earnest in 1970 as the administration articulated its strategy for peace. Two factors shaped the public themes the administration pushed. First, the Cold War provided the cultural context in which to frame China as a pragmatic counter to the Soviet Union. China's move from intransigence to a more flexible approach provided opportunities for a Sino-American rapprochement that changed the balance of forces in East Asia.[60] Second, the Vietnam War shook U.S. attitudes enough that many were ready for an opportunity for peaceful change. Nixon's rapprochement illustrated that the larger Cold War frame was general enough to construct multiple meanings and interpretations. There would be a symbolic struggle to build specific meanings out of larger Cold War symbols.

Speeches, background briefings, and most of all, visual images such as Nixon's historic trip to China set the stage to explain the China policy under review. Critical of the administration's efforts, author Steven Mosher concluded that Nixon engaged in an all-out lobbying campaign to convince the U.S. public there was no shame in gambling with the likes of Mao Zedong and Zhou Enlai and that he had resorted to various "fictions" about the Communist Chinese in order to succeed.[61] These fictions or framing efforts paved the way for a dramatic shift in people's reference points regarding China and effectively undercut potential opposition by dramatically changing the terms of debate on U.S.-China relations. The hierarchical nature of the advisory system and back-channel negotiations that excluded potential critics inside the administration allowed dramatic surprises like this to be sprung on the public. Table 3.1 illustrates strategic framing in the Nixon administration.

The Difficult Road to Normalization: Domestic Politics, Taiwan, and the Record of President Gerald Ford

While the opening to China was a dramatic shift in the general approach to China, it left specific issues unresolved. The most controversial of these as normalization proceeded proved to be the future status of Taiwan. In late 1973, indications began to appear that China wanted progress on Taiwan in order to keep the relationship with the United States on track. Deng Xiaoping, pressured by left-wing critics, argued publicly that no forward movement could be achieved without U.S. severing of political relations with Taiwan.[62] Additionally, the domestic

Table 3.1   Components of Richard Nixon's China Policy Frame

Problem diagnosis	• Need to redefine China from threat to essential ally in struggle with the Soviet Union
Themes that resonated with president and public	
Presidential beliefs	• PRC a priority and seen as useful counter to USSR
	• Personal confidence in his foreign policy expertise solidified his efforts
Policy themes	• China as strategic opportunity and anti-Soviet
	• Peace and stability in East Asia
Political considerations	• Need to move carefully between opposition from political left (critics of Vietnam policy) and right (original China lobby or Taiwan lobby)
	• Spring "opening" to China to undercut opposition
Supporting conditions/tactics	• Back-channel negotiations essential to "spring" the surprise
	• Incremental change to prepare domestic ground

attacks on President Nixon related to Watergate caused the Chinese to worry that the United States might become more isolationist at a time when it was needed to counter the Soviets.[63]

After Richard Nixon's resignation, President Ford tried to reassure the Chinese that he would follow the same basic approach to the international system as Nixon's. His retention of Kissinger as secretary of state signaled this continuity. Ford stated there would be no higher priority during his time in office than accelerating the normalization process. In an early report to the new president, Kissinger explained that the United States had agreed to achieve normalization by 1976, which would entail some form of representation on Taiwan, peaceful resolution of cross-strait issues, and U.S. exercise of great restraint in its military supply policy.[64] To make progress on normalization, it became important to balance domestic needs with Chinese demands. Several factors influenced the domestic debate in the United States. Normalization proposals previously moved to Nixon's second term for domestic reasons were now left for President Ford to resolve, but his lack of foreign policy credentials, the Nixon pardon, and events such as the April 1975 fall of Saigon complicated the domestic picture.

Concrete efforts to normalize relations were immediately controversial because the policy change would directly impinge on Taiwan's interests (and thus members of the Taiwan lobby and their sympathizers in Congress). In his talks with China, Kissinger worked to find a mutually acceptable way to handle Taiwan's future, as a basis for establishing formal diplomatic relations.[65] The task of negotiations with China was to move the relationship forward by using Chinese geopolitical concerns about the USSR for leverage. When normalization occurred, the White House would need to take congressional consultations against the risk that Congress would raise objections later if a timetable and formula were worked out without their notification.[66]

The administration had to find how to supply arms to maintain Taiwan's security in ways that pleased Taiwan and her congressional allies while avoiding actions that indicated to China the United States did not have an important interest in the island's security.[67] In 1975, Kissinger's State Department evaluated various options regarding levels of U.S. weapons sales to Taiwan in a memo, NSSM 212. It argued that the extreme options of (1) a complete cutoff of arms or (2) substantial new weapons for Taiwan would both be unacceptable. The option not to sell beyond existing technology levels also was rejected as a drastic departure that would be read as a lack of U.S. concern for Taiwan's security. The State Department, however, advocated limiting Taiwan's access to new weapons because that would balance concerns about accommodating PRC sensitivities and fulfilling Taiwan's psychological needs and deterrence requirements.[68] The Defense Department also preferred this option, observing that it was unlikely the PRC would be able to mount a successful nonnuclear invasion of Taiwan before 1980. Even though Taiwan would struggle to keep up with the PRC's military capacity, a major military confrontation was seen as unlikely. The administration sought a balance between continuing to offer great flexibility in maintaining Taiwan's confidence while not advancing sales that would be a major obstacle to normalizing relations with the PRC.[69]

Although China pressured for progress, the domestic political situation in the United States rendered a major move toward normalization politically impossible. Instead, the administration resorted to unilateral steps in this direction, such as not actively resisting Taiwan's expulsion from international financial institutions and delaying construction of a new Taipei chancery and residence.[70] While President Ford mentioned his intention to accelerate the relationship in a message to Congress, he also responded to conservative pressure to acknowledge the importance placed on U.S. relations with Taiwan.[71] This meant that Ford straddled two contradictory trends: the push to fulfill the objectives of the Shanghai Communiqué, and the domestic and international forces that raised obstacles to this shift. The difficult decisions to come would be less likely to evoke a substantial degree of support. Issues like Taiwan would provoke a negative reaction from some members of Congress, members of the media, and the public. Even Ford's visit to China in December 1975 could not break the downward slide.[72]

The United States and China agreed that maintaining the relationship was in both countries' interests—a factor that made Ford's trip important but more as a symbol of defeat than of momentum in the relationship. On the Chinese side, the strain was caused by Chinese doubts about U.S. capabilities to play a major role in the world (as a counterweight to the Soviets), concerns over détente, and tensions caused by the stalling of normalization. On the U.S. side, the administration did not expect the Chinese to be forthcoming on U.S. concerns or to be ready to move beyond the symbolism of Ford's trip. This meant it was only a sustaining visit.[73] After the trip, at the congressional leadership briefing, Kissinger emphasized that the trip "helped clear the air." Both sides agreed relations were good and that they would gradually get better if differences were handled in a noncontentious manner.[74]

A core component of President Ford's foreign policy strategy had been halted by domestic politics. Ford and Kissinger recognized that the short-term costs to move toward normalization were too great in the context of the fall of Vietnam and the approaching 1976 election. An opportunity had been lost. In response, China's approach to Taiwan became tougher the longer normalization was delayed. Their hard-line message included arguments that Taiwan's liberation could only be achieved through force of arms. If the United States did not disengage from Taiwan, it would be caught in the eventual military showdown.[75]

Conclusion

Changes in the international context and new domestic opportunities helped Nixon reframe the China problem, and these became the basis for his policy changes. The international context provided Nixon with the chance to reframe U.S. policy in geostrategic and positive terms. At the domestic level, the Nixon administration constructed its message to address diverse but potent interests in the Congress and the public. Both liberals desiring peace and conservatives fearful of the Soviet Union saw positive aspects of the opening to China. By the time of Nixon's visit to China, the dominant frame had shifted from perceiving China as a threat to U.S. interests to seeing the opportunity for peace and stability that China posed.

The Nixon administration successfully took advantage of changing strategic circumstances to help legitimate a corresponding change in policy. Their strategic framing efforts emphasized the opportunities presented by the change in circumstances, making that change an advantage rather than a risk to basic values. As these efforts prepared the groundwork to handle potential opposition, they succeeded in preparing the U.S. public for the change.

The administration had to cultivate the domestic ground carefully. The hierarchical advisory system helped them put out a consistent message, and the gradualist approach undermined potential opposition, as it created expectation for the change to come. The major themes in their framing message that linked the China policy to the overall "structure for peace" provided a general framework for specific policies. From this the administration built broad acceptance for themes that guided the general U.S. relationship with China for the next quarter century. These new themes emphasized that the two countries could work together to respond to East Asian problems, that China could help the United States deal with the Soviet Union, and that the United States should not challenge Chinese Communist Party (CCP) rule.

Measuring the long-term implications of strategic framing requires a focus beyond the Nixon administration. We have seen in this chapter that the increased favorable ratings of the Chinese in U.S. public opinion polls, the president's high approval ratings, and the general backing for Nixon's February 1972 visit were not sustainable beyond a certain point. President Ford's inability to solidify Nixon's gains (i.e., to finish normalization) showed the limitations on a president to push his policy agenda. The complex U.S. political context allowed other forces to challenge the president's definition of policy problems. It would take a sustained effort to maintain the dominant engagement frame.

Notes

1. Nixon, "Asia After Vietnam."
2. Report from Department of Defense to NSC, "Response to NSSM #9: Review of the International Situation—as of 20 January 1969, Vol. II:

Communist China," February 19, 1969 (Doc. no. 00040), Special National Intelligence Estimate no. 13–69, "Communist China and Asia," Director of Central Intelligence, March 6, 1969 (Doc. no. 00067), National Security Archives Collection: China and the United States.

3. Henry Kissinger, *White House Years,* 165–167.

4. An earlier version of this analysis by the author appeared in *Asian Perspective* as "Framing the National Interest in U.S.-China Relations: Building Consensus Around Rapprochement." Unlike that paper, this chapter has been reorganized to reflect a discussion of different components of strategic framing and to include a section on President Ford. This chapter also includes new data from the National Security Archives and various interviews unavailable in 2000.

5. George, *Presidential Decision Making in Foreign Policy*; Johnson, *Managing the White House.*

6. Morton Abramowitz, interview by the author, Washington, D.C., June 14, 2002.

7. Garthoff, *Détente and Confrontation,* 248; Kissinger, *White House Years,* 179–182. Movement toward a strategic triangular approach began when the president directed a study on policy options in light of the intensifying Sino-Soviet rivalry. See National Security Study Memorandum (NSSM) 63, "U.S. Policy on Current Sino-Soviet Differences," July 3, 1969 (Doc. no. 01373), National Security Archives: National Security Memorandum Collection from Truman to Clinton.

8. Department of State, "Draft Opening Statement and Contingency Guidance for Possible Warsaw Meeting" (drafted by East Asia and Pacific Bureau [EAP]), December 23, 1969 (Doc. no. 00100), National Security Archives Collection: China and the United States.

9. Department of State, "Summary of U.S. Strategy in Current Sino-U.S. Talks," January 21, 1970 (Doc. no. 00120), and Memo from Marshall Green in East Asia (State Department) to Undersecretary Elliot Richardson, "Next Steps in China Policy," October 6, 1969 (Doc. no. 00079), National Security Archives Collection: China and the United States. See also Garthoff, *Détente and Confrontation,* 256; Kissinger, *White House Years,* 687; Richard H. Soloman, The *U.S. PRC Political Negotiations, 1967–1984: An Annotated Chronology* (unclassified, U), National Security Archives Collection: China and the United States, 8

10. Department of State Telegram, "Sino-U.S. Relations: Significance of the 135th Sino-U.S. Meeting in Warsaw," January 21, 1970 (Doc. no. 00122), National Security Archives Collection: China and the United States.

11. Memos from Marshall Green (EAP) to the Secretary of State, February 4, 1970 (Doc. no. 00127) and March 5, 1970 (Doc. no. 00148), National Security Archives Collection: China and the United States. See also John Holdridge, oral history interview, December 14, 1989; Kissinger, *White House Years,* 686.

12. Memo from Winston Lord to Henry Kissinger, "Issues Raised by the Nixon Doctrine for Asia," January 23, 1970, in Folder: "Selected Lord Memos," Box 335, in Policy Planning Council (S/PC) Director's Files

(Winston Lord 1969–1977), Winston Lord Chronological File, December 1970–September-December 1972, pp. 1–2, Record Group (RG) 59, General Records of the Department of State, National Archives.

13. Policy Paper, "The New American Approach to Asia," ca. January 1970, in Folder: "Selected Lord Memos," Box 335, in Policy Planning Council (S/PC) Director's Files (Winston Lord 1969–1977), Winston Lord Chronological File, December 1970–September-December 1972, pp. 15, 26, Record Group 59, General Records of the Department of State, National Archives.

14. Kissinger, *White House Years,* 693, 733–784; see also Holdridge interview, December 14, 1989; Garthoff, *Détente and Confrontation,* 259–261; Vernon Walters, *Silent Missions,* 526–550.

15. Holdridge interview, December 14, 1989, and Chas W. Freeman, oral history interview, April 14, 1995. See also Memorandum from Winston Lord to John Holdridge and Dick Kennedy, "China Policy Group," November 10, 1970 (Doc. no. 00193), National Security Archives Collection: China and the United States; Robert Nichols, oral history interview, August 30, 1988.

16. Issues Paper on NSSM 124, "Next Steps Toward the People's Republic of China," by Winthrop Brown, Acting Chairman NSC Interdepartmental Group for East Asia and the Pacific, May 1971 (Doc. no. 00210), National Security Archives Collection: China and the United States.

17. National Security Council Memorandum, "Response to NSSM 124: Next Steps Toward the People's Republic of China," June 1, 1971 (Doc. no. 00211), National Security Archives Collection: China and the United States.

18. By October 1971, the number of countries favoring Taiwan's position had eroded to the point that the U.S. ability to preserve Taiwan's seat had ended. Kissinger's second visit to China that month corresponded with the General Assembly vote to seat the PRC (Kissinger, *White House Years,* 719).

19. Memo from Henry Kissinger to the President, "My August Meeting with the Chinese Ambassador in Paris," August 16, 1971 (Doc. no. 00215), and Memo from Winston Lord to Henry Kissinger, "Your Meeting with the Chinese Ambassador in Paris," July 27, 1971 (Doc. no. 00213), National Security Archives Collection: China and the United States.

20. William Burr, *The Kissinger Transcripts: The Top Secret Talks with Beijing and Moscow,* 17, 49.

21. H. R. Haldeman, *The Haldeman Diaries: Inside the Nixon White House,* 316, 409–422; Soloman, *U.S. PRC Political Negotiations, 1967–1984: An Annotated Chronology,* National Security Archives Collection: China and the United States, 11–15.

22. Marshall Green, oral history interview, 1998.

23. Memo from Winston Lord to Henry Kissinger, "Your Meeting with the Chinese Ambassador in Paris," July 27, 1971 (Doc. no. 00213), National Security Archives Collection: China and the United States.

24. Some concern was voiced in the early 1960s that a nuclear-capable China would use its position to weaken the will of Asian countries, to stir up divisions between the United States and its allies, and to put political pressure

on the U.S. military presence in Asia. The Johnson administration even explored with the Soviet Union the possibility of preventive military action against Chinese targets. See Memorandum from McGeorge Bundy for the Record, September 15, 1964 (Doc. no. 00019), and the Secret Special National Intelligence Estimate, "Chinese Communist Capabilities and Intentions in the Far East," U.S. Office of the Director of the CIA, March 13, 1961 (Doc. no. 00007), National Security Archives Collection: China and the United States.

25. *The Gallup Poll: Public Opinion 1935–1971*, Vol. 2, 2053. For a discussion of public opinion toward China during this time period see Leonard Kusnitz, *Public Opinion and Foreign Policy: America's China Policy, 1949–1979*, 108–120.

26. *The Gallup Poll*, 2032–2033.

27. Ibid., 2308; see also Kusnitz, *Foreign Policy and Public Opinion*, 162–168, for U.S. public opinion data from 1954–1971 on the PRC entrance into the UN.

28. Richard Nixon, *RN, the Memoirs of Richard Nixon*, 343.

29. Ibid., 340.

30. Kissinger, *White House Years*, 171.

31. Ibid., 173–179.

32. Holdridge interview, December 14, 1989; Memo from Robert Osgood to Henry Kissinger, "Memorandum on the Nixon Doctrine with Attached Draft Presidential Statement," November 19, 1969, Folder: Planning Staff, Box 343, UN Actions to General Purpose Forces, Winston Lord RG 59, National Archives.

33. "The Nixon Doctrine: A Foreign Policy for the 1970s" (draft presidential statement), Folder: Planning Staff, Box 343, UN Actions to General Purpose Forces, Winston Lord RG 59, pp. 1–2, 6, National Archives.

34. Ibid., 8.

35. Nixon, *RN*, 545.

36. "U.S. Foreign Policy for the 1970s: A New Strategy for Peace." See also Richard Nixon, "State of the Union," 145–147; "A Conversation with William Rogers with Eric Severaid," 53–58; "National Foreign Policy Conference for Editors and Broadcasters with Secretary Richardson."

37. "U.S. Foreign Policy Report for the 1970s: Building For Peace"; see also Garthoff, *Détente and Confrontation*, 257–258; Nixon, *RN*, 548.

38. "National Foreign Policy Conference for Editors and Broadcasters with Secretary Richardson."

39. "U.S. Foreign Policy for the 1970s: The Emerging Structure for Peace"; "State of the Union Excerpts," 141; "Address to Accompany the 1971: A Year of Breakthrough Toward Peace in the World (Third Annual Foreign Policy Report)"; Garthoff, *Détente and Confrontation*, 266; Haldeman, *Haldeman Diaries*, 322.

40. James Mann, *About Face: A History of America's Curious Relationship with China, from Nixon to Clinton*, 13–14.

41. Memorandum from Henry Kissinger to the President, "Your Meeting with the Congressional Leadership on Your China Trip," February 28, 1972,

Folder: February 1972, Lot no. 770112, Winston Lord RG 59, Box 340, May 1971–February 1972, pp. 2–4, National Archives.

42. Haldeman, *Haldeman Diaries,* 368; Kissinger, *White House Years,* 770–774; Patrick Tyler, *A Great Wall: Six Presidents and China*, 90–92.

43. Haldeman, *Haldeman Diaries*, 319–320; "President Nixon Announces Acceptance of Invitation to Visit PRC," 121. Even before Kissinger's secret trip, Nixon used a gathering of midwestern news media executives, on July 6, 1971, to place on record an outline of reasons for approaching China. Downplaying any accomplishment, Nixon challenged China to open other doors. See "President Nixon Briefs Media Executives from 13 Midwest States," 93–97.

44. John W. Finney, "Congress Chiefs Pleased," 1, 3.

45. Tad Szulc, "Move by President Seems to Outflank His Potential Foes," 1–2.

46. See, for example, *New York Times* editorial, "The Opened Door," July 17, 1971; Tyler, *A Great Wall*, 108.

47. Haldeman, *Haldeman Diaries*, 409, 424.

48. Robert Semple Jr., "Two Senate Leaders Will Go to China; Invited by Chou," sec. 1, 16.

49. *The Gallup Poll: Public Opinion 1972–1977,* Vol. 1, 25, 39–40.

50. Nixon, *RN*, 545.

51. For a discussion of limitations Nixon's and Kissinger's styles placed on their policies, see Robert Beisner, "History and Henry Kissinger"; Sutter, *The China Quandary.*

52. Briefing Paper from the Department of State on Taiwan (February 1973 Talks), October 1973 (Doc. no. 00270), National Security Archives Collection: China and the United States.

53. Zeev Maoz, "Framing the National Interest: The Manipulation of Foreign Policy Decisions in Group Settings."

54. President Nixon's News Conference of January 27, 244; Kissinger, *White House Years*, 169.

55. "U.S. Foreign Policy: Some Major Issues—Statement by Secretary Rogers."

56. Kissinger, *White House Years*, 712; National Security Decision Memorandum (NSDM) 105, "Steps Toward Augmentation of Travel and Trade Between the People's Republic of China and the United States," April 13, 1971, Presidential Decision Directives (Various), Box 10, Folder NSDM, National Security Archives; Soloman, *U.S. PRC Political Negotiations, 1967–1984: An Annotated Chronology (U),* National Security Archives Collection: China and the United States, 8. See also National Security Decision Memorandum 17, "Relaxation of Economic Controls Against China," June 26, 1969 (no. 01179), National Security Memorandum Collection from Truman to Clinton, National Security Archives. Just prior to Nixon's trip to China on February 17, 1972, the categorization of the PRC was transferred on the Commodity Control List. The secretary of the treasury was asked to eliminate the regulations that subsidiaries of U.S. firms obtain a Treasury Department license in addition to a host country license for exporting strategic goods to China, including the export of foreign

technology. This placed trade with the Soviet Union and China on an equal basis. See National Security Decision Memorandum 155, "Relaxation of Restrictions on Trade with People's Republic of China," February 17, 1972, Presidential Decision Directives (PDD) (Various), Box 10, Folder NSDM, National Security Archives.

57. Richard Nixon, "America's Role in the World."

58. Richard Nixon, "Presidential Address: Strengthening the Total Fabric of Peace."

59. Policy Paper, "The New American Approach to Asia," ca. January 1970, in Folder: "Selected Lord Memos," Box 335, in Policy Planning Council (S/PC) Director's Files (Winston Lord 1969–1977), Winston Lord Chronological File, December 1970–September-December 1972, pp. 12–13, RG 59, General Records of the Department of State, National Archives.

60. National Intelligence Estimate, "Communist China International Posture," November 11, 1970 (no. 13-7-70), National Security Archives postpublication Collection: China and the United States.

61. Steven Mosher, *China Misperceived: American Illusions and Chinese Reality*, 140–141.

62. Department of State Telegram from David Bruce to Secretary Kissinger, October 23, 1973 (Doc. no. 00275), National Security Archives Collection: China and the United States. In his talks with Zhou Enlai, Kissinger was asked about U.S. support for the production of planes in Taiwan. He drew a distinction between supplying parts for short-range fighter aircraft rather than giving Taiwan the aircraft, stating there was an assembly plant in Taiwan, not a production plant. Kissinger assured China that Taiwan would not be allowed to attack the mainland. See Memorandum of Conversation Between Henry Kissinger and Zhou Enlai, November 12, 1973 (Doc. no. 00279), National Security Archives Collection: China and the United States.

63. Memo from Henry Kissinger to the President, "My Visit to China," November 19, 1973 (Doc. no. 00285), National Security Archives Collection: China and the United States.

64. Top Secret Cable from the White House to David Bruce, August 9, 1974 (Doc. no. 00306), National Security Archives Collection: China and the United States; Memo from Henry Kissinger to the President, "Our Future Relationship with the PRC in 74/75," National Security Archives postpublication Collection: China and the United States.

65. Department of State Scope Analysis, "U.S.-PRC Normalization at a Turning Point," November 1974 (Doc. no. 00316), National Security Archives Collection: China and the United States.

66. Briefing Paper for President Ford on the People's Republic of China, August 14, 1974 (Doc. no. 00307), National Security Archives Collection: China and the United States.

67. Memo for General Brent Scowcroft, "Submission of Response to NSSM 212," November 12, 1974 (Doc. no. 00318), National Security Archives Collection: China and the United States.

68. Memo for General Brent Scowcroft from the Department of State, "Department of State's Comments and Recommendations on NSSM 212,"

January 29, 1975 (Doc. no. 00336), National Security Archives Collection: China and the United States.

69. Memo for the National Security Adviser from the Secretary of Defense, April 12, 1976 (Doc. no. 406), National Security Archives Collection: China and the United States.

70. Memo for Secretary Kissinger, "Indicators of PRC Internal Debate and Desire for Movement on the Taiwan Issue," May 23, 1974 (Doc. no. 00299), National Security Archives Collection: China and the United States.

71. Secret Briefing Paper on Bilateral Relations to Henry Kissinger, May 1975 (Doc. no. 00344), National Security Archives Collection: China and the United States.

72. Memo for Secretary Kissinger, "U.S.-PRC Relations and Approaches to the President's Peking Trip: Tasks for the Rest of 1975," July 3, 1975 (Doc. no. 00357), National Security Archives Collection: China and the United States.

73. Memo from Henry Kissinger to the President, "Your Trip to the People's Republic of China," November 20, 1975 (Doc. no. 00391), National Security Archives Collection: China and the United States.

74. Briefing Memo from Winston Lord and William Gleysteen to Secretary Kissinger, "Your Briefing of the Congressional Leadership on the Asian Trip," December 9, 1975 (Doc. no. 00400), National Security Archives Collection: China and the United States.

75. Memo from Harold Saunders, Intelligence and Research Bureau (INR), to Secretary Kissinger, "Peking's Hard Line on Taiwan," October 4, 1976 (Doc. no. 00427), National Security Archives Collection: China and the United States.

4

Normalization Realized: Carter and the Institutionalization of Engagement

The formal recognition of the People's Republic of China on January 1, 1979, shifted the balance in the U.S., Soviet, and Chinese triangular relationship. When it formally recognized the PRC, the Carter administration moved away from its early foreign policy agenda emphasizing détente with the Soviet Union toward an alliance with the Chinese that included controversial military ties to counter a shared perception of the Soviet threat. This shift in President Carter's thinking was a dramatic change for a president who initially sought deep cuts in nuclear weapons with the Soviets.

As the United States conducted its sensitive negotiations with China, strategic, domestic, and internal considerations influenced how negotiations proceeded. There were trade-offs at the international level because as the United States pursued normalization, the Soviet Union could be alienated. At the domestic level, given the shared nature of power between the president and the Congress, any change in policy toward China faced challenges from members of Congress and other domestic critics who strongly supported the Republic of China on Taiwan. Public opinion polls highlighted the domestic controversy to come vis-à-vis Taiwan. In an April 1977 poll, respondents were asked how important it was for the United States to continue its interest in the security of the Taiwan people after diplomatic relations with the mainland were established. Thirty percent felt it was very important, 31 percent fairly important, and only 22 percent responded not particularly important or not important at all. In a related question only 27 percent strongly or fairly strongly favored establishing diplomatic relations with the PRC (compared to 47 percent fairly or very strongly opposed) if that meant ending diplomatic and defense treaty relations with Taiwan.[1] Carter's efforts to balance Chinese expectations and demands with the constraints posed by the domestic political context as normalization proceeded were complicated further by infighting between two different bureaucratic factions.

How and why the tilt toward China occurred is the central question of this chapter.[2] Because Secretary of State Cyrus Vance and National Security Adviser Zbigniew Brzezinski held different policy agendas and beliefs about the possibilities of when and how normalization should be approached, manipulating the problem definition became a means to influence the timing and content of policy toward the PRC. The changes in Carter's policy corresponded to the increasing dominance of the national security adviser over the secretary of state in making foreign policy. This chapter begins with an overview of the normalization process struggle within the open advisory structure adopted by President Carter.

Jimmy Carter, His Advisers, and the Struggle over the Normalization Agenda

Stalled talks over normalization of U.S.-China relations during the Ford administration left unfinished business for Jimmy Carter. Although Carter and his advisers did support the Shanghai Communiqué and the principle of one China, normalization was not a pressing priority for the new president. In these circumstances the policy issue was open to differing interpretations. What began as a collegial advisory system devolved into a classic case of bureaucratic politics, as policy discussions turned into a big turf war. The open organization of the advisory system meant that competing policy priorities were much more visible than they had been in the Nixon administration.

Organizing the Open Advisory System and Players in Positions

In contrast to President Nixon's advisory system, President Carter entered office determined to open up the foreign policy making process to bring some accountability back into the system. In Presidential Directive NSC-1 he authorized an open, spokes-of-the-wheel system that placed the president in the center of divergent foreign policy voices. As noted in other work, Carter's system allowed both of the central foreign policy advisers—the secretary of state and national security adviser—open access to him and created two committees that dealt with different issues within the NSC. The first, the Policy Review Committee, designed to be chaired by the relevant departmental secretary, developed policies that fell within one department's jurisdiction but had implications for other areas. Vance coordinated early China policy in this committee. The second, the Special Coordinating Committee that Brzezinski chaired, dealt with crisis management and arms control. In general, Brzezinski's cabinet-level posting, chairmanship of this committee, close physical proximity to the president in the White House, and his close personal relationship with Carter gave him more than equal footing with the secretary of state. Secretary of Defense Harold Brown also proved influential in the open arrangement because he headed the largest foreign policy bureaucracy with a stake in Sino-American relations and was largely Brzezinski's ally on China policy.[3]

The open advisory structure of the Carter administration was designed to foster collegial discussion of policy alternatives. However, as the policy priorities of the central advisers diverged, the advisory system with its competing committees created two centers of power within the administration. Early discussions on the appropriate policy approach toward China illustrated that bureaucratic differences and competition existed between the NSC and State Department principals and their staffs. These differences arose early because of the question of how to handle the triangular relationship with the Soviet Union and the timing of normalization. Vance saw hope for improved relations with the Soviets, with the Strategic Arms Limitation Talks (SALT) as his first imperative. Brzezinski, however, saw the Soviet Union as increasingly threatening to U.S. interests, thus giving the relationship with China strategic meaning.

Because Brzezinski's agenda was not the same as Vance's, this meant that those of their deputies (Michel Oksenberg for Brzezinski and Richard Holbrooke in the East Asian Bureau for Vance) also differed. According to some State Department sources, Holbrooke and Oksenberg personally disliked one another and each worked to protect his own bureaucratic turf behind the other's back. Both also took a strong interest in moving the policy forward (but on different terms), and each controlled policy at different points with different implications.[4]

In the State Department the Policy Planning staff put together the administration's initial China strategy (PRM-24). Alan Romberg and Stapleton Roy, specifically, were tasked with reviewing the record of the Kissinger–Zhou Enlai talks and formulating policy memos first for Vance and then the president.[5] The major issues of contention were how to break relations with Taiwan (and what sort of relationship would result) and how to handle relations with the Soviet Union. Vance, along with Anthony Lake in Policy Planning, wanted to proceed slowly, and initially he attempted to maintain some sort of official representation with Taiwan to avoid uncharted territory with an informal relationship. However, Holbrooke and others convinced Vance that China would not accept the United States retaining an official consulate relationship with Taiwan.[6]

During the first Policy Review Committee meeting on China policy, which Vance chaired on June 27, 1977, the differences between the NSC and State Department on the timing question became apparent. The State Department was charged with preparing two alternative approaches. The first, which was supported by Brzezinski, would have Vance push the U.S. position in detailed terms during his August 22–25 visit. The second, supported by Vance, would have him only sound out the Chinese.[7] The president's instructions to Vance reflected Vance's preferences. Instead of moving forward on normalization, Vance was to emphasize the need for reciprocal movement from China. Carter required assurances that Beijing would not "publicly contradict expressions of our expectations that the Taiwan problem will be resolved peacefully." Vance was to engage China on areas of mutual self-interest in global policy, such as Korea, southern Africa, the Horn of Africa (Ethiopia and Somalia), Southeast Asia, and South Asia, but not mention the Soviet Union directly. Carter also was willing to explore new cultural and economic ties that communicated forward movement in the relationship, but he simultaneously intended to sell defensive equipment to Taiwan.[8]

The Chinese expressed their impatience over the slow process of normalization and the low priority it had within the administration vis-à-vis SALT. Foreign Minister Huang Hua and other officials went so far as to accuse the administration of appeasing the Soviets, calling Vance's presentation a "retreat" from President Ford's 1975 position.[9] Following Vance's visit and through the fall of 1977, China maintained its distance from the United States. The PRC even moved to shift its intended scientific relationship to France, Canada, and West Germany and announced it would buy wheat from more dependable sources. Chinese leaders refused to discuss Taiwan further and told the administration "perhaps Mr. Carter will learn and decide China has a special importance to the economy of the U.S. We are very disappointed in him. He and Mr. Vance were superficially friendly in NYC recently but their words are empty of meaning."[10]

In spring 1978, the deteriorating relationship with the Soviets over the Horn of Africa provided an opportunity for Brzezinski to change President Carter's focus on reaching a SALT agreement before pursuing normalization; he convinced the president to send Vance to Moscow to discuss SALT while granting Brzezinski a freer hand in negotiating with China with a trip in May.[11]

A Department of State briefing paper for Brzezinski's trip noted that normalization was not supposed to be the centerpiece but that the national security adviser's attitude would affect Chinese attitudes toward the talks. In a much-excised account, the State Department briefing paper reveals the thinking of the administration at that point. It acknowledged that both sides saw a mutual benefit, but in the absence of "acute Soviet provocation" both sides would have been reluctant to cooperate. It noted, "among the most important deterrents on each side has been the concern that collaboration would result in damaging Soviet counteractions, which could in our case undermine existing bases for cooperation with the USSR." In addition, there already were asymmetries in the relationship with China such as more U.S. visits to China than vice versa, more restrained rhetoric on the U.S. side, and trade and exchanges that favored the Chinese while China used the United States as a residual supplier of grain only when their crops failed, and Chinese textiles created problems for U.S. producers.[12]

Unlike Vance's trip, when Carter sent Brzezinski to Beijing, he went with the authority to play the China card. Brzezinski's trip was an opportunity to reframe the initial policy discussion and to deepen the consultative relationship through an exchange of views on wider global issues, notably on U.S.-Soviet relations.[13] In a memo to the president, the national security adviser put it in the context of maintaining better relations with both China and the Soviet Union than either had with the other country.[14]

The warm reception Brzezinski received in China (in contrast to the secretary of state) gave him a bureaucratic advantage over Vance and his agenda.[15] According to Raymond Garthoff, China intentionally worked to "reward Brzezinski and further his influence to the detriment of Vance" because it saw in the national security adviser a friend to its agenda. For example, Brzezinski joked that the first one to the top of the Great Wall would take on the Russians in Ethiopia. This reflected the shared anti-Soviet banter that characterized his trip to China.[16] According to one press report, Brzezinski seemed to have "fallen victim

to the Chinese genius for overwhelming guests with hospitality and getting them to make exorbitant statements." Brzezinski's visit sent the
message to both Moscow and Beijing that the U.S. position had tilted
toward alignment with China. After his return, in interviews and on
Meet the Press the national security adviser noted that the United States
and China had many "parallel interests."[17]

Vance, fearing that SALT would be set aside in favor of normalization, became leery of expanding the security relationship with China.
The State Department and its European bureau, in particular, saw little
utility in building up the Soviet fear of China by strengthening a U.S.-
China global strategic alliance. To counter Brzezinski's fast-paced
move for normalization before SALT, Vance and Holbrooke proposed to
move first with Vietnamese normalization rather than China. According
to Paul Kreisberg, on the policy planning staff during the normalization
period:

> It wasn't that he was so engaged on Vietnam, but he was engaged with
> the Soviet Union. And he would have preferred to put off the China
> connection until after the meeting that he had scheduled with
> Gromyko in December [1978]. But Vance kept losing each time with
> the President who clearly wanted to move ahead on China as the great
> new, fresh capstone in his foreign policy initiatives.

The Vietnam-first agenda directly threatened Brzezinski's goals.[18]

The question of how fast the United States should move toward
normalization with Vietnam had an effect on the pace of U.S.-PRC relations and brought out the differences between the State Department and
NSC on this issue.[19] China, Brzezinski claimed, saw Vietnam as veering
toward the Soviets. The State Department efforts to normalize relations
with Vietnam came at the wrong time, in the wrong context, and would
reinforce China's concerns and complicate the more important task of
normalizing relations with China. Brzezinski asked and gained the president's approval to postpone the State Department's efforts with
Vietnam.[20]

Despite this conflict Brzezinski succeeded in getting a consensus to
move ahead as quickly as possible to normalize relations. He
declared:

> We wanted, in 1978 to facilitate Chinese acquisition of nondefense
> and possibly even defense-oriented Western technology, by 1979 to
> host a visit by a leading PRC political figure, sign trade and cultural
> agreements, and lay the basis for a long-term cooperative relationship.

> At the same time we were determined to maintain adequate security, economic, and cultural relations with Taiwan.[21]

While early normalization would cause complications in concluding SALT II, it would improve the administration's position domestically, showing congressional doubters that the administration could play hardball and power politics and be in a better position to do so with China.

Moving Forward with Normalization

In the month following Brzezinski's trip, normalization was pursued vigorously in back-channel contacts. Over that summer and fall, Leonard Woodcock, chief of the liaison office in China, became the main conduit for these secret negotiations. All communications would go through this channel and would automatically be sent to the president, the national security adviser, and the secretary of state. Woodcock was instructed to meet with the Chinese every two weeks, with the goal of having a final agreement around mid-December. The president, per Brzezinski's suggestion, kept the circle closed to avoid leaks that could jeopardize the whole process; these instructions were known only by Walter Mondale, Brown, Vance, Brzezinski, Holbrooke, and Oksenberg.

In the negotiations Taiwan remained the main obstacle. When a basis could be found to maintain U.S.-Taiwanese cultural and commercial contacts while peacefully resolving the question, then the president was willing to normalize relations. The United States was prepared to abide by the Shanghai Communiqué and acknowledge the view that all Chinese on either side of the Taiwan Strait maintain there is but one China and that Taiwan is part of China.[22] On December 4, 1978, China accepted the contents of the draft joint communiqué for normalization, with the target date of January 1, 1979, for reciprocal recognition. On December 15 it was announced that diplomatic relations would be established as of January 1 and that Deng Xiaoping would visit the United States at the end of January 1979.[23]

Oddly enough, public opinion seemed primed for these changes. In November 1978, a poll sponsored by the Chicago Council on Foreign Relations reported that 25 percent agreed strongly and 39 percent agreed somewhat that the United States should try to expand trade and technical exchanges with the PRC, while 21 percent disagreed somewhat strongly or strongly to that notion. The sentiment on Taiwan still sent confusing signals, however. In the same poll, respondents were asked how the United States should respond if China invaded Taiwan—

25 percent said do nothing; 27 percent, try to negotiate; 5 percent, refuse to trade; 7 percent, send military supplies; and only 20 percent said send U.S. troops. Ironically, these responses came in the same poll where 53 percent of those polled agreed that the United States did have a vital interest in Taiwan.[24] By February 1979, just after normalization, on a +5 to −5 scale only 30 percent had a favorable opinion of the PRC while 64 percent had an unfavorable opinion (24 percent rated it −5, the lowest rating possible). In contrast, Taiwan was rated favorably by 60 percent and negatively by 31 percent.[25]

Congress reacted by challenging the administration's agreement with the PRC in legislation known as the Taiwan Relations Act (TRA). After much wrangling, on March 13, 1979, with a 90 to 6 Senate vote and a House vote of 345 to 55, Congress passed the TRA and made it a matter of law that the United States would maintain "extensive, close and friendly relations" with Taiwan and help it maintain its military capacity to resist any threat. It asserted the continuing U.S. interest in Taiwan's de facto independence from China and that any threat to Taiwan would be "of grave concern to the United States." Both the administration and leaders of Congress declared a victory—the president for his policy of normalization of relations with Beijing and key members of Congress for their success in toughening the language of the administration's original legislation. The Chinese for their part expressed "grave concern" about the TRA but did not suggest its passage would interrupt normalization of relations.[26] Taking the language from the president's executive order that established diplomatic relations with the PRC (and terminated diplomatic relations with Taiwan), the TRA created a corporation under the laws of the District of Columbia called the American Institute on Taiwan (AIT) to handle unofficial relations with Taiwan.[27]

The internal political process leading up to normalization set a certain tone that allowed a broad new relationship to develop. By studying how the domestic political situation and the international context converged to influence presidential decisionmaking, we will see how the basis for the new relationship developed.

The Internal Fight over Policy Definition and Timing

The previous section described Carter's shift in focus but not how and why it proceeded. Competing visions of the proper approach to U.S.-China relations and how differences should be resolved internally illustrate how the decisionmaking process shaped particular policy choices.

Competing Diagnoses of the Problem

The debate leading up to normalization illustrated the points of contention among the central decisionmakers. As noted, when Cyrus Vance had the upper hand with this issue early in the policy review process, he emphasized gradual normalization so that it would not threaten his arms control agenda. The conclusions reached in PRM-24 reflected his caution in developing diplomatic relations with the Chinese because it might harm negotiations with the Soviets. Brzezinski's trip to China helped him to take control of the agenda, however, and change the terms of the debate. His and Vance's positions were based on very different views of the Soviet Union and two different sets of assumptions about the way the world worked.

The evenhanded position. From the beginning, Vance's reference point looked beyond the U.S.-Soviet equation. Rather than seeing the Chinese as a counter to Soviet power, the secretary of state saw the possibility of China playing an important independent role in world and regional affairs. China policy had to be pursued in a way that strengthened the balance of power in Asia and globally without alienating the Soviets. On April 15, 1977, Vance sent the president a memo insisting "the Chinese must also be made to understand that we do not perceive our relations with them as one-dimensional (i.e., vis-à-vis the USSR), but that we also look at our relationship in the context of key bilateral and international issues."[28] According to Morton Abramowitz, Vance went to China with the concern that China would be a hindrance to his diplomacy with the Soviets, and he felt the United States should keep the Soviets in the loop on U.S. efforts.[29]

Vance argued for an evenhanded approach that emphasized improved relations with both the Soviets and the Chinese even as Brzezinski gained control. During congressional hearings in June 1978, the secretary of state emphasized that the consistent policy to improve relations based on the Shanghai Communiqué was not a function of U.S.-Soviet relations. He also downplayed Brzezinski's trip and emphasized that it was an opportunity for a wide-ranging discussion of global issues with Chinese leadership, not a negotiation over normalization.[30]

After the establishment of formal relations with the PRC, the secretary of state still argued that the administration should pursue an "evenhanded" policy toward both China and the Soviet Union that moved policy forward "in tandem, granting trade privileges to both, especially the most-favored-nation [MFN] privilege, but not engage in a military relationship with either."[31] From Vance's perspective, the United States needed to realistically appreciate the limits of cooperation, especially in security matters, and to carefully manage triangular relations with the Soviets and the Chinese. He especially remained opposed to providing military technology or arms to China.

The balanced position. By the time of Vance's August 1977 trip, Brzezinski had become convinced it was impossible to treat both China and the Soviets in an evenhanded manner. Since it was the Soviets who militarily threatened the United States and not the Chinese, he did not want the president to mechanically equate Beijing with Moscow. In Brzezinski's terms the Soviets actively sought to expand their sphere of influence and encourage war by proxies. They also conducted a world-wide propaganda campaign against the United States and threatened to link the question of China to SALT. As a result, Brzezinski believed the United States should stress it wanted a balanced relationship with Beijing and Moscow. Mechanical equality could result in rewarding intransigence by one party and ignoring restraint or accommodation by the other. Balancing recognized the need to refrain from allying with one against the other but also saw the reality of existing differences between the Sino-American and U.S.-Soviet relationships. The U.S.-China relationship had strategic value because it shared a common concern about the Soviets, but it also had a broader basis that included extensive commercial, scientific, and cultural relations. One of Brzezinski's tactics was to create flexibility on the MFN question for China specifically to de-link it from MFN for the Soviet Union.[32]

On the security front Brzezinski understood that Deng Xiaoping had to be convinced that the United States would remain a credible counterweight to Soviet military power in Asia.[33] Part of the answer was to promise a substantial security relationship. First, it was in the U.S. interest to understand what the Chinese military was doing, and second, from a Department of Defense perspective, it was important to be able to use China as a foundation against the Soviets in terms of base access, electronic reconnaissance, and intelligence facilities.[34] After the Iranian revolution in 1978, the loss of intelligence capacity in Iran accelerated the push for normalization with this in mind. It would be impossible to verify Soviet missile launches without the China solution. Additionally, the NSC and Defense Department persisted in this focus because they saw it as an opportunity to have good relations with China and Japan that decreased the military contingencies the United States would have to face in the Pacific.[35]

Themes That Resonated: Understanding the President's Choices

President Carter's value structure made him receptive to certain themes at different points. Eventually, he hardened his attitude toward the Soviets and responded differently as political circumstances changed.

President Carter's beliefs and priorities. Jimmy Carter entered office committed to arms control first and with a desire to push for deep cuts in nuclear weapons. As a result, the president accepted the evenhanded approach early on because it fit with his desire to improve relations with the Soviet Union and push for a SALT agreement. At this point Carter still gave higher priority to maintaining détente and agreed that an immediate opening to China would damage his arms control objectives.[36] Thus his lack of urgency can be explained, in part, because he found Vance's policy arguments and domestic concerns compelling. SALT was the president's central priority, and domestically his foreign policy plate was quite full at the time. He sought "to improve our relationship with China without reneging on our commitments to the well-being of Taiwan and without further affecting our already strained relations with the Soviet Union."[37] On the question of flexibility to transfer technology to China, Carter noted, "I'm concerned about transferring advanced electronics and other technology to PRC if it can later be used for military purposes. Also a policy of favoring PRC over Soviet Union."[38]

Carter's support for Brzezinski's trip, however, began a fundamental shift in his emphasis to make relations with China a central facet of U.S. global policy and to acknowledge the shared, long-term strategic concerns. The United States was determined to seek peace with the Soviets but also to deter their military challenge as well as protect the interests of friends and allies. Brzezinski stressed that he envisioned a primarily competitive relationship with the USSR with some cooperative aspects. "My concern is that the combination of increasing Soviet military power and political shortsightedness, fed by big-power ambitions, might tempt the Soviet Union both to exploit local turbulence and to intimidate our friends."[39]

Anti-Soviet policy themes. Brzezinski's push to reframe the U.S. China policy with the president in anti-Soviet terms had success because of the hostile context of Soviet activities. Events in the Horn of Africa, in particular, made China an attractive strategic counterweight to the Soviet Union. According to Brzezinski, Soviet behavior showed they were indifferent to U.S. interests. He did not believe they were sincere on SALT, and he felt the United States should increase the pace of normalization with China against Soviet wishes. Brzezinski raised these issues with the president and in important committee meetings in order to move his agenda forward. For example, the Special Coordinating Committee meeting of February 22, 1978, that he chaired, which focused on problems in the Horn of Africa, moved the administration in this direction. In it steps were taken with respect to space cooperation and technology transfers to the Chinese.[40] On March 2, Brown and Brzezinski even suggested that the Chinese be approached to issue a joint statement on the Horn to place pressure on the Soviets. Brzezinski argued that "Soviet disregard for our concerns, . . . made me feel that we should not be excessively deferential to Soviet sensitivities about U.S.-Chinese collaboration. If we should make no linkage between SALT and Soviet misconduct—as Vance strongly argued—then why should we let the Soviets link (negatively) SALT and better U.S.-Chinese relations?" For this reason he gave the Sino-American relationship a great deal of his personal attention.[41]

Political circumstances and domestic timing of normalization. The president's reluctance early on to move China forward on the agenda reflected the pragmatic reality that he had a number of foreign policy matters (such as the Panama Canal treaties) that had to be gotten through Congress first. This fact precluded his taking any important initiative on China that might further energize conservative opposition in Congress.[42] Timing became the most important factor. Through Brzezinski's efforts the president began to see how normalization in the first term could become politically advantageous. Emphasizing trade and expanded commercial contacts with China, while maintaining arms sales to Taiwan, had domestic appeal with Taiwan supporters and a popular anti-Soviet tinge for the policy hawks. By balancing SALT, the Chinese would be reassured and the administration could demonstrate domestically their attempts to enhance the U.S. strategic position. After the Panama Canal treaties were completed, the administration began highlighting China in public statements. It proceeded carefully and attempted to recreate the sense of inevitability that had been so successful for President Nixon.[43]

There was a window of opportunity to exploit, from late 1978 until summer 1979, if electoral politics were to be avoided. Hard-liners argued that a SALT agreement should not be reached first because normalization would be seen as weak by conservatives rather than as anti-Soviet. Holbrooke saw the administration's strategy as one to recreate the phenomena of 1971–1972, when simultaneous movement toward both China and the Soviets was seen as reinforcing and politically beneficial. Brown thought that if normalization did not come by early 1979, it might have to wait.

Working together to cut off domestic debate for a time, the administration proposed a series of interrelated executive-branch moves—Brzezinski's trip, secret talks conducted by Leonard Woodcock, a possible second Vance trip, and a presidential announcement—and only then followed by congressional action. The hope was that this combination would increase the chances for normalization to be completed no later than mid-1979, when domestic political concerns would again emerge.[44] First, Brzezinski's visit to Beijing signaled to China that the administration was ready to devote significant attention to normalization. Second, secret talks accompanied by minor public actions such as reducing troops on Taiwan would take place. Third, an agreement with Vance would be followed by consulting with Congress and informing Taiwan. Finally, there would be a presidential announcement and a visit of Huang Hua or Deng Xiaoping to the United States. The real decision involving timing was to proceed in fall 1978.[45]

After Brzezinski's trip, two options were proposed. First, a sequential negotiating strategy was proposed, supported by Vance, in which Woodcock would broach the easiest issue with the Chinese first (postnormalization representation on Taiwan) and then move to more difficult issues such as arms sales to Taiwan. A second option, supported by Brzezinski, was to have Woodcock lay out the position comprehensively, even including a possible draft of the communiqué. The advantage of the first approach was that it lengthened the negotiating process; its disadvantage was that the Chinese might see it as insufficiently serious. Brzezinski's concern was that Vance's approach would give the president little opportunity to turn back without high political costs and damage to future relations with China.[46] During a June 20 meeting of the president, Vance, Brzezinski, Brown, and Chief of Staff Hamilton Jordan, Brzezinski got many of the things he wanted, including keeping the group small and the talks confidential, and designating December 15 as a possible target date. As Woodcock entered negotiations, however, he proceeded in a step-by-step fashion, focusing in order on the nature of the U.S. postnormalization presence on Taiwan, the statements on the occasion of normalization, U.S. trade with Taiwan, and the nature of the joint communiqué.[47]

Assuming success in its negotiations, the administration's congressional strategy was to pursue a lean, vague version once legislation to change Taiwan's status was presented to Congress. "The Chinese weren't going to like anything, so the less it looked as if we were perpetuating the language of the treaties, particularly those relating to security, the one that bothered them the most, and the less there was that implied a continuing U.S. commitment to Taiwan, the better off we would be. So that was the version that eventually the president signed off on." The initial draft taken to the Hill had no congressional input. It was put together in secret with Brzezinski, Oksenberg, Holbrooke, and Lake driving the simple version that caused so many problems from a domestic perspective.[48]

Jimmy Carter's official statement following the December 15 announcement was designed to sell normalization as a win-win scenario. The administration argued that the establishment of diplomatic relations would "contribute to the welfare of the American people, to the stability of Asia where the United States has major security and economic interests, and to the peace of the entire world." Carter also maintained that his policy would not jeopardize a SALT agreement with the Soviets or expose Taiwan to an attack from the PRC. In fact, this offered a chance "to bring diplomatic relations into line with political reality and give the United States a vast new market and political partner in Asia and elsewhere in the world."[49] Taiwan itself lived by trade, and the best guarantee of its security was access to foreign markets.

To bolster his position with Congress, Carter insisted that China intended to resolve the Taiwanese situation peacefully. The administration was helped by the PRC because it did not publicly challenge the president's pledge to protect Taiwan and avoided threats to use armed force to liberate Taiwan. The president noted to Deng, "Any reference to patience or peaceful resolution on your part to the Congress or to the public would be very helpful." For his part, Deng wanted the United States to be very prudent on future arms sales to Taiwan and to urge Taiwan to engage in negotiations with the Chinese government.[50] Repeatedly, the president argued that Taiwan's security was adequately protected and emphasized that the strong relationship with Taiwan would continue in commercial, cultural, and other matters without official government representation. The administration would seek special legislation to permit this kind of exchange with the people of Taiwan.[51]

The administration asserted it was a no-lose situation because

Taiwan had a strong military, and the pragmatic new leadership of China (which had moved past radicalism toward a policy of aggressive modernization and foreign trade) understood that any attempt to militarily take over Taiwan would threaten U.S. interests and jeopardize relations with its friends and allies. The administration emphasized that it was almost impossible for China to take control of Taiwan by force except at so great a cost it would be the sole Chinese foreign policy objective at the expense of others, including their concern over the Soviets and Vietnam.[52]

In his statement following the January 31, 1979, formal signing, Carter argued it was time to make interaction with the PRC routine rather than a matter of headlines: "We've charted a new and irreversible course toward a firmer, more constructive, and a more hopeful relationship." He noted that he shared many common perspectives with Deng and in many areas shared similar goals, including "a world of security and peace, a world of both diversity and stability, a world of independent nations free of outside domination."[53] Talking points on China normalization stressed that this relationship served the best interests of the United States through constructive, nonmilitary, economic and cultural involvement with the nation that governed a quarter of the world's population. Already over a hundred other nations including Japan and all of Europe recognized China's reality. Normalization would bring stability to the world where the United States had fought three wars in thirty-five years.[54]

The failure to consult prominent congressional leaders during the decision process, however, created immediate trouble. Most controversial, the United States signed the agreement with China without an explicit guarantee that force would not be used to retake Taiwan. With the formal change of status for China and Taiwan, opponents worked hard to block the president. Gerald Ford voiced "terse" approval while Senator Barry Goldwater called it a "cowardly act." The criticism from angry conservative (and some moderate) senators indicated the president would face a fight in Congress.[55] Hard-liners like Goldwater challenged the president on the grounds that he had not obtained congressional permission to terminate the mutual defense treaty with Taiwan, but the courts upheld that the president did not need congressional approval to abrogate the treaty.[56]

Not consulting Congress proved costly. According to Harry Thayer, country director for China during the normalization period, members of Congress felt the administration had not consulted them adequately: "It simply was a case of just not estimating correctly how this package that we put together would sell." The abrogation of the defense treaty created the most outrage, with "many of those opposed to the administration policy absolutely convinced that the administration was engaging in an immoral act by breaking relations with Taiwan."[57] Herbert J. Hansell, who was the legal adviser at the State Department, agreed that mistakes were made in the administration's dealings with Congress. He noted that disagreements between Vance and Brzezinski over how bound they were by political commitments to Congress or Taiwan exacerbated the situation. The national security adviser felt the United States had to move ahead without prior notification to Congress or to the Taiwanese (even though some commitments were made to Congress that there would be ample prior notice). The administration proceeded with Brzezinski's recommendation against Vance's advice.[58]

Ultimately, the urgent lobbying of the administration and Carter's veto threat mitigated congressional outrage over the change in Taiwan's status. This halted the harshest language suggested by the ranking Republican on the Foreign Relations Committee, Senator Jacob Javits (NY), who wanted the legislation to read that Taiwan was separate from China and that the United States "would consider any use of force by Peking against Taiwan a direct threat to American security." Once congressional leaders removed explicit terms of the U.S. commitment to Taiwan, the president accepted the language that declared a continued U.S. interest in Taiwan's security. Carter went so far as to say that he and future presidents retained the option of using force to protect Taiwan.[59]

Supporting Conditions—Controlling the Procedures of Debate and Building Coalitions

In the two years leading up to normalization, Brzezinski gained greater control of the foreign policy agenda and the president's ear. Once he secured his May 1978 trip, he could more directly shape China policy and determine who was involved. As Woodcock's negotiations proceeded, Brzezinski increased his personal consultations with the head of the Chinese liaison office in Washington and provided briefings to them on U.S. policy.[60]

Brzezinski also became more proprietary and nervous about the activities of the State Department as normalization negotiations proceeded. For example, reports that *Time* magazine's Strobe Talbott had learned at the time of normalization of the State Department's consultations about the best way to end the mutual defense treaty with Taiwan led Brzezinski to call for tighter control.[61] Knowledge of what went on was restricted to the East Asian Bureau in the State Department (i.e., excluding entities like Policy Planning).[62] In one specific example, the national security adviser also convinced the president to move up the public announcement by two weeks to December 15 while Vance was on a trip to the Middle East. According to Vance, Brzezinski excluded his aides (Warren Christopher and Dick Holbrooke) from the decision-making process, and they were unable to inform him of the changed announcement date until after the decision had been made. The announcement came at an inopportune time for arms control supporters—just one week before Vance was to meet with Andrei Gromyko in Geneva to discuss a possible summit. The move effectively pushed SALT back with the Soviets.[63] In addition, Herbert Hansell claims that if Vance had been in Washington, Congress would have been consulted and the resulting domestic problems might have been avoided.[64]

An important reason Brzezinski was able to push forward was that he received early support from important players like the Department of Defense and prominent members of Congress who shared his concerns over SALT and the Soviets. Secretary of Defense Brown shared Brzezinski's belief that China was strategically important as a counter to the Soviet threat. Prominent members of Congress such as Senator Henry M. "Scoop" Jackson (D-Washington) supported Brzezinski's efforts because approaching China was corrective action for a policy that was weak toward the Soviets.[65] On issues such as the sale of dual-use technology to China, the Department of Defense worked in concert with Brzezinski. They both were prepared to support the sale of select items to the PRC that were not sold to the Soviets.[66] This did not mean abandoning Taiwan, because they also supported a close tie to Taiwan in the form of selling it more advanced fighters (the debate centered on the more advanced F-4 versus the F-5E) because it would keep Taiwan going for ten to fifteen years and allow the United States to finish its previous commitments.[67]

Brzezinski's efforts broadened the nature of contact with the PRC and naturally opened the door for multiple departments and offices to be involved in shaping postnormalization cooperation in such areas as developing China's energy resources, student exchanges, launch services to space, and agriculture, medicine/public health, and the geosciences.[68] Science and technology cooperation served as a means to deepen U.S. relations with the PRC (i.e., exerting influence on the PRC's future domestic and international orientation) while potentially moderating Soviet foreign policy conduct. Simultaneously, U.S. commercial opportunities would broaden, and major development projects could prepare the domestic political ground.[69] A trip Brzezinski arranged in July 1979, led by Frank Press, Carter's science and technology adviser, and including the heads of NASA, the National Institutes of Health, and other science and technology leaders, followed by Secretary of Energy James Schlesinger's trip, gained him new bureaucratic allies. The strategy to secure executive approval for the U.S.-China trade agreement (October 2, 1979) included on the executive side broad involvement from the State Department, the Commerce Department, the U.S. Trade Representative (USTR), NSC, the Office of Management and Budget (OMB), the Treasury Department, the Export Import Bank (EXIM), the Agriculture Department, and the Overseas Private Investment Corporation (OPIC).[70]

The strategy to deepen Sino-American cooperative relations after normalization included scheduling a number of trips to China by various members of the cabinet, "thereby involving every key policy maker and every major bureaucracy in a constructive relationship with China" and effectively creating a wider constituency favoring a broadened relationship.[71] Charles (Chas) Freeman, country director for China from 1979 to 1981, stated that the purpose was to knit the two bureaucracies in Beijing and Washington together. "But I have to say that, politically, the motivation for doing all this was very clear, and that is that those of us charged with promoting U.S.-China relations wished to ensure that the relationship was sufficiently broad and engaged a sufficient number of bureaucracies and special interests on both sides so that it would be insulated, to some extent, from political cross currents."[72] Beyond the executive branch, governors, congressional delegations, and business delegations made trips to China. The high-level travel had the effect of concentrating the mind of the bureaucracy on that task and the need to make progress. In the words of Chas Freeman, "Trip-driven diplomacy accelerated the negotiation of framework agreements and the like."[73] Table 4.1 outlines strategic framing of China policy in the Carter administration.

Understanding the Postnormalization Tilt Toward China

After normalization, the series of high-level contacts dramatically increased the scope of interaction between China and the United States.

Table 4.1   Components of Jimmy Carter's China Policy Frame

Problem diagnosis	• Competing priorities on arms control led one faction to see China as a threat to détente and the other to see China as a source of leverage against the Soviets
Themes that resonated with president and public	
Presidential beliefs	• China and East Asia a secondary priority • Personal priority was arms control with Soviets
Policy themes	• Brzezinski argues Soviets cannot be trusted and normalization needs to be early priority • Vance sees PRC normalization as a threat to arms control values
Political considerations	• Full foreign policy agenda • Brzezinski bolsters position by linking normalization to domestic SALT discussion • Decision not to consult Congress until after normalization agreement made with PRC • Opportunity taken before electoral politics a factor
Supporting conditions/tactics	• Bureaucratic infighting until Brzezinski gains control of policymaking agenda and discussions • Brzezinski involves broad group of cabinet-level actors to widen the coalition of support

Once Treasury Secretary Michael Blumenthal's negotiations in March 1979 resolved the thirty-year-old dispute on Chinese assets in the United States and U.S. assets confiscated by the Chinese Communists, the door was open for trade negotiations. During her trip in May, Commerce Secretary Juanita Kreps made progress in bilateral commercial relations, with particular focus on a trade agreement. Both efforts were integral to the trade agreement, signed on July 7, 1979, that opened the door to more forward, expansive trade ties and possible most-favored-nation status for China.[74] By midsummer the president was willing to consider MFN for China alone (thus de-linking it from the Soviets) once the Senate had begun considering the SALT II Treaty.

On his August 25–September 1 visit to Beijing, Vice President Walter Mondale announced the expansion of economic ties, including granting MFN status to China in the near future. To show his commitment, the president ordered the State Department to expedite the opening of consulates in Shanghai and Guangzhou and to conclude the civil aviation and cultural exchange agreements during the vice president's visit.[75] From this point forward a distinction was made between technology transfers for the Chinese and for the Soviets.

The expanded commercial relationship—exemplified by the trips of Michael Blumenthal and Juanita Kreps—and the evolving strategic relationship simultaneously made the U.S.-China partnership an essential one with positive overtones. Juanita Kreps's talking points reveal these dynamics. First, China was seen as an important market that other competitor nations such as Japan, Germany, and Britain had already tapped. A trade agreement was needed to foster MFN and reciprocity in reducing trade barriers and to establish procedures to facilitate business growth. Second, closer commercial relations were presented as a potential benefit to both countries that could aid efforts for worldwide peace and security.[76] Her media guide noted that voicing optimism for a successful outcome of the talks was important. Throughout her trip, Kreps was to use press conferences to make clear the importance of the kinds of agreements under discussion and also to emphasize the interrelationship of those agreements and their importance to the "totality" of relations between the two nations.[77]

NSC efforts to develop security relations with China included encouraging the PRC to join Geneva arms control talks, negotiating a hot-line agreement, and engaging China in more sophisticated discussion than before concerning nuclear strategy, as well as discussing in greater depth Soviet combat capabilities and strategies. Regarding technology transfer, the administration discussed making China subject only to the controls applied to non-Communist countries. This "Yugoslavia exception" would ensure a separate and less restrictive list than that applied to the Soviet Union. It would also require amending the formal regulations of the Coordination Committee for Multilateral Export Controls (COCOM) so that cases in particular categories approved for China would not set a precedent for export of the item to other Communist countries. A list of items that could be sold to China but not the Soviets was established.[78] These steps would be taken to secure a friendly relationship and to successfully modernize China into a force that could contribute to global balance and peace in Asia. Economic, political, and cultural ties with China would be expanded to bolster ties to the Organization for Economic Cooperation and Development (OECD) countries and to ensure maximum U.S. benefit. The question was how to promote the relationship. Steps would begin by liberalizing export control procedures, differentiating China from the Soviets in COCOM controls, and approving U.S. dual-use technology and military support equipment for export. The United States would support bringing China into the arms control dialogue, help develop key industries, support trade expansion, and normalize commercial relations.[79]

Harold Brown's trip in January 1980 (suggested as early as July 1979 by Brzezinski), coming just after the Soviet invasion of Afghanistan, signaled the greatest movement to date toward strategic and military collaboration with China.[80] Following the trip, the Pentagon announced that it would consider selling certain kinds of military equipment to China, including the Landsat D and Western Geophysical radar systems and the Over-the-Horizon Radar that would provide an early warning in case of Soviet attack. On Afghanistan, the United States intended to supply the Afghan rebels with weapons covertly and proposed formal intelligence exchanges with the Chinese on this subject. These announcements came just as the administration publicly acknowledged its willingness to consider selling China high-technology items, such as computers, on a case-by-case basis. The Pentagon called this change an "incremental step" in broadening ties between the two countries, in light of changed circumstances.[81]

The talking points provided for Harold Brown's visit to China further reveal how the emphasis on the shared anti-Soviet intellectual framework helped move forward sales of dual-use technology. Brown argued "the Soviet threat is serious, Afghanistan is a historically significant development, but the strength of the U.S., our allies and China is sufficient to cope with the Soviet Union if we all exhibit will and carry out our respective responsibilities."[82] Brown's visit initiated high-level, formal military contacts similar to those conducted previously in the economic, scientific, and cultural realms. The basis for shared interests now focused on the global military balance, respective security planning, and the shared interest in limiting the growing Soviet threat. The increased bilateral contacts and consultations between the two defense establishments would expand their capacity to act in mutually reinforcing ways when their interests coincided.[83]

In his January 9 news conference, Brown pointed to Mondale's August trip as the point where the basis of common strategic objectives began. Brown discussed U.S. willingness to transfer technology to the

PRC on a case-by-case basis, even civilian technology that had potential military applications, and he did not rule out selling arms to the PRC.[84] The Soviet invasion of Afghanistan was the framing event that most helped the Pentagon's cause with a reluctant Congress and public. The administration and congressional leaders now shared the same reference point in regard to China policy and saw the Soviets as the primary threat to U.S. interests.

To placate potential domestic critics, on his return Harold Brown gave a "full and candid" briefing to a select group of congressional leaders, including some administration critics such as Senator Javits. Given the Soviet invasion of Afghanistan, the administration now anticipated no hostility on the issue of technology transfers to the Chinese. They attributed the full congressional support they received for the policy to the fact that Brown stressed the "step-by-step and cautious approach to development of the relationship. No one in the room openly advocated an alliance with China and none of the members suggested by their comments and questions that they would be concerned if our relationship with China developed too fast." Congressional leaders were fully reassured on this point.[85] To illustrate the change in political climate, MFN status for China drew support even from Senator Jackson, author of earlier trade restrictions that affected both China and Russia. To Jackson the new policies were a proper antidote to the "misguided policy of evenhandedness" toward the two Communist powers. MFN tariff status for China went into effect on February 1, 1980.[86]

Conclusion

The essential task for this chapter has been to discuss how and why the advisers' frames, along with other factors, influenced the tilt toward China. The multiple levels in the consensus-building game (international, domestic, and internal) show how considerations on one level directly affected outcomes on other levels. At the international level, Chinese hostility and threats softened as Soviet hostility increased. Defining Soviet behavior as aggressive, and arguing for closer relations with the PRC, was made easier for hard-liners in the Carter administration by Soviet activities in the Horn of Africa and their invasion of Afghanistan. China also lowered its hostile rhetoric at the most crucial point—when Congress considered the Taiwan Relations Act. (Passage of the TRA temporarily took a potentially volatile issue off the table.) As members of Congress began to see the Soviet Union as a strategic threat, they came to accept the administration's frame of the situation and thus the need for a strategic relationship with China. These circumstances made it easier for the administration to go forward as it desired. By looking inside the administration it is possible to see the process by which the anti-Soviet frame came to dominate the internal policy agenda. By 1979, the national security adviser had gained the upper hand in making China policy. Once the president adopted Brzezinski's hard-line foreign policy frame, Brzezinski was in a stronger position vis-à-vis Vance.

The Carter administration case illustrates how characterizing the international situation as threatening was used to justify the administration's approach to the PRC. From Vance's "evenhanded" strategy based on the need to balance the administration's China policy with initiatives toward the Soviets, the policy eventually evolved into an anti-Soviet one. As noted, on the domestic front Brzezinski gradually built the basis of the strategic relationship by taking positions on MFN that set the groundwork to de-link U.S. policy toward the Chinese from the Soviets as it broadened his basis of support. Once China was treated as a separate case on MFN, it also could be treated separately on arms transfers and in other areas. Interestingly, Brzezinski used growing commercial ties (or "low" policy) as a means to bolster his strategic, "high" foreign policy goals.

Throughout this process, President Carter seemed particularly vulnerable to the influence of his advisers. He displayed the characteristics of an uncommitted thinker. Because he had little experience or knowledge in this area, he was more likely to exhibit fragmented and contradictory beliefs.[87] These circumstances also made the president more open to change. During the framing struggle, Zbigniew Brzezinski gained the upper hand by playing to Carter's fears about the Soviet threat and by cultivating allies inside the administration and within Congress. Soviet behavior itself also played a role in that Brzezinski's negative frames of Soviet motives seemed to be confirmed. The doves could not overcome this frame because of an increasingly conservative domestic audience and an international context that seemed to support hard-line interpretations of Soviet behavior. Following the Soviet invasion of Afghanistan, Carter became unwilling to give the USSR the benefit of the doubt in any area.

In the climate that developed, it cannot be ignored that China also played the "American card." Particularly as Brzezinski gained ascendancy, the Chinese used the media as an important part of the negotiating process. Richard Soloman describes Deng Xiaoping's efforts before and during his January 1980 visit as "pump priming" or setting the discussion agenda. The Chinese did this by discrediting Vance after his visit, playing up to Brzezinski on his visit, and by Deng Xiaoping's statements that helped undermine domestic fears about the Chinese approach to Taiwan.[88] Their efforts effectively placated many of Carter's domestic critics.

By implication the relationship seemed ready to move beyond generalities to an alliance in response to the invasion of Afghanistan. According to Chas Freeman, however, "the Chinese, rather quickly, I think, . . . concluded that in fact the Soviets were more likely to become bogged down and regret their Afghan adventure than to use it as a springboard for further advance."[89] Additionally, after Carter's electoral defeat, a new U.S. president came into office with a much different attitude toward the PRC.

Notes

1. Gallup Poll conducted in April 1977.
2. An earlier version by the author of this case study focusing on advisory manipulation in China policymaking appeared in *Asian Affairs: An American Review* as "Explaining Change in the Carter Administration's China Policy: Foreign Policy Advisor Manipulation of the Policy Agenda." Unlike that paper, this chapter directly links China policymaking in the Carter administration to an analysis of strategic framing; it also benefits from new sources such as the oral histories from the Association of Diplomatic Historians.
3. Garrison, *Games Advisors Play,* 11–15.
4. Paul Kreisberg, oral history interview, April 8, 1989; Thayer interview.
5. Presidential Review Memorandum (PRM)/NSC-24 to the Vice President, Secretary of State, and Secretary of Defense, "PRC," no date, USSR-US Conference, March 1995, Briefing Book 1, Vertical File, USSR-US Conference, May 6–9, 1994 (2) through USSR-Vienna Summit (Box), Carter Presidential Library. See also Thayer and Kriesberg interviews.
6. Cyrus Vance, *Hard Choices: Critical Years in America's Foreign Policy*, 45–46, 77–78; Zbigniew Brzezinski, *Power and Principle: Memoirs of a National Security Advisor*, 199.
7. "China Policy Review: Recent Developments," no date, NSA Staff Materials, Box 4, Armacost Chron File, July 1–14, 1977, Carter Presidential Library.
8. Letter from President Carter to Cyrus Vance, NSA Staff Materials, Box 4, Armacost Chron. File, August 16–25, 1977, Carter Presidential Library.
9. Charles Mohr, "Carter Orders Steps to Increase Ability to Meet War Threats," *New York Times*, August 26, 1977, A7; Fox Butterfield, "Vance Finishes Visit with Peking Leaders," A1; Memo from Dennis Chapmann to

Rick Indefurth, "Secretary Vance's PRC Trip," Chief of Staff Jordan, Camp David, 1979 (changes, etc.) through Iran, March 1980, Box 34, File: China, 1977, Carter Presidential Library; Soloman, *U.S. PRC Political Negotiations, 1967–1984: An Annotated Chronology (U)*, National Security Archives Collection: China and the United States, 62–63; Richard H. Soloman, *U.S. PRC Political Negotiations, 1967–1984*, National Security Archives Collection: China and the United States, 72.

10. Memo from Peter Bourne to Dick Holbrooke on the PRC, November 2, 1977, Box: Staff Offices, Special Assistant to the President—Bourne, Box 33, File Holbrooke, Dick, June 14–November 2, 1977 (CF, O/A 154), Carter Presidential Library.

11. Memo from Zbigniew Brzezinski for the President, "Trip to Northeast Asia," no date, USSR-US Conference, March 1995, Briefing Book 1, Vertical File, USSR-US Conference, May 6–9, 1994 (2) through USSR-Vienna Summit (Box), Carter Presidential Library; Brzezinski, *Power and Principle*, 187–190; Jimmy Carter, *Keeping Faith: Memoirs of a President*, 193–194; Garthoff, *Détente and Confrontation*, 766; Vance, *Hard Choices*, 84–92.

12. Department of State Briefing Paper and Memo for Zbigniew Brzezinski, "U.S.-PRC Relations: Consideration for Your Trip," no date, National Security Archives postpublication Collection: China and the United States.

13. Memo from Zbigniew Brzezinski to Leonard Woodcock, no date, Leonard Woodcock response memo, November 22, 1977, and Memo from Zbigniew Brzezinski to the President, "Possible China Visit," November 22, 1977, Zbigniew Brzezinski Collection, File: China, PRC—Brzezinski's Trip: November 19, 1977–May 14, 1978, Box 9, China, PRC—Alpha Channel: February 1972–November 1978, Carter Presidential Library.

14. Memo from Michael Armacost and Michel Oksenberg to Zbigniew Brzezinski, "Your Trip to Japan, China and Korea," and Memo from Zbigniew Brzezinski to the President, "Trip to the Far East," February 27, 1978, Zbigniew Brzezinski Collection, File: China, PRC—Brzezinski's Trip: November 19, 1977–May 14, 1978, Box 9, China, PRC—Alpha Channel: February 1972–November 1978, Carter Presidential Library; Abramowitz interview.

15. Soloman, *U.S. PRC Political Negotiations, 1967–1984: An Annotated Chronology*, National Security Archives Collection: China and the United States, 64.

16. Garthoff, *Détente and Confrontation*, 772–773.

17. Fox Butterfield, "Brzezinski in China; The Stress Was on Common Concerns"; see also Soloman, *U.S. PRC Political Negotiations, 1967–1984: An Annotated Chronology*, National Security Archives Collection: China and the United States, 64; Vance, *Hard Choices*, 80–83.

18. Kreisberg interview.

19. Thayer interview.

20. Memo from Zbigniew Brzezinski to the President, NSC Weekly Report no. 66, July 7, 1978, ZB Collection, Box 41, Subject file, File: Weekly

Report to the President, 61–71: June 1978–September 1978, Carter Presidential Library.

21. Brzezinski, *Power and Principle*, 53–54; see also Vance, *Hard Choices*, 114–116.

22. Memo from Cyrus Vance to Leonard Woodcock, June 22, 1978, Memo from Cyrus Vance to Leonard Woodcock, June 28, 1978, and Leonard Woodcock, "Report to the White House," July 5, 1978, Zbigniew Brzezinski Collection, Geographic File, Box 9, China (People's Republic of)—Alpha Channel: February 1972–November 1978, Carter Presidential Library; Briefing memo from Herbert Hansell to the Secretary of State, "The Legal Dimensions of Normalization," Staff Offices Counsel Lipshutz, Box 7, File: China Briefing Book Tabs 1–10, undated (CF, O/A 715), Carter Presidential Library.

23. Soloman, *U.S. PRC Political Negotiations, 1967–1984: An Annotated Chronology*, National Security Archives Collection: China and the United States, 70; Garthoff, *Détente and Confrontation*, 776–777; Vance, *Hard Choices*, 117–120.

24. Gallup Poll, released January 1979.

25. Gallup Poll, AIPO, released February 26, 1979.

26. Jay Mathews, "China Warns Factions Against Change So Rapid That Stability Is Threatened"; Robert G. Kaiser, "House and Senate Adopt Taiwan Bills," A10.

27. Herbert J. Hansell, oral history interview, March 29, 1995.

28. Vance, *Hard Choices*, 76.

29. Abramowitz interview.

30. Memo from David Anderson to Christine Dodson (State) with voluminous attachments, "Re: Vance Testimony at Zablocki Hearings," June 17, 1978, WHCF, Subject File, Box FG-151, File: FG33-11, January 20, 1977–January 20, 1981, Carter Presidential Library.

31. Brzezinski, *Power and Principle*, 415–419; Garthoff, *Détente and Confrontation*, 777; Vance, *Hard Choices*, 390–391.

32. Memo from EA to ZB, "Evening Report," June 2, 1978, Box: National Security Affairs, Staff Material, Far East, Box 1, File Armacost Evening and Weekly Reports File March–April 1978, Carter Presidential Library.

33. Memo from Brzezinski to the President, "The Meeting with Deng," no date, Zbigniew Brzezinski Collection, File: China, PRC—President's Meeting with (Vice Premier) Deng Xiaoping: December 19, 1978–October 3, 1979, Box 9, China, PRC—Alpha Channel: February 1972–November 1978, Carter Presidential Library.

34. Kreisberg interview.

35. USSR-US Conference, March 1995: Transcript (II), Transcript of the Proceedings of a Conference of Russian and U.S. Policymakers and Scholars, March 24, Session 4, China, held at Harbor Beach Resort, Fort Lauderdale, Fla., March 23–26, 1995, edited by Svetlana Savranskaya and David Welch (uncorrected 1st draft), sponsored by the Carter-Brezhnev Project, Thomas J. Watson Jr. Institute, Brown University, Carter Presidential Library.

36. Garthoff, *Détente and Confrontation*, 764–765.

37. Carter, *Keeping Faith,* 188–191; Garthoff, *Détente and Confrontation,* 761–762.

38. Memo from Brzezinski to the President, "Summary of April 11 Meeting on Korea and China," April 18, 1978, Box 7, NSA Staff Material, Far East: File Armacost Chron File, April 11–18, 1978, Carter Presidential Library.

39. Memo from the President to Brzezinski on purpose of sending ZB to China, May 17, 1978, USSR-US Conference, March 1995, Briefing Book 1, Vertical File, USSR-US Conference, Mary 6–9, 1994 (2) through USSR-Vienna Summit (Box), Carter Presidential Library.

40. Minutes of SCC Meeting on the Horn of Africa, February 22, 1978, Cable News Network Cold War Series.

41. Brzezinski, *Power and Principle*, 196; Memo from Brzezinski to Jimmy Carter, "Meeting with Senator Jackson on China," May 4, 1978, and Memo from Brzezinski to the President, "Meeting with Senator Kennedy on China," May 5, 1978, USSR-US Conference, March 1995, Briefing Book 1, Vertical File, USSR-US Conference, May 6-9, 1994 (2) through USSR-Vienna Summit (Box), Carter Presidential Library.

42. Fox Butterfield, "Mr. Vance Will Find the Main Topic in China Is Still Taiwan"; see also Brzezinski, *Power and Principle,* 199; Carter, *Keeping Faith,* 190–191; Garthoff, *Détente and Confrontation,* 762; Vance, *Hard Choices,* 78–83.

43. Memo from Michel Oksenberg and Michael Armacost to Zbigniew Brzezinski, "Strategy for Trying to Normalize Relations with the PRC in 1978," NSA Staff Materials, Box 6, Armacost Chron File, March 22–31, 1978, Carter Presidential Library; Memo from Cyrus Vance, Harold Brown, and Zbigniew Brezinski for the President, May 10, 1978, National Security Archives postpublication Collection: China and the United States.

44. Memo from Michel Oksenberg and Michael Armacost to Zbigniew Brzezinski, "Strategy for Trying to Normalize Relations with the PRC in 1978," NSA Staff Materials, Box 6, Armacost Chron File, March 22–31, 1978, Carter Presidential Library.

45. Memo from Holbrooke, Abramowitz, Armacost, and Oksenberg to Vance, Brown, and Brzezinski, "Issues for Decision on Korea and China," April 4, 1978, NSA Staff Materials, Box 6, Armacost Chron File, April 1–10, 1978, Carter Presidential Library.

46. Memo from Zbigniew Brzezinski to the President, "Next Moves on China: Woodcock's Approach," June 13, 1978, NSA Staff Materials, Box 7, Armacost Chron File, June 14–30, 1978, Carter Presidential Library.

47. Brzezinski, *Power and Principle*, 224–228.

48. Kreisberg interview.

49. Soloman, *U.S. PRC Political Negotiations, 1967–1984: An Annotated Chronology*, National Security Archives Collection: China and the United States, 73; Carter, *Keeping Faith*; Vance, *Hard Choices*, 110–120; China Talking Points, January 11, 1979, Memorandum from Jerry Rafshoon to members of the cabinet and senior staff, Staff Offices Counsel Lipshutz, Box 7, File: China, Goldwater v. Carter, 1979 (CF,O/A 710), Carter Presidential Library.

50. White House Memorandum of Conversation on the President's Third Meeting with PRC Vice Premier Deng Xiaoping, January 1979, pp. 2–4, 10, National Security Archives postpublication Collection: China and the United States.

51. United States Statement, "Diplomatic Relations Between the United States and the People's Republic of China," and President Carter's Remarks following the Address to the Nation, December 15, 1978, (Doc. no. 00448), National Security Archives Collection: China and the United States.

52. China Talking Points, January 11, 1979, Memorandum from Jerry Rafshoon to members of the cabinet and senior staff, Staff Offices Counsel Lipshutz, Box 7, File: China, Goldwater v. Carter, 1979 (CF,O/A 710), Carter Presidential Library.

53. Agreement Between the Government of the United States of America and the Government of the People's Republic of China on the Mutual Establishment of Consular Relations and the Opening of Consulates General, January 31, 1979 (Doc. no. 00453), National Security Archives Collection: China and the United States; Don Oberdorfer, "Teng Hints Use of Force Along Vietnam Border."

54. China Talking Points, January 11, 1979, Memorandum from Jerry Rafshoon to members of the cabinet and senior staff, Staff Offices Counsel Lipshutz, Box 7, File: China, Goldwater v. Carter, 1979 (CF,O/A 710), Carter Presidential Library.

55. Jay Mathews, "Sudden Shift Stuns Taiwan; Leaders Embittered: Chiang Says U.S. Broke Assurances," A1; David S. Broder and Bill Peterson, "U.S. to Normalize Ties with Peking."

56. Department of State Action Memorandum to Deputy Secretary from Herbert Hansell regarding the strategy to deal with plaintiffs of the Mutual Defense Treaty with Taiwan, and Memo for Brzezinski on Goldwater v. Carter, Staff Offices Counsel Lipshutz, Box 7, File: China, Goldwater v. Carter, 1979 (CF,O/A 710), Carter Presidential Library; Hansell interview.

57. Thayer interview.

58. Hansell interview.

59. Kaiser, "House and Senate Adopt Taiwan Bills," A10.

60. Brzezinksi, *Power and Principle*, 226.

61. Memo from Brzezinski to the President, "NSC Weekly Report no. 74," October 6, 1978, Zbigniew Brzezinski Collection, Box 42, Subject File, File: Weekly Reports to the President, 71-81: September 1978–December 1978, Carter Presidential Library.

62. Thayer interview.

63. Carter, *Keeping Faith*, 234; Vance, *Hard Choices*, 110–120; Soloman, *U.S. PRC Political Negotiations, 1967–1984: An Annotated Chronology*, National Security Archives Collection: China and the United States, 73.

64. Hansell interview.

65. Memo from Brzezinski to Jimmy Carter, "Meeting with Senator Jackson on China" May 4, 1978, and Memo from Brzezinski for the President, "Meeting with Senator Kennedy on China," May 5, 1978, USSR-US

Conference, March 1995, Briefing Book 1, Vertical File, USSR-US Conference May 6–9, 1994 (2) through USSR-Vienna Summit (Box), Carter Presidential Library.

66. Memo from Far East Bureau for Zbigniew Brzezsiniki, March 9, 1978, weekly report; Memo from Oksenberg to Brzezinski Only, no date; Memo from Oksenberg to Brzezinski, March 1978, Box: National Security Affairs, Staff Material, Far East, Box 1, File Armacost Evening and Weekly Reports File March–April 1978, Carter Presidential Library; Garthoff, *Détente and Confrontation*, 784.

67. Memorandum of Conversation, "Summary Minutes of the April 11, 1978, Meeting on Korea and China," White House Situation Room, NSA Staff Materials, Armacost Chron File, April 11–18, 1978, Carter Presidential Library.

68. Presidential Directive/NSC-43, "US-China Scientific and Technological Relationships," November 3, 1978 (Doc. no. 00447), pp. 1–3; National Security Archives Collection: China and the United States; see also Memorandum of Understanding on Agricultural Exchange Between the United States of America and the People's Republic of China, September 1978 (Doc. no. 00446), pp. 1–3, National Security Archives Collection: China and the United States. An accord focusing on scientific and technological cooperation was finalized on January 31, 1979, when diplomatic relations were established (this agreement is available in the National Security Archives Collection: China and the United States, Doc. no. 00452).

69. Memo from Frank Press to the President Through the National Security Adviser, "Chairman of PRC China S&T," Staff Offices Science and Technology Adviser to the President—Press; Box 6, File US-China Science and Technology, May 1977–August 1979, Carter Presidential Library.

70. Legislative Action Plan—U.S.-China Trade Agreement, October 1, 1979, National Security Affairs Staff Material, Far East, Box 8-64; File Albright (Madeline), Ad Hoc China Group, October 1979, Carter Presidential Library; Brzezinksi, *Power and Principle*, 226.

71. Brzezinski, *Power and Principle*, 417.

72. Freeman interview.

73. Ibid.

74. Confidential Briefing Paper from Department of Commerce to Juanita Kreps, January 1979 (Doc. no. 00449), Confidential Cable from Roy Stapleton, U.S. Embassy to Department of State, "Secretary Blumenthal's March 1 Press Conference," March 2, 1979 (Doc. no. 00458), Itinerary for Visit of Secretary of Commerce Juanita Kreps, "Media Briefing Schedule," May 1979 (Doc. no. 00463), National Security Archives Collection: China and the United States; see also Brzezinski, *Power and Principle*, 415–419; Garthoff, *Détente and Confrontation*, 777; Vance, *Hard Choices*, 390–391.

75. Memorandum for Secretary of State, et al., from Zbigniew Brzezinski, "Preparations for Vice President Mondale's Visit to the People's Republic of China," July 21, 1979 (Doc. no. 00466), National Security Archives Collection: China and the United States.

76. Media Briefing Schedule for Secretary of Commerce Juanita Kreps's

Trip to China, May 4–16, 1979 (Doc. no. 00463), p. 6, National Security Archives Collection: China and the United States.

77. Media Briefing Schedule for Secretary of Commerce Juanita Kreps's Trip to China, May 4–16, 1979 (Doc. no. 00463), pp. 1–9, National Security Archives Collection: China and the United States. The U.S. position is further detailed in the Issue Briefing Book for the Visit of Secretary of Commerce Juanita M. Kreps to the People's Republic of China, May 1979 (Doc. no. 00462), National Security Archives Collection: China and the United States.

78. Memo from Oksenberg to ZB on need for orderly decisional process for developing our security rel w/China, Box 68, National Security Affairs, Staff Material Far East; File: Platt Chron File, October 1979, Carter Presidential Library. At the time, there was confusion over the difference between weapons and the military equipment that could be sold to China. All those involved concluded it was important to make the criteria for such sales explicit because without it China would not know what the United States would sell and U.S. businesses would have no guidelines. Memo from Michel Oksenberg on Item for V-B-B Luncheon, "Sale of Military Equipment but Not Arms to the PRC," January 23, 1980, Zbigniew Brzezinski Collection, File: Meetings—Vance/Brown/Brzezinski: January 1980–February 1980, Box 34, Subject File, Carter Presidential Library; Memo from Richard Holbrooke, Nicholas Platt, and Michel Oksenberg to the Secretary of State, Secretary of Defense, and National Security Adviser, "Sale of Sensitive Equipment to China," January 22, 1980, Zbigniew Brzezinski Collection, File: Meetings—Vance/Brown/Brzezinski: January 1980–February 1980, Box 34, Subject File, Carter Presidential Library.

79. Memo from the Secretary of State for the President, "Your Meeting with Chinese Premier Hua Guofeng at Ohira Memorial Service," no date, National Security Archives postpublication Collection: China and the United States.

80. Memorandum for Zbigniew Brzezinski from Michel Oksenberg and Don Gregg, "NSC Meeting on China/Brown Trip," January 2, 1980 (Doc. no. 00480), pp. 1–2, National Security Archives Collection: China and the United States; see also "SCC Meeting, Afghanistan: Harold Brown's Trip to China," January 2, 1980 (Doc. no. 00481), pp. 1–2, National Security Archives Collection: China and the United States; Brzezinski, *Power and Principle*, 418–423; Garthoff, *Détente and Confrontation*, 782.

81. Talking Points for Harold Brown for Geng Biao–First Session, January 1980 (Doc. no. 00478); Talking Points to Harold Brown from NSC, January 1980 (Doc. no. 00479); Memorandum from Michel Oksenberg and Don Gregg for Zbigniew Brzezinski, "NSC Meeting on China/Brown Trip," January 2, 1980 (Doc. no. 00480), pp. 1–2; SCC Meeting, Afghanistan: Harold Brown's Trip to China, January 2, 19890 (Doc. no. 00481), National Security Archives Collection: China and the United States; Brzezinski, *Power and Principle*, 418–423; Garthoff, *Détente and Confrontation*, 782.

82. Objectives and Talking Points from NSC to Harold Brown, January 1980 (Doc. no. 00478), p. 1, National Security Archives Collection: China and the United States.

83. Talking Points for Harold Brown for Geng Biao–First Session, January 1980 (Doc. no. 00478), pp. 1–8; Banquet Speech of the Secretary of Defense, January 3, 1980 (Doc. no. 00482), pp. 1–5, National Security Archives Collection: China and the United States.

84. News Conference by Secretary of Defense Harold Brown—Beijing, China, January 9, 1980 (Doc. no. 00490), pp. 1–4, National Security Archives Collection: China and the United States; Soloman, *U.S. PRC Political Negotiations, 1967–1984: An Annotated Chronology*, National Security Archives Collection: China and the United States, 78–79.

85. Memorandum from Richard Holbrooke to the Secretary of State, January 23, 1980 (Doc. no. 00493), p. 1, National Security Archives Collection: China and the United States.

86. Helen Dewar and Richard L. Lyons, "Congress Begins Weighing China Trade Favors"; Michael Getler, "Pentagon Willing to Sell Chinese Some Equipment."

87. John Steinbrunner, *The Cybernetic Theory of Decision.*

88. Soloman, *U.S. PRC Political Negotiations, 1967–1984*, National Security Archives Collection: China and the United States, 70.

89. Freeman interview.

5

Developing a Strategic Partnership: Reagan and the China-Taiwan Balancing Act

Ronald Reagan ran for president determined to restore U.S. strength vis-à-vis the Soviet Union and U.S. honor around the world. A strong critic of the Nixon and Carter administrations' détente record, he also opposed Carter's normalization agreement with China. In his campaign and early rhetoric, Reagan called for the Taiwan Relations Act (TRA) and not the 1978 joint communiqué to be the basis for U.S. China policy. In one press statement before the election, Reagan stated, "I would not pretend . . . that the relationship we have now with Taiwan . . . is unofficial."[1] Any hint of abandoning Taiwan "offended his sense of the loyalty that old friends and longtime allies owed to one another."[2] This sympathy for Taiwan made it difficult to maintain a positive relationship with China in the early days of his administration.

To the Chinese the president's statements and commitment to Taiwan challenged the one-China policy established by Richard Nixon and "interfered" in China's internal affairs. In fact, Reagan's statements on Taiwan and the administration's arms sales policy created a recurring political crisis with China that remained unresolved for several years. The immediate issue was the potential sale of arms to Taiwan, particularly of advanced aircraft such as the F-5G, and how this influenced negotiations for a communiqué with China. According to Chas Freeman, Reagan's support for arms sales to Taiwan was a "conjunction of Ronald Reagan's . . . gut feeling that it was wrong to deprive a former ally and a friend of access to this very potent weapons system with the economic and political muscle that was behind it from Texas and

California."[3] Domestically two companies, Northrop (California) and General Dynamics (Texas), competed for the contract to sell the next generation of advanced fighters to Taiwan.

Many inside and outside the White House seemed to believe the sale would be approved with no questions asked. The problem was that even the least-sophisticated option, Northrop's F-5G, was a quantum leap above the other fighters previously sold to Taiwan, and its sale was guaranteed to give China fits. China's threat to downgrade relations if advanced fighters were sold convinced some that the United States faced the same situation as had the Dutch, whose relationship with China was downgraded when it sold Taiwan diesel submarines.[4] This was intolerable for a group in the State Department led by Secretary of State Alexander Haig who worked to formulate a policy that acknowledged China's central importance in U.S. strategic foreign policy goals—sometimes to the detriment of Reagan's Taiwan objectives. For conservative Taiwan supporters, such as National Security Adviser Richard Allen, Secretary of Defense Caspar Weinberger, and several members of the White House staff, the sale was a way to shore up the U.S. commitment to Taiwan in the wake of normalization.[5]

These competing orientations on the importance of China and Taiwan, respectively, to East Asian policy formed the basis for internal policy disagreements surrounding the arms sales issue and communiqué negotiations. What emerged was a dual policy that tried to balance support for Taiwan with a broadened relationship with China that included expanded commercial, cultural, scientific, military, and cooperative intelligence ties. How and why a president who was initially so committed to Taiwan could pursue such a broad and cooperative relationship with China is the central question for this chapter. This story of change can be explained by focusing on the internal realities of Reagan's decisionmaking process, in which China policy was fought over by two distinct groups within his administration. Different factions—specifically the China-first, or geostrategic perspective, and the Taiwan-first, or pan-Asian perspective—fought to control competing definitions of the United States' East Asian priorities.[6] Eventually a new consensus emerged on China as the Taiwan issue temporarily faded from view.

The Struggle to Balance Policy Priorities

The Early Advisory System and Deep Bureaucratic Differences

The Reagan administration structured its advisory process specifically to reverse the Carter and Nixon trend that established a strong national

security adviser and NSC staff. Reagan formed a cabinet-style government, with a White House–centered, chief-of-staff system that strengthened the position of White House staff vis-à-vis other policy advisers.
The position of national security adviser was weakened purposefully,
leaving Richard Allen without the stature to design the administration's
foreign policy. Unlike his predecessors, Allen had no direct access to
the president and instead reported to him through Edwin Meese (coun-
selor to the president). When William Clark took Allen's place as
national security adviser in November 1981, he was able to gain direct
access to the president, but his lack of foreign policy experience still
left the White House in control. This chief-of-staff system meant that
Ed Meese, as the only other person with direct access, controlled who
saw the president and what information reached him.[7]

This weakening of the national security adviser combined with the
hands-off leadership style that Reagan employed set the stage for
Secretary of State Alexander Haig's attempt to fill the void and the
bureaucratic conflicts this generated. Haig's power play coupled with
his acerbic style further alienated members of the White House staff—
particularly when he set himself up as the "vicar" of foreign policy, its
chief formulator, and main spokesman. To many, including the president, Haig overstated his power in foreign policy at the expense of the
president's interests. In his memoirs, Reagan recalled that Haig did not
want the White House or the president involved in foreign affairs. "He
didn't want to carry out the president's foreign policy; he wanted to formulate it and carry it out himself."[8] On this issue one press story concluded: "Ron Reagan doesn't want any one of his key people out in
front of anyone else. If someone does get out in front, he gets sawed
off. People learned to be careful not to elbow one another. Al wanted to
put his mark on the tree and got out in front."[9]

From the beginning Ed Meese, Chief of Staff James Baker, and
Deputy Chief of Staff Michael Deaver countered Haig's influence. For
example, when Haig submitted a draft copy of the National Security
Decision Directive (NSDD)-1 to the president (through Ed Meese),
which assigned the secretary of state central authority in foreign policy,
it was not passed on to the president. Meese, Baker, and Deaver considered the move a power play attempt by Haig, and they chose to shelve
the directive to undermine the secretary of state's design.[10]

Struggle over the East Asian Agenda: Taiwan or China First?

On policy issues like priorities in East Asia there were deep policy differences over the status of China and Taiwan that reinforced the bureaucratic conflict. By June 1981, Haig had successfully hammered out a

policy that moved the United States toward an anti-Soviet strategic association with Beijing and laid the groundwork for U.S. sales of lethal, offensive weapons to the PRC. The secret offer to sell lethal weapons on a case-by-case basis went a step beyond the Carter administration's support for nonlethal sales.[11] Haig seemed to have in mind weapons that included antitank and air defense systems that would make them more formidable against the Soviets and would relieve pressure from Beijing on the Taiwan arms sales issue. Part of Haig's instructions for his June 1981 trip to China was keep the decision to sell arms to China secret until the U.S. Congress, Taiwan, Japan, and other allies could be advised. The decision would be made public in advance of a visit to the United States by China's deputy chief of staff, General Liu Huaqing.[12]

Other steps supporting this shift toward China included changing China's trade status to friendly but nonallied. This move took China out of the potential enemy category it had shared with the Soviet Union and placed it in the same class as Yugoslavia (China moved from Country X to Country Y classification in export control regulations in 1983). Substantively, the change would make it possible to transfer to China more advanced and dual-use technology, with both civilian and military applications. Haig argues he also was charged with finding a solution on Taiwan that included parameters for unofficial relations and arms sales.[13]

On the other side of the coin, Haig's detractors felt he took the strategic association with China too far. Officials in both the Pentagon and White House felt that it made little sense to sell sophisticated weapons to China. Weinberger generally mistrusted the tilt toward China and believed instead that strengthening the security pact with Japan was the appropriate strategy to curb the immediate Soviet threat.[14] Representing this perspective in the Pentagon, Weinberger argued that Japan could provide the answer for the new power configuration in Asia that would counter Soviet influence. "Japan's geography, industrial base and security treaty with the US were the factors which convinced him of the validity of this approach."[15]

Additionally, China was not the priority that Taiwan was to East Asia policy.[16] Weinberger soon resented what he saw as the State Department taking over Pentagon prerogatives on issues such as arms sales and technology transfers to the Chinese. Haig's critics also saw sales of advanced aircraft to Taiwan as a tool to maintain commitments to Taiwan and to downplay China's importance. Richard Allen, in particular, was confident he could guarantee a new fighter to Taiwan; he had the president's agreement and apparently leaked the story periodically to the press.[17]

An opportunity to undercut Haig's position came when Haig became the first Reagan official to visit China in June 1981. In Haig's final press conference there he confirmed to reporters—without White House permission—that the United States proposed arms sales to China.[18] This unauthorized announcement led James Lilley (the NSC China specialist) and Richard Armitage (an aide to Secretary of Defense Weinberger) to quickly cable the White House reporting Haig's breach of policy. After prompting from his White House staff, the president held a news conference to clarify that while arms sales to Beijing would be part of U.S. policy, the TRA and arms sales to Taiwan were still the basis of U.S. policy.[19] In his memoirs, Haig acknowledges that the timing of Reagan's statement showed that the president felt he had "gotten out in front of him in our China policy."[20]

One interpretation for the premature announcement, consistent with other events, is that Haig was going public to circumvent his White House opposition. John Holdridge hints that Haig might have announced the change because he wanted to better position the Department of State in the China policy debate, but he also acknowledges Haig might have been tipped from the White House that he could make the announcement.[21] William Rope, director of the China Desk at the State Department during this period, asserts that Haig's gaffe was merely the product of fatigue after a long day of negotiations, banquets, and ceremonies. Rope notes that Haig initially "stuck to the White House script and only confirmed the story after being repeatedly badgered by Washington-based reporters."[22]

In either case, the administration's early mixed signals led the Chinese to ratchet up the pressure on Taiwan arms sales. Beijing delivered a démarche to Ambassador Arthur W. Hummel stating that if arms sales went forward, it would have grave consequences for the strategic situation. The establishment of areas of joint cooperation, such as modernizing industrial plants and energy resources, mining, and agricultural production proposed during Haig's visit, were ultimately stalled by the Taiwan arms sale question. Eventually, China even canceled the proposed visit of Deputy Chief of Staff Liu Huaqing to Washington because of U.S. inability to agree on what the arms sale list would entail.[23] Apparently, the list was delayed because the Pentagon raised obstacles to selling the sophisticated weapons systems Haig wanted on the list.[24]

In Cancun at the North-South Summit in October 1981, the Chinese reiterated their desire for a long-term strategic relationship but argued that Taiwan arms sales remained a critical problem to be addressed and that U.S. "interference in Chinese internal affairs" must end. In Beijing's view arms sales were unacceptable as a matter of principle, and also in practice they discouraged Taiwan from accepting the PRC's nine-point reunification offer of complete autonomy for Taiwan as a special administrative region with its own social, political, economic, and cultural relations. Going beyond previous demands, Foreign Minister Huang Hua delivered an ultimatum that Taiwan arms sales must decline each year and then end. If Washington refused to enter negotiations to set that date, China would recall its ambassador, thus downgrading the Sino-American relationship. This demand placed Taiwan arms sales at the center of the Chinese relationship with the United States. When Huang visited Washington after Cancun, Haig told him Reagan could not accept a deadline (a "date certain") for ending arms sales, but added that the administration would limit sales to defensive weapons that would not exceed the quality or quantity of the previous high arms sales levels in the last year of the Carter administration.[25] Critics of the State Department claimed that Haig and his staff leaned toward greater accommodation with the Chinese, with some even trying to set a date certain for the end of arms sales—an accusation denied by members of the "China-first" crowd.[26]

The combination of a weak national security adviser, a determined secretary of state, an independent secretary of defense, and a strong White House staff opened the door to a pattern of vicious infighting. Although Haig tried to be "the principal developer of options," his efforts faced strong opposition.[27] John Holdridge recalls "the whole relationship was from the very beginning extremely tense. Michael Deaver, Ed Meese, and Dick Allen, none of them was going to allow Al Haig unimpaired access to the president or unimpaired definition of foreign policy for the United States." Comparing these three to Kissinger and Brzezinski, Haig referred to them as the "hydra-headed monster" at the White House.[28] In this situation the administration operated on an ad hoc basis, shifting its stance with each decision and creating considerable confusion.

Consistent internal divisions over the proper approach to Taiwan arms sales while maintaining the PRC relationship created competing networks that reflected the differences discussed above. Haig and the State Department's East Asian and political military bureaus placed highest priority on close ties with China not only for strategic reasons vis-à-vis the Soviets but also as the linchpin of a strong, secure, peaceful, and developing Asia.[29] The second group, composed of the White House, NSC, Defense Department, and the State Department policy planning staff led by Paul Wolfowitz, maintained a pan-Asian perspective that placed greater emphasis on relations with Taiwan and Japan in regional security and economic terms.[30]

Through the first year of the administration there were no agreed-upon objectives and little clarity on East Asian priorities. Despite the president's ultimate decision not to sell an advanced fighter to Taiwan, there was continued deterioration in the U.S.-China relationship. An early 1982 op-ed piece by Richard Holbrooke, the former assistant secretary for East Asia during the Carter administration, captured the concern many felt for the slippage in the relationship. He argued the administration's failure to clarify its policy on Taiwan had led China to stiffen its position on arms sales. Such strained relations benefited only Moscow and rolled back the strategic gains of the last decade. Holbrooke concluded that campaign rhetoric, minor decisions favoring Taiwan that made China feel the United States was promoting a two-China policy, delays in promised exports, and the lack of comment on China's nine-point proposal to Taiwan (its plan to negotiate a Taiwan settlement) had the cumulative effect of reducing maneuvering room for both sides.[31]

Explaining How and Why the Taiwan Question Was Brought Under Control

The relationship with China deteriorated to the point that even routine announcements such as a spare parts sale to Taiwan—$60 million in spare parts and $37 million in services to stockpile the parts—in December 1981 led China to accuse the United States of a two-China policy. The policy challenge at this point was the need to set U.S. priorities in East Asia. Explaining how and why the Taiwan question was resolved requires a closer look at the struggle over policy definition and the shifting fates of the central players involved.[32]

Diagnosing the Problem

Diagnosing Reagan's China policy problem is deceptively straightforward. Focusing on the president's early rhetoric, one might have expected Taiwan to have priority over China. As we will see, however, since there were potential negative implications for the president's priority of enlisting China as an ally in the struggle against the Soviets, Taiwan could not be focused on blithely at the expense of the PRC.

The president's conflicting inclinations, coupled with the fact that he was seldom centrally involved in day-to-day foreign policy making, facilitated bureaucratic competition. Central to this competition was the issue of how to define and present the problem to the president. The struggle throughout the Haig period remained the diagnosis of the problem based on the solution to the Taiwan arms sales issue and the terms of the joint communiqué.

The geostrategic position.   Alexander Haig's China-first strategic approach, noted above, focused on the need to rejuvenate the U.S.-China alliance in order to counter the Soviet threat, and was perceived by the pan-Asia group as a means to elevate China above other East Asian interests such as Taiwan or Japan.[33] However, the anti-Soviet component also made the China relationship salient for many in the administration and even Taiwan's supporters in particular circumstances. For example, even hard-liners such as Weinberger warned that if the Soviet Union invaded Poland, "the United States might retaliate by opening its military arsenal to China." The crux of the problem was that decisionmakers such as Weinberger wanted China to be strong enough to fight the Russians, but not strong enough to threaten Taiwan.[34]

Taiwan arms sales were the crux of the problem for Haig. The geostrategic group pushed for a decision on arms sales so that China policy could be settled. A draft presidential directive memo authorizing the State Department to enter negotiations for a communiqué in December 1981 became Haig's decision-forcing mechanism to solidify an understanding on China. Because the communiqué developed language on future arms sales to Taiwan, it forced the administration to decide on the scope of pending sales of advanced fighters.[35]

The conclusions of a Defense Intelligence Agency (DIA) study adopted by the intelligence community as a National Intelligence Estimate (the NIE commissioned earlier by James Lilley) partially aided Haig's cause. It confirmed that Taiwan did not need an advanced fighter and that the F-5E already in its arsenal created a sufficient deterrent capability to raise the costs of a potential PRC attack.[36] Once the Defense Department concluded that Taiwan's defense needs could be met through continued coproduction of the F-5E, a major roadblock was removed. The January 11, 1982, announcement by State Department spokesman Alan Romberg that the administration would not sell the FX (F-5G or F-16/79) or an upgraded F-5E but would instead extend coproduction for the F-5E did not completely settle the matter. Although Holdridge handled the announcement in Beijing carefully to emphasize that this was a decision *not* to sell rather than one to sell, Chinese pressure did not abate.[37]

While Haig's objectives succeeded, in part, because of the conclusions of the National Intelligence Estimate, at least some of his success can be attributed to the departure of two major White House players. Richard Allen was forced to take a leave of absence on November 19 and James Lilley left the NSC to go to Taiwan in January 1982. This situation led to a breakdown in the chain of policymaking in the White House and a dearth of expertise on East Asia. William Clark, who replaced Richard Allen as national security adviser, was no expert in foreign policy. Additionally, no China expert replaced Lilley on the NSC staff.[38]

The draft communiqué produced that spring of 1982 reaffirmed Beijing's commitment to a peaceful resolution of the Taiwan problem, restated the U.S. commitment to the one-China policy, and offered language on arms sales meant to placate the Chinese. Haig recalled that "the United States does seek to carry out a long-term policy of arms sales to Taiwan and affirms the ultimate objective of ending arms sales to Taiwan. In the meantime, it expects a gradual reduction of its arms sales, leading to a final resolution of this difficult issue."[39] With minor changes this became the basis for the August 17 communiqué.

The Taiwan-first/pan-Asian position. White House aides and the Pentagon prioritized a solid, stable relationship with Taiwan as more important to the stability of East Asia and U.S. credibility in the region. The emphasis that Taiwan was a long-term ally who had been betrayed by the 1978 communiqué informed their push for Taiwan arms sales (noted above) and also their moves to reinterpret the Sino-American communiqué.

Although the communiqué reflected Haig's priorities, the Taiwan-first/pan-Asian faction had a greater influence over how it would be interpreted. The president's commitment to its terms seemed open to interpretation because those most opposed to the communiqué had a hand in writing a one-page codicil that linked the decline in arms sales to maintaining the balance of power in the Taiwan Strait. Although arms sales decreased every year, they were never eliminated as the Chinese desired.[40] In his book Alan Romberg reprints part of the codicil that outlined a new understanding of the communiqué. He notes that U.S. willingness to reduce arms sales to Taiwan was "conditioned absolutely upon the continued commitment of China to the peaceful solution of the Taiwan-PRC differences." The quantity and quality of arms were "conditioned entirely on the threat posed by the PRC" and "Taiwan's defense capability relative to that of the PRC will be maintained."[41] James Lilley concludes that Reagan's codicil righted the balance across the Taiwan Strait that had tilted too far toward the PRC under Haig's policy approach. Explaining the president's thinking, Lilley reports that the president felt the communiqué hit him "at the last minute." For Reagan, the important point was to maintain the balance of power between China and Taiwan.[42]

Just as Richard Allen and James Lilley's departures had made Haig's efforts easier, Haig's resignation in June 1982 strengthened the bureaucratic position of the Taiwan-first faction.[43] George Shultz, the new secretary of state, seemed to align himself with the White House view that Haig had gone too far in treating China as the strategic linchpin of U.S. policy and agreed that the former secretary of state had made too many concessions to Beijing. As a businessman and former secretary of the treasury, Shultz saw Asia's importance in economic terms, unlike Haig who had placed China's importance under the rubric of U.S. strategic interests. Shultz's emphasis on economic and industrial strength rather than military power seemed to make Japan, not China, the primary focus for U.S. policy in Asia.[44] Although Shultz supported the communiqué, his reluctance to go to China, despite the urging of the China specialists, reflected his overall caution.

Themes That Resonated with President Reagan and the Public

President Reagan's beliefs and priorities. Because President Reagan held important beliefs about the Soviet Union and Taiwan salient to the question of closer ties to the PRC, the stage was set for conflicting frames to trigger conflicting schema. The president's uncertainty represented fertile ground for bureaucratic actors within his administration.

As a strong anti-Communist, Reagan's world was divided into two camps: good versus evil, with winning or losing the only two possible outcomes. A critic of arms control efforts such as SALT I and II, Reagan argued that arms control had weakened the U.S. military position in relation to the Soviet Union. He felt that détente had been interpreted by the Russians "as a freedom to pursue whatever policies of subversion, aggression, and expansionism they wanted anywhere in the world."[45] His anti-Soviet rhetoric, in conjunction with larger defense budgets and the need to reestablish U.S. strength around the globe, demonstrated his belief that the United States was in a constant test of wills with the USSR. The Soviets could not be trusted, and if the United States failed to man the line against them, they would exploit the gap. Reagan felt they had exploited U.S. weakness to pursue their agenda of a Communist-dominated world. Thus negotiation with the Soviets was not a viable option in the first years of the administration until, in his terms, the United States negotiated from a position of strength.[46]

Reagan also had long supported Taiwan and the position of the Taiwan lobby. During the 1950s and 1960s, he even hoped the Chinese on Taiwan would help retake mainland China from the Communists. Throughout the 1970s, he remained an advocate for U.S. support for Taiwan. Given his stance, Nixon used Reagan as his emissary to Taiwan in 1972 to reassure the Taiwanese about rapprochement with China. When Carter normalized relations with the PRC, however, Reagan characterized it as a betrayal of an old, loyal friend to whom the United States "owed unqualified support. . . . I felt we had an obligation to the people of Taiwan, and no one was going to keep us from meeting it."[47]

During his campaign and through the inauguration, Reagan seemed committed to elevating Taiwan's diplomatic status. Eventually, his strong campaign rhetoric concerned advisers enough that they sent his running mate George H.W. Bush to reassure the Chinese that Reagan supported the one-China policy. When Reagan and the pro-Taiwan crowd put long-time Taiwan supporter Anna Chennault on the Reagan-Bush Inaugural Committee, the first symbolic crisis with China was created. When the Chinese learned Chennault had invited Taiwan officials to the inauguration, China's ambassador stated he would refuse to attend if Taiwanese officials attended the event as well. Although Taiwan's invitations were rescinded, this situation was a harbinger for the difficult times to come.[48]

Both sets of Reagan's beliefs represented well-defined schemata that had persisted for at least thirty years—his anti-Soviet stance since the McCarthy era and his stance on Taiwan since the "fall" of China in 1949. Furthermore, the personal tenor of those beliefs was tied to his image of himself as a man who did not abandon friends or back down from a life-and-death struggle. These factors illustrate the need to understand what led to the triggering and persistence of a particular schema and its corresponding policy priorities.

Policy themes that resonated with President Reagan. It is clear that Secretary Haig had to overcome Reagan's preexisting beliefs about China and tap into his anti-Soviet core beliefs to convince the president that gains from ties to China did not mean betraying Taiwan. The goal was to make the relationship with China a positive-sum game rather than one involving difficult trade-offs.

Chas Freeman recalls that he worked with Haig to "educate" the president by writing short memos and providing Reagan with briefing material that emphasized the anti-Soviet pitch. On this score Haig arranged for the president to be briefed early on about the secret intelligence alliance between the United States and China with regard to the Soviets and the secret cooperation to provide arms to the guerrillas in Afghanistan. This helped Reagan rethink his early push to restore an official relationship with Taiwan because he began to realize the importance of China to the overall U.S. international strategy.

The State Department team also helped the president get a more personal feel for and sophisticated understanding of China. They brought in Ji Chaozhu, a mid-ranking Chinese official, to see Reagan. Ji, who had gone to Harvard, presented Chinese views in terms the president could understand, which began to break down Reagan's anti-Chinese stereotype and put a human face to Chinese Communists. Haig gained some ground with the president on these fronts as he convinced him the real enemy was the Soviet Union, not China.[49]

The talking points prepared for Haig's trip to China built a rationale for closer relations based on the Soviet threat and the commonality of U.S.-Chinese aims in Asia. Once in China, Haig focused on the positive outcomes from his meetings when he reported back to the president. In one cable to the White House, he reported that China's upbeat attitude toward Sino-American relations had dominated the sessions, confirming to the president the overriding value of strategic coordination with China as a basis for strong relations. Haig concluded his efforts had gone well, despite the Taiwan issue, and that relations were ready to move ahead.[50] He argued that "our policies can complement each other; and that China's strength, security, and well-being are fundamental to the global balance that is the basis for our own security."[51]

Haig's arguments were bolstered by both the strategic context and the possibility for broader ties. He pointed to Afghanistan, Pakistan, and India as areas that benefited from Sino-American coordination and explored similar goals in regard to Vietnam and Kampuchea.[52] An expansion of strategic and consultative ties was accompanied by the offer to loosen export controls on technology transfer and to hold a series of prospective cabinet-level visits. Haig's only concern was China's export of sensitive nuclear materials, which he argued would hurt mutual strategic interests without appropriate safeguards. Haig succeeded in getting the president to talk with the Chinese (despite Reagan's early disinclination to do so) and to make them a prominent piece of U.S. global military strategy. Through these efforts Haig understood that maintaining a good relationship with China meant that the United States would have to go through a certain level of contortion on the Taiwan issue.[53]

China's warnings about Taiwan convinced Haig to push for a tenth-anniversary communiqué that sought a reduction in Taiwan arms sales, which could take the issue off the table. William Rope, who first proposed this document to Haig, says its aim was "to reiterate all the key elements of the U.S.-China relationship and commonly held U.S. and Chinese positions on geostrategic issues" and to incorporate in it "a brief section in which the United States would express its intention gradually to reduce arms sales to Taiwan, clearly linked to a Chinese statement of intent to pursue a peaceful policy toward Taiwan." To justify this policy, Reagan could single out the nine-point reunification offer to Taiwan as evidence of China's peaceful and constructive approach to reconciling with Taiwan.[54]

Although the president was receptive to the importance of China for his anti-Soviet strategy, he remained committed to Taiwan as well. Pursuing a dual policy of closer ties to the Chinese and arms sales to secure Taiwan's future seemed to address his concern for Taiwan. The ambiguity over exactly how the reduction in arms sales to Taiwan would proceed in the August 1982 communiqué allowed him to avoid the trade-offs implied in these policy choices.[55] When Reagan was convinced the communiqué came at the expense of Taiwan, he wrote his understanding of the agreement in a codicil. Several of Haig's critics argue that the secretary of state tried to sell out Taiwan up to the end.[56] William Rope, on the other hand, writes that Reagan looked over the communiqué thoroughly and agreed to its major components; only the normal give-and-take of the negotiating process with China, he asserts, explained the compromises that were made.[57] By adopting the codicil, Reagan could feel he was stepping back from Haig's language and could argue, as he often did after compromising on an issue, that in fact he had done no such thing. According to Weinberger, the communiqué that was signed was a vague agreement on Taiwan, as well as the agreement to disagree on Taiwan that Haig sought.[58]

After the 1982 communiqué was finalized, Taiwan and the arms sales issue faded from view. This occurred, in part, because arms sales did go down throughout the 1980s and because defense technology and defense services—as opposed to weapons—were frequently transferred to Taiwan. A new tactic emerged to build up Taiwan's manufacturing capabilities and its indigenous defense program, which would eventually lead to reduced arms sales. It also meant there would be no visible exports to Taiwan and no congressional or public debate.[59]

Domestic political considerations. Given White House interests and Taiwan's strong supporters in Congress, Haig had to proceed prudently while encouraging the Chinese to exercise restraint. In China, his efforts to convince the Chinese that less tension would allow the United States to assess requests more cautiously in a less politically charged atmosphere were only partially successful. He bought some time with China by reassuring them no decision was expected on the advanced fighter before the end of 1981.[60]

Haig also tried to develop a new political base with key lawmakers, the press, and business leaders outside the administration to counter the Taiwan lobby. The State Department made a huge effort to keep the Hill informed. To members of Congress and U.S. allies, Haig emphasized the strategic convergence of views that would build a strong and lasting relationship. For example, in a letter to Howard Baker, Haig argued that Taiwan would not distract the discussion from the overall strategic imperative of the relationship. In his briefing before the Association of Southeast Asian Nations (ASEAN), the secretary again repeated his optimism that the visit had provided momentum to the relationship.[61] As he had throughout his trip, Haig claimed that his visit to China had cleared the air between Washington and Beijing and had taken the U.S.-Chinese friendship to "a new plateau."[62]

John Holdridge also regularly consulted Congress and invited congressmen to staff meetings as a means to build congressional support. To avoid Carter's debacle over the TRA, before the communiqué was signed it was taken to the Senate Foreign Relations Committee for consultation. This effectively committed members of the committee to the policy, and if it went wrong, they were partially responsible. Gaston Sigur, the NSC staffer who handled East Asia from 1982 to 1983, states that "the fact that Reagan had done it in some ways muted some of the critics up there from the more right wing of the Republican Party who would have, if it had been another president, really been much more loud than they were. They didn't like it, but they didn't want to come out against him."[63]

With Reagan, Haig needed to bring a domestic political component to his frame. In his memoirs, Haig admits,

> I told the President and Bill Clark that if the President faltered in his relations with China, the Democratic opposition would leap on this question and turn it into a major issue in the 1984 elections. The refusal to search for a compromise on the issue of Taiwan could result in the most significant diplomatic disaster since the "loss of China" in 1949, and the party judged responsible for this failure would, and should, pay heavy political consequences.[64]

Art Hummel recalls that Haig's clinching argument with Reagan was that "we Republicans cannot have, in our first year in office, a foreign policy disaster like a rupture with the PRC. This would hurt us domestically."[65]

Once Taiwan arms sales were put to bed, even White House aides could see the domestic advantages in closer Sino-American relations. As the 1984 election season approached, they were behind the plans for timing the U.S.-China summit to be held during the primary election to take the issue off the Democratic agenda.[66]

Supporting Conditions:
Manipulating the Agenda to Gradually Commit the President

Despite Haig's resignation and the purging of his pro-China constituency, his efforts set a new tone that gradually transformed the dialogue on Sino-American relations within the administration. Haig successfully worked out a greater balance in the arms sales issue and got the president to agree to his strategy for the 1982 communiqué.[67] Although Haig's detractors argued that he accomplished this task by "tricking" the president, his submission of a series of decision memos to the White House successfully committed the president to a fundamental change in priorities that brought stability back to the U.S.-China relationship. In those memos Haig convinced Reagan what had to be done to win concessions from the Chinese, and the president checked off issue after issue until he eventually conceded to China's demands.[68]

Haig, however, did push the envelope too far, too often—a fact demonstrated by his resignation and Reagan's codicil to the communiqué. In practical terms, his resignation meant that concentration of control over policy in the White House immediately increased, as loyalty to the White House became the basis for evaluating new appointments. Documents focusing on Haig's resignation show that the White House personnel office made sure new appointees had a philosophical commitment to Reagan's programs and were loyal to the administration. The White House also ordered a careful review of "all regional bureaus and senior non-career positions with an eye toward ensuring that they are filled by the most competent people and that they reflect your philosophy."[69] George Shultz was chosen as the new secretary of state precisely because he seemed the kind of team player Haig never was. The strategy to minimize the political costs of Haig's leaving included using the imagery of Shultz working well with the White House and the NSC.[70]

Most blatantly, those who had sided with Haig were accused of being willing to abandon Taiwan and were purged from the administration. John Holdridge was sent off as ambassador to Indonesia, and once William Rope had completed his time on the China Desk, he was transferred from the East Asia Bureau. Paul Wolfowitz, a consistent critic of close ties to China, replaced Holdridge and became Shultz's right-hand man on East Asian policy. Although a hawk on the Soviet Union, Wolfowitz seemed to believe his predecessors had been too eager to accommodate the Chinese and had handled the Taiwan issue badly. The new Asian team also included Gaston Sigur, a Japanologist in charge of East Asia at the NSC, and Richard Armitage, the architect of Weinberger's Japan policy at the Pentagon. Unlike the previous infighting, this group worked well together to formulate policy. Once a week it gathered to work out the administration's Asia policies and to see that arms sales to Taiwan continued. The group seemed a harbinger for a new shift in China policy.[71]

Despite his resignation, Haig's efforts to prioritize China set a baseline for the administration's policy. Once the question of Taiwan arms sales was put to bed, a closer relationship was more palatable even to Haig's critics. Table 5.1 illustrates the major components of Reagan's China policy approach discussed in this section.

The Shultz Era and the Emerging East Asian Consensus: New Definitions and Priorities?

The lull in relations following the 1982 communiqué was a time when the administration reassessed its East Asian policy objectives. Without Haig the personal nature of the bureaucratic fight with the White House diminished because the Taiwan arms sales policy was set. On the surface, Haig's resignation and the appointment of George Shultz seemed to highlight the triumph of the pan-Asia faction in the Reagan administration. Once Shultz became secretary of state, East Asian policy shifted to prioritize economic issues and Japan more centrally. Paul Wolfowitz

Table 5.1   Components of Ronald Reagan's China Policy Frame

Problem diagnosis	• Competition between prioritizing strategic importance of Sino-American relationship and broader pan-Asian focus emphasizing relations with allies such as Japan and Taiwan
Themes that resonated with president and public	
Presidential beliefs	• Taiwan seen as East Asian priority and initially hostile toward China • Strong anti-Soviet stance/anti-Communist perspective changes president's emphasis
Policy themes	• Haig argues there is an opportunity for strategic association with PRC vis-à-vis the Soviets; prioritizes China relationship over Taiwan • Pan-Asian group argues for need to focus on relationship with Taiwan and Japan as cornerstone of political, economic, and military policy in East Asia • Shultz prioritizes economic relations
Political considerations	• Haig sought PRC acquiescence to avoid domestic politicization and argued Reagan could not be the president who disrupted relationship with PRC • White House advisers saw usefulness of China summit as election approached • President's Cold War credentials helped mitigate criticism from the Taiwan lobby
Supporting conditions/tactics	• Bureaucratic infighting led to confusing signals in East Asian priorities • Incremental commitment of president to strategic association position • Elimination of pro-China crowd seems to weaken strategic position

also urged the new secretary of state to manage China in a more mature and effective way. He claimed the United States had been chasing after the Chinese and the administration needed to stop doing this for a while.[72] This argument convinced Shultz to wait to visit China (and then only in the context of a trip to Japan and Korea), even though pro-China holdovers—William Rope and John Holdridge—argued for an earlier trip to China (as did Richard Nixon, who—after returning from a visit to China—passed this message to Shultz through Holdridge and Rope in September 1982).[73]

Shultz's February 1983 East Asian trip set a new tone for China that seemed to make it only a small part of the overall strategy to promote economic and security developments in Asia.[74] During his February 2–5 visit, Shultz emphasized first the global recession and underdevelopment as hindrances to global stability and only secondly, Soviet military expansion and involvement in regional conflicts. Countering the Soviet threat was discussed in new terms that elevated strengthening the defense budget, economic ties with European allies, and the relationship with Japan over expanding relations with China.[75] Shultz's priority with regard to China was to build a solid framework for expanding economic and commercial relations (trade, civil aviation, shipping, EXIM Bank, OPIC, and other areas).[76] Weinberger remained concerned that the technology might be used for military purposes and urged extreme caution; simultaneously, however, he courted the Chinese with offers of military-to-military cooperation and weapons sales to get them to line up with the United States against the USSR.[77] A corresponding lowering of expectations surrounded Shultz's visit to China and Sino-American relations, which was in stark contrast to Haig's prominent visit in 1981. Press reports argued that China was an "Asian giant lagging far behind Japan" whose importance should not be oversold.[78]

Reporting to Washington on his progress in China, Shultz emphasized the interconnectedness of major actors in the "complex and interrelated world." In the evolving economic relationship China had potential, but there would be a certain degree of growing pains and trade problems among them. Opportunities did expand and by that point China had become the fourteenth largest trading partner and fourth largest market for U.S. agricultural products.[79] Shultz reported that both sides recognized the potential benefits of good relations. Frank Carlucci, later named secretary of defense to replace Weinberger, argued that the United States accepted that helping China modernize was the best way to protect U.S. interests and to avoid confrontation in dealing with Taiwan issues.[80]

The new emphasis on the opportunities of interdependence came at the same time that internal reports from sources like the State Department's Bureau of Intelligence and Research (INR) noted that China had distanced itself from the United States and sought to balance relations with the Soviets and the United States in the years leading up to 1984. "China wanted the benefit of ties to the United States without the appearance of a close relationship with the Americans, thus avoiding the appearance of joining forces against the Soviets."[81] Still, the report concluded that China's emphasis on Western economic and technological help as an essential part of modernization illustrated that economic needs would fuel their future foreign policy. China's new priorities redirected budget resources to the civilian economy, leaving the military to convert factories to civilian production. Ironically, these plants began to produce weapons for export and eventually sought international markets for those goods with Saudi Arabia, Syria, Iraq, Iran, Libya, and Pakistan in order to produce hard currency. Just four years later the administration would work to get China to end missile proliferation.[82]

Two policy documents in quick succession in 1984 illustrate that China remained an important part of the U.S. East Asian priorities. The major thrust of NSDD 120, dated January 9, 1984, was U.S. readiness to lend support to China's modernization efforts (liberalizing technology transfer). It emphasized the conclusion of an agreement on peaceful uses of nuclear energy (after nonproliferation assurances) and the need to move forward on a bilateral grain agreement, while encouraging the Chinese to look to the long-term potential of the economic relationship. In strategic cooperation the emphasis was on upgrading China's defensive capabilities with appropriate technology.[83] Similar goals were outlined in NSDD 140 for the president's trip to China. First and foremost, the trip was seen as a chance for U.S. leaders to carry the message of friendship directly to the Chinese, while sending a quiet signal to U.S. allies and the Soviets that the Sino-American relationship could thrive on a foundation of realism and mutual interest. "Our overall strategy should be to develop our relationship by highlighting the areas of agreement and potential cooperation, while maintaining a firm but quiet stance on issues involving our own principles and commitments not subject to compromise."[84]

Gaston Sigur claims that these meetings "pushed the relationship very far ahead. But at the same time, we were continuing to live up to the obligations that we believed we had to fulfill, under the terms of the Taiwan Relations Act, with Taiwan in terms of the sale of weapons and high-technology."[85] Art Hummel felt Zhao's and Reagan's presidential trips signaled to the bureaucracy on both sides that the relationship was stable and that routine business would be conducted more smoothly. "You could sense a little loosening up every time we'd have a high-level exhibition of the value of this relationship. The same effect was perceptible on the Chinese side."[86]

The March 1984 trip was a watershed for Ronald Reagan's way of thinking. He became convinced that the PRC was moving slowly but steadily toward acceptance of a free-market system. The fact that the Chinese invited investment and that China's farmers were given long-term leases and permission to sell goods for a profit above their quotas provided examples of the regime's commitment to this change. Reagan told Zhao that China and the United States could contribute jointly to stability of the Pacific region.[87] His shift was dramatic in comparison to his early rhetoric and even the communiqué. Chas Freeman notes that "he had entered office with an ideological stereotype of China really untempered by any human contact with the Chinese. . . . When Reagan actually came to China, he suddenly discovered very warm, reasonable human beings, who spoke in pragmatic, nonideological terms." En route back to the United States, Reagan claimed that the Chinese really weren't Communists at all. "What he meant," explains Freeman, was "that they were decent human beings, rather than ideological fiends."[88]

Now that Reagan's position was clarified, the politicization of the U.S.-China relationship diminished. Sigur argues that a domestic consensus for the relationship developed on two points: (1) the need to preserve the community of interests with Asian states that included meeting the Soviet challenge and maintaining the one-China policy, and (2) the conviction that U.S. interests were met by continued PRC economic modernization, internal reform, and expanded relationships with others. By this theory, if China had a greater stake in regional stability, it would be less vulnerable to outside influences and become better integrated into the world economy.

The administration influenced this domestic consensus by emphasizing the tangible benefits that resulted from Reagan's trip. For example, cooperation in the peaceful uses of nuclear technology with China opened negotiations for U.S. companies to build eight nuclear reactors. Such negotiations also provided other opportunities for U.S. companies and appealed to the business side of the equation.[89] One *Washington Post* editorial commented that the Zhao summit and Reagan's trip to China sealed the normalization process and ended it as a domestic political issue. It seemed that the Sino-American relationship had finally matured beyond the stage of alternating bouts of euphoria, where differences were forgotten, and depression, where leaders became so overwhelmed by differences that it seemed the whole relationship was in jeopardy.[90]

Encouraging high-level congressional delegations to travel to China was one means to influence congressional opinion. Chas Freeman, the deputy chief of mission who coordinated these trips, saw them as an opportunity to build "a bit of enthusiasm for the relationship. There were a lot of things that the Congress people might not have asked about, which I put them up to asking about, precisely because I wanted them to have their stereotypes shaken and to get a more accurate view of China."[91]

By the mid-1980s, relations had matured beyond Nixon's strategic focus to develop a broader-based and complex web of interactions that solidified the United States as China's third largest trading partner after Japan and Hong Kong. The United States had $4 billion in investments in China, over 30,000 Chinese students were in the United States, and about 300,000 U.S. tourists visited China annually. U.S.-PRC science and technology cooperation was the largest bilateral program of its kind, and military cooperation assisted the development of defensive capabilities without posing a threat to U.S. friends and allies. Common ground had been found in strategic interests in Afghanistan, Cambodia, and Korea. Challenges remained in ballistic missile proliferation (e.g., concern over sales to Saudi Arabia), but with Secretary of Defense Frank Carlucci's September 1988 trip to China, the administration was reassured that China would act responsibly. Concerns remained about the evolution of a peaceful resolution of the Taiwan question, PRC tariff and nontariff barriers, and tension in technology transfers desired by China, but these did not trigger major anxiety. The gradual trend was toward liberalization, with the United States playing an important role in China's long-term modernization program.[92]

Conclusion

Comparing Haig's style to his opponents reveals how much the U.S. China policy was driven by personal politics and the internal dynamics of the Reagan administration. Haig's forceful style allowed him to set the policy frame but not to be there to guide the specifics as the policy was implemented. The active set of White House advisers who shared the president's focus on Taiwan blocked many of his efforts, but Haig's message focusing on China as a counter to the Soviets made headway regardless because of the president's anti-Soviet stance. This meant that Haig accomplished less than he might have if he had been able to fully align the president to his strategic thinking. However, the fact that the relationship broadened into new areas—particularly in trade and economics, based on the efforts of George Shultz—showed that Haig's baseline interpretation of the relationship became part of the foundation for their policy through Reagan's second term.

Not unlike Jimmy Carter, President Reagan demonstrated mixed foreign policy goals when he entered office that led to early mixed signals and to policy shifts later. This fact seems unusual in a president who is better known for his ideological rigidity and hard-line stances. Some scholars such as Keith Shimko have noted that Reagan held contradictory beliefs about the Soviet Union—a hard-line, anti-Soviet theme on the one hand and a liberal faith in the harmony of interests among men on the other—that helped him react to new circumstances in the Soviet Union in 1985.[93] In Barbara Farnham's terms, the dual nature of Reagan's goals illustrated that he saw the problem of the Soviet threat as having more than one dimension. Regarding the Soviet Union, Farnham argues that Reagan did not waver between contradictory policies—he concentrated on the nuclear threat and attempts to negotiate with the Soviets only after he had neutralized the threat by rebuilding U.S. military strength. By her analysis Reagan's open-mindedness, sense of optimism, and orientation to the future helped him perceive and thus react to changed circumstances.[94]

Similar to Farnham's conclusions, this study shows there was more than one dimension to Reagan's China policy. His flexibility on China policy reflected his competing and contradictory definitions of how China should be categorized. The process by which one or another priority gained the upper hand depended on which adviser dominated at what point in time. Reagan seemed to react to arguments that fit his pre-existing belief structure, based on what beliefs had been primed. For example, mixed signals dominated while the Taiwan arms sales were unresolved. But as soon as the Taiwan issue seemed resolved satisfactorily, the anti-Soviet theme accompanied by the economic interdependence theme provided a new basis and language for engagement with China.

This analysis adds impetus to the notion that how advisers framed problems influenced the president's perceptions, his interpretation of the stakes involved, and the relevance of particular policy choices. While Reagan's beliefs helped determine his policy, his lack of foreign policy experience and involvement in the process are a better explanation of the policy process and results surrounding U.S. China policy. Reagan gave his advisers a lot of room to maneuver in and increased the bureaucratic political games that shaped Sino-American relations.

Notes

1. Soloman, *U.S. PRC Political Negotiations, 1967–1984, An Annotated Chronology (U)*, National Security Archives Collection: China and the United States, 83.
2. Alexander M. Haig Jr., *Caveat: Realism, Reagan and Foreign Policy*, 198.
3. Freeman interview.
4. John Holdridge, oral history interview, July 20, 1995; John Holdridge, *Crossing the Divide*; Tyler, *A Great Wall*, 309; Arthur Hummel, oral history interview, April 4, 1994.
5. Richard Halloran, "New Jets for Taiwan: An Issue Surrounded by Nettles."
6. James Mann in *About Face: A History of America's Curious Relationship with China, from Nixon to Clinton* labels Alexander Haig and the State Department as the pro-China faction, while the group that emphasized the importance of Taiwan, Japan, and Asian relations more regionally was labeled the pan-Asia faction. These labels are useful in that they outline the primary orientation of each group toward East Asia. My interviews and research support these labels and groupings.
7. Holdridge interviews, July 20, 1995, and December 14, 1989; see also Robert Gates, *From the Shadows*, 175; Larry Speakes, with Robert Pack, *Speaking Out: The Reagan Presidency from Inside the White House*, 264–288; Talking Points for Presentation on WH Office, Folder: Cabinet, Services I: Memorandum File, Subseries A—1980–1981 (Baker/Hodsoll), Box 1, James Baker III Files, Reagan Presidential Library. For an overview of the foreign policy process, see Haig, *Caveat,* and *The Tower Commission Report*.
8. Reagan, *An American Life*, 270.
9. Leslie Gelb, "How Haig Is Recasting His Image."
10. Haig, *Caveat*, 73–77.
11. China ultimately made specific requests for armored personnel carriers, antitank weapons, torpedoes, over-the-horizon radar, and U.S. assistance in improving their F-8 interceptor aircraft. See Holdridge interview, July 20, 1995; Memorandum to the Secretary and Deputy Secretary of Defense for the Special Assistant, "Status Report on PRC Munitions and Commodity Export Cases," February 24, 1981 (Doc. no. 00542); Summary of June 15 Meeting between Secretary Haig and PRC Vice Premier and Foreign Minister Huang Hua, June 17, 1981 (Doc. no. 00592), National Security Archives Collection: China and the United States.
12. Tyler, *A Great Wall*, 298–300.
13. Haig, *Caveat*, 204–206; see also "Opening Presentation—Strategic Overview for Secretary Haig," June 1981 (Doc. no. 00553); Memo to the Secretary from John Holdridge, May 28, 1981 (Doc. no. 00548), and "China–Iran/Iraq Conflict Talking Points," June 1981 (Doc. no. 00550), National Security Archives Collection: China and the United States.
14. Caspar Weinberger, *Fighting for Peace: Seven Critical Years in the Pentagon*, 220–253.

15. Richard Nations, "Why the Pentagon Pumps for Japan"; see also Garthoff, *Détente and Confrontation*, 637; George Shultz, "United States and East Asia: A Partnership for the Future," March 5, 1983, Current Policy no. 459, Department of State, Bureau of Public Affairs.

16. Weinberger, *Fighting for Peace*, 220–253.

17. Tyler, *A Great Wall*, 308.

18. Presidential Decision Memoranda on U.S. Policy Toward China, June 6, 1981 (Doc. no. 00567), National Security Archives Collection: China and the United States.

19. Tyler, *A Great Wall*, 301; Mann, *About Face,* 121–122.

20. Haig, *Caveat*, 208.

21. Holdridge interview, July 20, 1995; Hummel interview.

22. Author interview with William Rope, June 2002.

23. Haig, *Caveat*, 208; Hummel interview; Soloman, *U.S. PRC Political Negotiations*, National Security Archives Collection: China and the United States, 86; Confidential Cable to Secretary Baldridge from Secretary of State, June 1981 (Doc. no. 00595), National Security Archives Collection: China and the United States.

24. Tyler, *A Great Wall*, 306.

25. Haig, *Caveat*, 209–210; Holdridge interview, July 20, 1995; Soloman, *U.S. PRC Political Negotiations*, 89–91; see also Tyler, *A Great Wall*, 316; Mann, *About Face,* 123–124.

26. Author interviews with former NSC and State Department officials in the first Reagan administration, June 2002, Washington, D.C., who wish to be unnamed. See also James Lilley, with Jeffrey Lilley, *China Hands: Nine Decades of Adventure, Espionage, and Diplomacy in Asia.*

27. Leslie Gelb, "Foreign Policy System Criticized by U.S. Aides." Apparently, situations like this frustrated Haig, and more than once he threatened to resign over policy control disagreements on this and other issues involving the Pentagon and the White House. Holdridge interview, July 20, 1995; Haig, *Caveat,* 202; Reagan, *An American Life*, 154–156; Tyler, *A Great Wall*, 302.

28. Holdridge interviews, July 20, 1995, and December 14, 1989; see also Gates, *From the Shadows,* 175; Speakes, *Speaking Out*, 264–288.

29. In his correspondence with the author in October 2003, William Rope asserted that Asian nations from Japan to Southeast Asia considered a stable U.S.-China relationship vital to their security; conversely, he stated they would have been alarmed by a U.S.-China "downgrading." For this reason, he personally, and sometimes secretly, kept the Japanese fully informed of communiqué negotiations so that—in the event of a breakdown—Tokyo would know Reagan had done all he could to avoid it.

30. Richard Nations, "Why the Pentagon Pumps for Japan," 37; see also Shultz, "United States and East Asia: A Partnership for the Future."

31. Richard Holbrooke, "A Crisis with China Must Be Avoided."

32. Michael Weisskopf, "Decade of Sino-U.S. Détente Has Woven Complex Relationship."

33. Department of State Telegram reporting on Secretary Haig's June 14, 1981, bilateral meeting with Huang Hua, June 12, 1981 (Doc. no. 00581), National Security Archives Collection: China and the United States.

34. Murrey Marder, "The China Policy That Isn't, Beyond Curbing the Soviets, Haig and Deng Have Little to Agree On."

35. Rope interview.

36. Rope interview, June 2002, and correspondence with the author, October 2003; author interview with former NSC official in the first Reagan administration, June 2002.

37. Haig, *Caveat*, 212; Hummel interview; Soloman, *U.S. PRC Political Negotiations,* National Security Archives Collection: China and the United States, 93.

38. Author interviews with former NSC and State Department officials in the first Reagan administration, June 2002; Mann, *About Face,* 120–131.

39. Haig, *Caveat,* 214–215; Art Hummel argues, "We persuaded the PRC leaders that, if we did not have an agreement on their ultimatum, the terms of which were public knowledge, we would then have to go ahead and make these sales to Taiwan, and the whole world would believe that we were just spitting in the eye of the PRC and ignoring their ultimatum" (Hummel interview).

40. Author interview with former NSC official from the Reagan administration, June 2002.

41. Alan Romberg, *Rein In at the Brink of the Precipice: American Policy Toward Taiwan and U.S.-PRC Relations,* 140.

42. Lilley, *China Hands,* 246–248.

43. While policy differences over the Middle East pushed his resignation, the differences over issues like China and Taiwan had simmered for too long. See Paper on Haig Resignation/Press Themes, Folder: Haig's Resignation—Classified Documents, Box 91643-44 (1 of 1), William Clark Files: Files 91643, Reagan Presidential Library.

44. George Shultz, *Turmoil and Triumph,* 382–386; Memo Edwin Harper (Assistant to the President for Policy Development for Secretary of State), October 6, 1982, Folder BE (121900-129578), Box 2, WHORM Subject file (BE, Business-Economics, BE 090000-140599), Reagan Presidential Library; Memo to the President from William Clark, "National Security Study Directive (NSSD) on U.S. Relations with China and Taiwan," with attached NSSD 12-82 December 7, 1982, Folder: DSDD; NSSD 12-82; NSDD 140, NSDD 120, Briefings and NSC Meeting January 5, 1983 [84], Box 1 (Loc: 151/08/7), Douglas Paal Files, Reagan Presidential Library.

45. Reagan, *An American Life,* 265.

46. Ibid., 266–268; see also Haig, *Caveat,* 96–99.

47. Reagan, *An American Life,* 361.

48. Tyler, *A Great Wall,* 303–305.

49. Freeman interview; see also Tyler, *A Great Wall,* 300.

50. Secret cable to State Department from USDEL Secretary in Beijing (Haig to the President), June 16, 1981 (Doc. no. 00587), National Security Archives Collection: China and the United States.

51. Department of State Telegram to the President from Alexander Haig, "Talks in Beijing: June 14 Opening Meeting," June 15, 1981 (Doc. no. 00579), National Security Archives Collection: China and the United States.

52. Briefing Memo to Secretary Haig from John Holdridge, "Your Meetings with Chinese Foreign Minister Huang Hua," June 3, 1981 (Doc. no. 00559), National Security Archives Collection: China and the United States. See also the Day Book of Secretary Haig's Visit to the Far East, June 16, 1981 (Doc. no. 00582); Briefing Memo to Secretary Haig from John Holdridge, "Your Meeting with Chinese Communist Party Vice Chairman Deng Xiaoping," June 3, 1981 (Doc. no. 00557); and Talking Points on Afghanistan, June 1981 (Doc. no. 00554), National Security Archives Collection: China and the United States.

53. Freeman interview. The Soviet threats to crack down on Poland during the first few months of the Reagan administration created a climate and audience receptive to Haig's anti-Soviet China alliance. Haig, *Caveat*, 103–107; Hedrick Smith, "Who's in Charge of Foreign Policy? Well . . ."

54. Rope interview, June 2002, and author's correspondence with Rope, October 2003.

55. Telephone interview by the author with former Secretary of Defense Caspar Weinberger, May 15, 2002.

56. Author interviews with NSC and State Department officials from the Reagan administration, June 2002.

57. Rope correspondence, October 2003.

58. Weinberger interview.

59. Freeman interview.

60. Secretary Haig's Talking Points on Taiwan, June 4, 1981 (Doc. no. 00561); Briefing Memo from John Holdridge to Secretary Haig, "Your Meeting with Chinese Communist Party Vice Chairman Deng Xiaoping," June 3, 1981 (Doc. no. 00556), National Security Archives Collection: China and the United States.

61. Letter from Secretary Haig to Senator Baker, June 17, 1981 (Doc. no. 00599); "Talking Points for Background Briefings on Secretary's Visit to China," June 19, 1981 (Doc. no. 00606), National Security Archives Collection: China and the United States.

62. Steven Weisman, "Haig Remark on China Puzzles White House Aides."

63. Assistant Secretary Gaston Sigur, oral history interview, April 24, 1990; author interview with former State Department official, June 2002.

64. Haig, *Caveat*, 214.

65. Hummel interview.

66. Michael Weisskopf, "Zhao's Nonproliferation Stand Seen as Path to U.S. Aid Pact."

67. Holdridge interviews, July 20, 1995, and December 14, 1989; for a more critical interpretation of these events see Lilley, *China Hands*, 246–248.

68. Author interview with former State Department official in the Reagan administration, June 2002.

69. Memo from the White House to President [author excised], June 25, 1982, Folder: Haig's Resignation—Classified Documents, Box 91643-44 (1 of 1), William Clark Files: Files 91643, Reagan Presidential Library.

70. "Scheduling Haig," June 26, 1982, ibid.

71. Richard Nations, "A Tilt Towards Tokyo" author interview with State Department official from the Reagan administration, June 2002; Mann, *About Face*, 120–131.

72. Briefing Memoranda from Paul Wolfowitz to Secretary Shultz, "Your January–February Trip to East Asia," January 26, 1983 (Doc. no. 00654), National Security Archives Collection: China and the United States.

73. Author interviews with former NSC and State Department officials, June 2002.

74. Briefing Memorandum from Paul Wolfowitz to Secretary Shultz, "Your First Meeting with Chinese Foreign Minister Wu Xueqian," January 26, 1983 (Doc. no. 00621); Briefing Memoranda from Paul Wolfowitz to Secretary Shultz, "Your January–February Trip to East Asia," January 26, 1983 (Doc. no. 00622); Briefing Memoranda from Paul Wolfowitz to Secretary Shultz, "Your January–February Trip to East Asia," January 26, 1983 (Doc. no. 00623); Briefing Memoranda from Paul Wolfowitz to Secretary Shultz, "Your January–February Trip to East Asia," January 26, 1983 (Doc. no. 00628), National Security Archives Collection: China and the United States.

75. Garthoff, *Détente and Confrontation*, 96, 624–625; Soloman, *U.S. PRC Political Negotiations,* National Security Archives Collection: China and the United States, 106.

76. Briefing Memoranda to Secretary Shultz from Paul Wolfowitz, "Your January–February Trip to East Asia," January 26, 1983 (Doc. no. 00623), pp. 4–5, National Security Archives Collection: China and the United States.

77. Clyde Farnsworth, "Trade Shift on China Seen Near"; Fred Hiatt, "U.S. Used China Trip to Press Its Courtship."

78. Leslie Gelb, "U.S.-China Ties: Lower Expectations."

79. Unclassified Cables to Washington, D.C. from USDEL Secretary in Beijing Through NSC Message Center, Subject: Shultz Toast at PRC Welcoming Banquet and Cable from USDEL to DC on Shultz's Business Lunch, February 1983, File: Secretary Shultz's Trip to China, Japan, Korea, February 1983 (2 of 3), Box 90621, Gaston Sigur Files, Reagan Presidential Library.

80. Author interview with former Secretary of Defense Frank Carlucci, June 6, 2002, Washington, D.C.

81. Department of State, Bureau of Intelligence and Research Confidential Report, "China's View of the US and the USSR," March 27, 1984, National Security Archives postpublication Collection: China and the United States.

82. Tyler, *A Great Wall,* 337.

83. National Security Decision Directive No. 120, "Visit to the U.S. of Premier Zhao Ziyang," January 9, 1984, Folder: DSDD; NSSD 12-82; NSDD 140, NSDD 120, Briefings and NSC Meeting January 5, 1983 [84], Box 1 (Loc: 151/08/7), Douglas Paal Files, Reagan Presidential Library.

84. National Security Decision Directive No. 140, "The President's Visit to the People's Republic of China," April 21, 1984, Folder: DSDD; NSSD 12-82; NSDD 140, NSDD 120, Briefings and NSC Meeting, January 5, 1983 [84], Box 1 (Loc: 151/08/7), Douglas Paal Files, Reagan Presidential Library; see also Secret Talking Points, "The Trip of President Reagan to the PRC," April 1984 (Doc. no. 00662), National Security Archives Collection: China and the United States.

85. Sigur interview.

86. Hummel interview.

87. Reagan, *An American Life*, 368–369.

88. Freeman interview.

89. Weisskopf, "Zhao's Nonproliferation Stand."

90. Philip Geyelin, "Reagan: The Best of Both 'Chinas.'"

91. Freeman interview.

92. U.S.-China Relations, Bureau of Public Affairs, Department of State, Folder: Presidential Trip to Japan, China, and Korea, February 1989, OA/ID [CF00867], Box 5 of 5, NSC Roman Popandiule [OA/ID CF 0067], NSC Doug Paal China-US, January–February 1990 [1] to Public Liaison James Schaefer OA/ID 01560, Bush Presidential Library.

93. Keith Shimko, *Images and Arms Control.* For a discussion of the uncommitted thinker, see John Steinbrunner, *The Cybernetic Theory of Decision*, 129–131.

94. Barbara Farnham, "Perceiving the End of Threat: Ronald Reagan and the Gorbachev Revolution."

6

Salvaging U.S.-China Relations: G.H.W. Bush and the Aftermath of Tiananmen Square

Since the opening to China in 1972, the U.S. policy of engagement with the PRC rested on a shared strategic interest to contain the Soviet Union. Deng Xiaoping's economic reforms added a second reason as China opened up to investment from the West. These circumstances led to the optimistic sense that China's economic revolution would eventually lead to political reform as well. By the late 1980s, Reagan's policy resembled Richard Nixon's dream of close Sino-American relations. Public opinion polls from early 1989 reflected this positive sense. When asked to rate their overall opinion of China, 72 percent of respondents in a March 1989 Gallup poll were either very favorable or mostly favorable toward the PRC while only 13 percent were mostly or very unfavorable.[1]

Upon entering office, President George H.W. Bush's initial policy goal was to strengthen engagement with China and to usher in a new level of stability in U.S.-China bilateral relations. He was determined to engage China aggressively and forge a broad U.S. role in the architecture of the emerging order in Asia (simultaneously countering the Soviets) and to expand ties to encourage economic and political progress.[2] Export growth was "where it was at" in the post-Soviet world, Asia was where it would occur, and China would be the president's central focus in Asia. However, the administration faced problems, namely the Tiananmen Square crackdown and its aftermath, which challenged the realization of presidential goals. Most pointedly, the crackdown and the end of the Cold War halted conservative euphoria over the Sino-American relationship. Domestically, friction arose due to long-ignored issues such as China's arms sales to other countries, problems in the trade relationship, and increasing U.S. criticisms of Chinese human rights abuses from the political left and right. Chinese leaders for their part began to blame the United States more than the Soviets for the arms race and remained unhappy about U.S. "interference" in their internal affairs.

Sustaining a dialogue with China, given this political climate, became President Bush's greatest challenge. To proceed, China policy needed to move beyond containment of the Soviet Union and be reconciled to the advancements in democracy that had occurred in other parts of the world.[3] How the president and his advisers strategically framed their policy to accomplish this task is the central focus of this chapter.

President Bush, His Advisers, and Maintaining the U.S.-China Relationship

In contrast to the infighting and ideological nature of the Reagan administration, President Bush became a hands-on administrator who authorized a stronger NSC system. Toward East Asia, Bush assertively pursued a strategic policy that elevated the PRC over other interests such as Japan or Taiwan. Given his previous experience as U.S. ambassador to the United Nations, head of the U.S. liaison office in China, director of central intelligence, and as vice president, Bush was comfortable directing foreign policy, and specifically China policy, from the White House.[4] According to James Baker, Bush understood the Chinese psyche and would use his talent to build personal relations with Chinese leaders and to generate his own policy initiatives. Baker argues that Bush was "so knowledgeable about China, and so hands-on in managing most aspects of our policy, that even some of our leading Sinologists began referring to him as the government's desk officer for China." Bush's choice of James Lilley as the U.S. ambassador to Beijing, replacing Winston Lord, signaled that the president intended to be involved directly. Lilley was an optimal choice because he had a good relationship with Bush from the days when Lilley was the CIA station chief in Beijing during Bush's tenure as the liaison officer. Lilley was to be Bush's eyes and ears and help him take charge of China policy more directly.[5]

Players and Their Positions

With the president's involvement the NSC became the principal forum "for coordinating Executive departments and agencies in the development and implementation of national security policy." The national security adviser chaired the NSC principals committee (made up of the secretaries of state and defense, among other central players), in which policy options were developed. At the staff level an NSC deputies' committee was established for principal deputies, and an NSC policy coordinating committee was established for each regional area including East Asia (subsequently chaired by individuals selected by the secretary of state).[6] In practice, the president relied on an informal system of advisers like National Security Adviser Brent Scowcroft and Secretary of State James Baker whom he knew well and trusted. Bush had worked with Scowcroft in the Nixon and Ford administrations and Baker was a long-time close friend. Scowcroft states that he managed the process to make sure the issues studied were ones that needed a presidential decision. He was uniquely able to perform this role because he was the only adviser with no institutional affiliation.[7]

The administration avoided some of the classic NSC–State Department infighting in previous administrations because of the president's direct involvement and the close ties among the advisers. For example, ties between the NSC and State Department were strengthened because Deputy Secretary of State Lawrence Eagleburger had worked closely with Scowcroft in Henry Kissinger's consulting firm, Kissinger Associates, and they shared many of the same policy orientations.[8] This meant the Bush administration represented a rare instance in the post-Vietnam context when there was a relatively harmonious relationship between the NSC staff and the secretary of state.[9]

The president's personalized system also meant that as the system was centralized at the top, the central players also isolated themselves from traditional sources of information coming from below and outside the bureaucracy. Baker's organization of the State Department repeated the closed nature of the president's inner circle and ignored the formal arm of the department that came up with policy papers. To bring something to the secretary of state's attention, it had to be channeled through one of his people.[10] Paul Russo, a State Department official in the Bush administration, argued that Baker's tendency to keep decisionmaking tightly held ignored the thousands of people who had years of experience with these countries. The consequence was that the United States missed the benefits of plugging into the system by cutting out a State

Department bureaucracy it did not trust.[11] One deputy assistant secretary for overseas citizen services characterized Bush's orders as "don't you trust those bureaucrats. Don't you trust them. You push them around. You do what you want. I don't want to hear you agreeing with them. I want you following our policies, and if you have to get rough with them, you get rough with them."[12]

Among the president's central advisers, Scowcroft took the greatest interest in China and wanted a meeting with the Chinese as soon as possible. For him "it was one of the most important relationships we had. It was especially useful in putting pressure on the Russians."[13] The death of Japanese Emperor Hirohito in February 1989 provided an early opportunity for George Bush to travel to China and take charge of his efforts to strengthen the Sino-American relationship—three months before Mikhail Gorbachev's scheduled May 15 visit. While in China, Bush emphasized that China had a friend in the White House committed to expanding the relationship. In return, Deng Xiaoping reassured Bush that Sino-Soviet rapprochement would not come at U.S. expense and that normalizing China's relations with the USSR would not entail a return to the Sino-Soviet alliance of the 1950s. The administration relied on the assumption that China's modernization goals necessitated a continued open door policy toward the United States and the West.[14]

During his February trip, President Bush downplayed issues that could generate domestic U.S. controversy (e.g., Chinese arms sales and references to China's dismal human rights record). He voiced confidence and optimism that the Chinese could be trusted on missile proliferation. Responding to reports of sales of Chinese Silkworm missiles and intermediate-range ballistic missiles routed through North Korea to the Middle East, the administration argued that China's "strict measures" on antiship missiles had been effective. On ballistic missiles it stated that on a number of occasions, including trips by George Shultz and Frank Carlucci in 1988, the United States had expressed its concerns and accepted Chinese assurances.[15] When the president was asked about proliferation during his visit, he told the *New York Times* that China would act responsibly. Comments on China's human rights record were to be avoided at all costs. However, the Chinese exclusion of astrophysicist Fang Lizhi, a noted human rights advocate, from attending a dinner President Bush hosted in Beijing forced the issue. Responding to the press, Bush downplayed the incident by explaining that human rights were but one aspect of the overall relationship. When Fang Lizhi was prevented from attending the dinner, the president did not lodge an official protest.[16]

Buildup to Tiananmen Square

In mid-April in China the death of Hu Yaobang, the former reform-minded general secretary of the Communist Party, generated huge crowds of mourners in Beijing's Tiananmen Square and in other cities around China. This demonstration of grief evolved into a diverse protest focusing on issues such as high inflation, government corruption, and economic stagnation. The protests became more antigovernment and escalated, with widespread hunger strikes by the eve of Gorbachev's May 15 visit. Taken by surprise by these protests, Chinese leaders were divided in their response, which heated up an internal power struggle between Deng's protégé Zhao Ziyang, who was sympathetic to the students, and the more cautious faction led by Premier Li Peng. On May 19, the leadership struggle resulted in Zhao being stripped of his authority and the next day the ordering of martial law.[17]

During this period Washington ignored the growing protests and instead prepared for the visit of Wan Li (chair of the National Standing Committee of the National People's Congress), scheduled just four days after Gorbachev's departure from China.[18] The preparation for Wan Li's visit to Washington provides specific evidence of the administration's single-minded pursuit of better relations with China despite the evolving crisis. The talking points provided to Secretary Baker and the president in anticipation of the visit by the State Department's Bureau of East Asian and Pacific Affairs point out that the administration would emphasize the U.S. commitment to strengthen bilateral relations, particularly in light of stronger Sino-Soviet ties. The president also was to express his personal commitment to further expand U.S.-PRC relations.[19]

According to one high-level embassy official who was in Beijing during the Tiananmen Square incident, it was hard to convince Washington that a crackdown was coming. Messages from Ambassador James Lilley in May went through official channels but did not make it to the president. The president also was predisposed to ignore the growing signs of unrest despite daily summaries from the embassy to the secretary of state speculating about a likely return to Leninist orthodoxy.[20] By June 3, the situation reached critical mass once notices published in Beijing warned that the People's Liberation Army (PLA) would impose martial law in Beijing.[21] Scowcroft himself admits that the administration was "fairly passive" about it and counted on the moderation of the Chinese.[22]

President Bush's response to the Chinese crackdown was more conservative than his critics demanded. Dismissing calls to break off formal relations, he remained careful not to isolate the Chinese leadership and threaten the broader U.S.-China relationship. The first round of limited sanctions he imposed focused on "suspension of all government-to-government sales and commercial exports of weapons, suspension of visits between U.S. and Chinese military leaders, [and a] sympathetic review of requests by Chinese students in the United States to extend their stay." He also offered humanitarian and medical assistance through the Red Cross to those injured during the assult and pledged to review other aspects of the bilateral relationship as needed.[23] With these sanctions the president resisted calls for a harsher reaction that included recalling Ambassador Lilley from Beijing and an immediate review of a full range of military and economic sanctions. Anticipating sanction legislation in Congress, the president announced a second wave of sanctions on June 20 that included the suspension of all high-level contacts with Beijing and postponed consideration of new international financial institution loans to China.[24] However, these failed to head off congressional sanction pressures. An alliance between hard-line anti-Communists such as Senator Jesse Helms (R–North Carolina) and liberals such as Representative Stephen Solarz (D–New York), chair of the House Subcommittee on Asia and the Pacific, formed a core of opposition to the administration's conservative response.[25]

Legislative attempts to attach amendments to the Foreign Aid Authorization Bill for fiscal year 1990/91 led to a combined comprehensive sanctions amendment that passed the House (418-0) in June and the Senate (81-10) in July. The sanctions suspended OPIC financial support in China, halted previously authorized funds for trade and development, mandated opposition for six months to liberalization of export controls, and banned the export of crime control equipment and nuclear equipment that could be used for military purposes.[26]

The comprehensive sanctions amendment allowed Congress to vent its outrage while still remaining within the bounds of the administration's preferences. Congress, in keeping with the wishes of the administration, did not rescind China's MFN status in retaliation for the crackdown. When the bill was revised to give the president greater leeway to waive sanctions, the president rescinded his veto threat and signed the legislation. According to Stephen Solarz, the chief sponsor of the sanctions package, "This amendment steers a very careful course between the two extremes—those who would like us to entirely sever diplomatic relationships with China and those who don't want us to take any action for fear of disturbing Deng Xiaoping and driving him into the arms of

Russia."[27] The sanctions bill became a bipartisan substitute for the two dozen bills, many of them harsher, that had been before the Congress.

Through this period the administration worked to maintain executive-branch control of China policy and to have one voice in policymaking in response to the tough domestic context. According to the national security adviser, there were no overwhelming differences because "everyone knew where the president stood."[28] Scowcroft's secret trip to China in early July is the best indication that policymaking became centralized under White House supervision; he went as the president's personal emissary. Although Eagleburger's presence on the two trips (one in July and one in December) demonstrated Baker's sensitivity to being cut out of policymaking altogether, for the most part policymaking during this period worked out as a division of labor, with the national security adviser taking the lead with the president.[29] Baker served only a limited role as the president's proxy with the Chinese and the Congress. Former administration officials argue that the president became the prime mover with Scowcroft rather than Baker because of their long record in dealing with China.[30] In addition, it seemed to work out this way because China was a sensitive domestic political issue that Baker was not interested in tackling, especially after Tiananmen. Baker was delighted not to have China on his personal agenda and avoided the policy because he regarded it as a loser.[31]

China's government, however, remained unwilling to accommodate the administration's efforts. For example, both publicly and privately, Bush's appeals for clemency for the students went unheard. In this context the president was forced to respond to domestic pressures for more sanctions. On November 16, with the proviso he could lift sanctions as needed for national security, he signed a bill that imposed a ban on arms sales and U.S. satellite exports, and clamped down on domestic export controls.[32] Despite the legislation, the administration sent signals through high-level meetings and made concessions to China that circumvented the imposed sanctions. For example, the president made exceptions for items such as the sale of Boeing aircraft, F-8 upgrades, and AUSSAT satellite launches. However, the next sanctions bill in fall 1989, Nancy Pelosi's Emergency Chinese Immigration Relief Act, raised the greatest challenge to the president's agenda. This legislation would grant a four-year extension on Chinese student visas and dropped the requirement that they had to return to China for two years before reapplying for a visa. Its veto by George Bush just as Scowcroft and Eagleburger made plans for a second visit to Beijing generated a new round of fights with Congress.

The fight over the Pelosi legislation and later, MFN debates set a pattern of executive-congressional wrangling that lasted through the Bush administration and beyond. The next section explores Bush's framing efforts in the context of the domestic challenge he faced.

President Bush's Public Framing Efforts

The high level of unity between the president and his advisers meant that the target for the framing game shifted outward to congressional critics who challenged the presidential foreign policy agenda. Bush's efforts to solidify and then reestablish the bilateral relationship with Beijing had to be reconciled with domestic political realities (i.e., the political firestorm the Tiananmen Square massacre had brought out). In his memoir, Secretary of State James Baker argues that it "forced a risky juggling act upon our new administration. Suddenly, we were challenged to defend a policy encompassing geostrategic, commercial, and human rights interests that in large measure conflicted." The dilemma faced by the president was dangerous to a policy that rested on a complex (and often conflicting) set of policy rationales.[33] Differences revolved around what emphasis to place on the strategic value of the Sino-American relationship and what the potential was for future reform in China. For an administration committed to strengthening bilateral relations, there were two problems—an assertive Congress and continued Chinese intransigence.

Diagnosing the Policy Problem

Bush's challenge was to make sure China did not close itself off from the rest of the world and thereby threaten the stable relationship his administration and his predecessors had worked hard to forge. To do this, the administration emphasized the long-term goals in the relationship and downplayed the immediate Tiananmen Square issue. Shifting focus, the administration's baseline emphasized Deng's courage in opening China, along with the historical change that had occurred since 1972, to draw attention away from the crackdown.[34] It argued that gains through engagement rather than isolation meant that, despite the events in Tiananmen Square, China's people enjoyed more freedom than in 1971, when China had a much more brutal regime. For example, in talking points following June 3, the administration hoped that China soon would return to a responsible role in world politics.[35] The president declared that given the emotional nature of the issue, it was time for "reasoned, careful action that takes into account both our long-term interests and recognition of a complex internal situation in China." The logical policy was for the United States to remain engaged if it was to have any influence to work for cooperation and restraint in China.[36]

The administration's metaphorical reference point for responding to events in China seemed to be a comparison to ones in Eastern Europe. In his memoirs, Baker likens the Tiananmen situation to Hungary in 1956, arguing that any rash action could trigger a more violent response that would really hurt bilateral relations.[37] In press reports, the situation was compared to the Solidarity movement in Poland. Although Poland instituted martial law, eventually Polish Communist leaders had been forced to share power.[38] If the Chinese troubles could be seen as being part of the same democratic cycle, then patience was the effective response. Bush's call for a limited response reflected the "hope that China will rapidly return to the path of political and economic reform and conditions of stability so that this relationship, so important to both our peoples, can continue its growth."[39]

As a body Congress was poised to take the initiative from the president. Members of Congress like Stephen Solarz saw the issue in different terms. The important issue was not the U.S. ability to influence the course of events in China, which he felt was very limited, but its capacity to credibly maintain leadership of the movement for democracy and human rights around the world. He thought the United States should manifest its concern by deeds as well as words.[40] He was joined by voices on the political right who accused Bush of kowtowing to the Communists. This made the central policy problem one about how to control the domestic political discussion.

Themes That Resonated with President Bush and Bolstered the Public Frame

Presidential beliefs and priorities. What motivated George Bush to be so conservative in his response to Tiananmen? One answer is that for Bush the Cold War anti-Soviet link was unmistakable. Specific examples such as the president's February visit to China and the points he raised in his discussion with Wan Li illustrate his concern about the deepening of ties between the Chinese and the Soviets. A second component of Bush's engagement policy rested on the assumption that expansion of economic ties with the Chinese (among others) would stabilize the relationship and lead to progress toward political reform. Baker explained in his memoir that "history shows that economic and political reform are but two sides of the same coin. Give someone economic freedom and they will want political freedom." During the president's visit to China, and again when Wan Li came to Washington, Bush felt reassured that economic reform would continue in China.[41]

Underpinning Bush's beliefs was a basic optimism reflecting the neoliberal assumption that trade and commercial ties promote reform. In talking points for the press for May 1989, the administration indicated it was working with Chinese leaders to expand trade opportunities and to emphasize the benefits of economic liberalization. On thorny issues such as intellectual property rights, market access, and China's membership in the General Agreement on Tariffs and Trade (GATT), administration officials emphasized the progress China had made over the previous several years, adding that regular contact would guarantee further progress.[42] Because the Chinese needed U.S. help to sustain their levels of economic growth, the administration felt it had some leverage to encourage political reform.

The president's emphasis on political reform, however, had clear limits if and when it came into conflict with his strategic interests and the overall stability of the relationship. For example, when Bush was in Beijing, he made sure he did not embarrass his hosts with the human rights question and specifically downplayed the issue when the Chinese prevented Fang Lizhi from attending Bush's Beijing banquet. Before the crackdown, Representative Solarz accused the president of not doing enough to help the students in their quest for freedom. Bush was accused of a double standard in regard to other Communist states because the administration asked less of China on human rights than it did the Soviet Union.[43]

Bush's measured response to Tiananmen Square illustrated a president committed to focusing on a longer time frame. It was important for him not to risk permanent damage to a mutually beneficial relationship built over two decades. Themes that reinforced the status quo relationship with the PRC resonated with a president deeply involved in the day-to-day decisionmaking.

Policy themes: Reinforcing China's strategic and economic value. The Cold War rationale lingered and new components became part of the strategic focus. Brent Scowcroft, in particular, reinforced George Bush's perspective that China served as an important strategic counterweight to the Soviet Union. Their concern that the Soviets would use rapprochement with China to score points against the United States lasted well beyond Tiananmen Square.[44] Bush and Scowcroft saw a strong and friendly China as an essential part of the administration's strategy for practical reasons, such as maintaining the network of secret U.S. listening posts across China that monitored military developments in the USSR.[45] During the second Scowcroft-Eagleburger mission, Scowcroft made sure he briefed the Chinese on the recently completed Malta Summit (before the Soviets had an opportunity to do so) as he worked on getting concessions from the Chinese not to sell missiles to the Middle East.[46] Even with the waning of the Cold War, Scowcroft saw China as a strategic player because it was a nuclear power and an arms exporter. Restraint would be gained on issues of interest to the United States like arms proliferation only with engagement at the highest levels. In January 1990, before the Senate Foreign Relations Committee, Lawrence Eagleburger repeated this argument, saying that the Cold War basis for strong Sino-Soviet relations was still "marginally important" but the real need was for cooperation on the proliferation of missiles, nuclear weapons, and chemical weapons.[47]

Scowcroft acknowledged that "when the Soviet Union disappears, then that sort of glue that held us together is gone and then the differences in perspective become overriding and the relationship gets more difficult to keep together." However, because China was destined to become a powerful influence in the Asian region, it was "important that we maintain a relationship with them and to steer them in ways which were not hostile to U.S. interests."[48]

The commercial theme gained some traction in Congress. Talking points for use with Congress reinforced the theme that the mutual interests of the United States and China were served best by continued bilateral commercial relations despite fundamental political differences.[49] Foreign trade and investment were seen as essential tools to keep China open to the outside world and encourage responsible behavior in areas like human rights and arms proliferation. Discontinuing MFN would make the administration's overall policy futile. If MFN was not renewed, it could reduce U.S. leverage in market-access and other issues, hurt U.S. exports and consumers, damage the nation's reputation as a reliable trade partner, hurt investors and business in Hong Kong, and set back meaningful reform in China.[50]

This perspective rested on the familiar assumption that "economic forces have been driving political and social change and encouraging a loosening of state control and more personal freedom. Withdrawing MFN would have the greatest adverse impact on [the] Chinese in the most dynamic, market-oriented coastal regions." The press guidance was very specific on the economic effects of MFN withdrawal. Major exports at stake included wheat ($511 million), aircraft ($749 million), fertilizer ($544 million), cotton ($259 million), timber ($281 million), computers and electronics ($860 million), and chemicals ($273 million). Hinting at domestic political costs, the press guidance noted that U.S. consumers would pay higher rates on footwear, clothing, toys, and electronic products.[51]

Domestic political considerations. Bush's arguments for presidential prerogative and the emphasis on his experience in foreign affairs were the central tactics used to overcome congressional sanctions pressure. As congressional criticism heated up on June 5, Bush declared, "I'm the President; I set the foreign policy objectives and actions taken by the executive branch. I think they know, most of them in Congress, that I have not only a keen personal interest in China, but that I understand it reasonably well."[52] As the comprehensive sanctions vote approached in late June 1989, he emphasized that the "appropriate" role for the president in foreign policy was for him to do what he thought was best for the country. He reminded members of Congress that he had many more factors to consider than did those who were his greatest critics.[53]

Bush's response to Tiananmen Square demonstrated that he was willing to follow his own views regardless of the opposition. Immediately following the massacre, Bush ignored the advice of his secretary of state to strongly denounce Beijing and put strong sanctions in place.[54] From the first, Baker proved more sensitive to the domestic political context and knew Congress would have to be dealt with carefully. On June 5 the president did agree with Baker's recommendations that the Chinese foreign minister's scheduled visit on June 12 should not proceed under the circumstances and that Secretary of Commerce Robert Mossbacher's trip to China should be postponed. An interagency working group had recommended it go forward, but Baker felt that it undermined the administration's message of outrage if Qichen Qian arrived for consultations.[55] An action memo to the secretary of state after Tiananmen Square noted it was critical for the president to "announce a strong, balanced reaction as soon as possible, both in order to express the United States' outrage and condemnation of the PLA's action and to preempt legislation that might do long-term damage to U.S.-PRC relations and be difficult to reverse."[56] These recommendations reflected the assumption that the United States could not conduct business as usual, but that the unstable situation in China called for a response that did not limit options.[57]

When Baker testified before the Senate Foreign Relations Committee, however, he reinforced the president's message on executive leadership in foreign policy. He focused on the risks of not having a unified approach to the problem and cited past examples where the United States had not spoken with one voice in foreign policy and thus failed to achieve its policy goals. To minimize congressional hostility, Baker also announced that the president had decided to cut off high-level contacts as an additional sanction on the Chinese. Baker's actions indicated he was sensitive to congressional demands and the need for a forceful reaction to Chinese intransigence.[58]

In the face of growing congressional pressure to react, the administration's strategy adjusted to compromise with Congress but only when it retained policy flexibility. When the initial sanctions bills were combined and MFN was off the table, Bush signed the legislation once he gained the authority to designate important exceptions. After signing sanctions legislation, he immediately announced a series of exceptions such as authorizing the licensing for three U.S.-built AUSSAT and AsiaSat satellites for launch on Chinese-built launch vehicles and waiving prohibitions on the Export-Import Bank's financing of trade with the PRC.[59]

In November 1989, Bush faced his greatest challenge in the face of legislation introduced by Congresswoman Nancy Pelosi (D-California) that would extend protection to Chinese students studying in the United States. The president pocket vetoed the Pelosi legislation, which he argued would unnecessarily tie his hands in the conduct of foreign policy.[60] In his memorandum of disapproval, he stated that he shared the objectives of the majority of Congress and had taken actions to protect Chinese students through an executive order.[61] The president argued the bill was not only unnecessary but that the long-term policy consequences were potentially great. Continued engagement showed that China more often chose peace over tension with its neighbors. Tiananmen Square was a setback to a people whose wealth and freedom were increasingly responsive to international standards of behavior. "My worry is that we not slam the door on this initial forward motion in US-China relations and in China's treatment of its own people."[62]

Controversial pictures showing the national security adviser toasting the Chinese leaders who had ordered the Tiananmen massacre just as the earlier secret mission to China was revealed galvanized liberal Democrats to attempt an override of the veto. Arguing for the benefit of the doubt, Bush told the Congress that more was at stake than had been revealed and that his strategy had led to a breakthrough in relations. To secure Republican support, the president added an argument for

Republican loyalty: "The bill is totally unnecessary, the long term policy consequences potentially great. Don't give the Democrats the first
perceived victory of the session with no substance to justify it." He
insisted that the successful policy of five administrations was at stake in
dealing with China, which meant a "China more often choosing peace
with its neighbors rather than tensions, a people whose wealth and freedom were increasing, an increasingly responsible standard of international behavior." Tiananmen set back reform but it had not been swept
away. He added, "This is a strong message. I want you to see it that
way. Don't stop the process. Don't vote with the Democrats and for
Pelosi."[63]

When Congress returned from its Christmas break, there was considerable momentum to override Bush's November 30 veto.
Disregarding the administration's appeals, the House, in particular, saw
the opportunity to show a bipartisan repudiation of Bush's China policy,
and on January 24, 1990, it voted 390-25 to override the veto. On
January 25, however, the Senate sustained the president's veto by four
votes (62-37). Bush took this as a signal that he could go ahead with his
policy approach.[64]

Supporting Conditions:
Agenda Control and Limits of the Back Channel

In the post–Cold War environment, Bush faced a growing domestic
challenge that made it difficult to successfully use past tactics like
Nixon's back channel. The Chinese refusal to make concessions made it
difficult to claim that any major success came from those negotiations
in the domestic arena. Justifying the back-channel moves in their memoirs, the president and his advisers argued that this way the Chinese
would understand his dismay at the violence, as well as the message
that the relationship could not return to normal until the repression
stopped; simultaneously, he could repeat his overall commitment to
maintaining the relationship.[65] U.S. concessions such as the decision to
move forward with the July sale of four Boeing aircraft to China
(delayed because of U.S. sanctions) and the decision in September to
allow U.S. contractors to proceed with upgrades to Chinese F-8 fighters
also did not change the Chinese response. The administration felt
efforts like these could give the United States leverage and encourage
the Chinese government to go easier on students.[66]

Former President Nixon and Henry Kissinger (on separate occasions) traveled in fall 1989 to China delivering private messages. After his return Nixon met with Bush and argued that it was time for the president to make a second move toward the Chinese.[67] Scowcroft planned a second trip for December 1989 with this in mind, explaining it indicated that if the United States would be responsive, the Chinese were ready to take action to seek the world's good graces again. He argued that the United States had not kowtowed to China.[68] According to Scowcroft, the second visit set in place a road map for improved relations. The administration subsequently claimed that the meeting brought about the end to martial law (lifted in January 1990) and the reopening of Tiananmen Square. In addition, the Chinese agreed to accept Peace Corps representation, accredit a Voice of America correspondent, release more Tiananmen detainees, and ban the sale of missiles to the Middle East (first announced in 1988). They also hinted there might be a solution to the Fang Lizhi issue.[69] More generally, the administration claimed the high-level mission had ended the backslide of the relationship and that the Chinese were convinced that goodwill begets goodwill.

For a limited time the back channel gave the president the autonomy to signal his resolve despite congressional sanctions. Once these efforts became public in fall 1989, however, it backfired domestically, fueling the Democrats' efforts to override the Pelosi legislation veto. The political context had changed so dramatically that back-channel contacts were hard to sustain. Table 6.1 lays out the major components of Bush's China policy frame.

The President, Congress, and MFN After 1989

Congressional opposition galvanized by Tiananmen settled into a predictable yearly pattern each time MFN renewal came up after 1989. The president used familiar themes, for instance, that not renewing MFN would harm rather than help U.S. interests and concerns.[70] He emphasized the promotion of freedom of emigration (China qualified under Jackson-Vanik),[71] the importance of commercial relations to promote reform, and the need to maintain engagement with the Chinese on issues of U.S. interest including human rights, nonproliferation, prison labor, exports, and trade issues. In black-and-white terms, a trade war would hurt business while a constructive relationship served world peace.

Reciprocal granting of MFN remained the essential element in

Table 6.1   Components of George H.W. Bush's China Policy Frame

Problem diagnosis	• Challenge to maintain stable relationship and not isolate PRC; need to overcome domestic pressure
Themes that resonated with president and public	
Presidential beliefs	• PRC strategically important vis-à-vis the USSR and given its position in East Asia • Remarkable economic reform in China harbinger for future liberalization
Policy themes	• Scowcroft reinforces strategic view that the Soviet threat is viable and given PRC's status as a growing power, its cooperation is needed in areas like arms proliferation • Baker reinforces link between economic reform and political reform; East European model of inevitable reform
Political considerations	• Administration united in presenting presidential prerogative arguments and referring to Bush's experience in foreign policy • Remain unresponsive to public calls for greater sanctions • Compromise only when they can maintain presidential flexibility on exceptions to sanctions • Baker argues for careful handling of Congress; placate Taiwan interests in context of 1992 election
Supporting conditions/tactics	• Centralized advisory system from the first; back-channel contacts had only limited utility

political and economic relations and reform within China. The president concluded that "MFN tariff status has given the Chinese the incentive to take into account U.S. interests—on fair trade practices globally, human rights, missile and arms sales, and cooperation on such regional issues as Cambodia and the Korean peninsula." Without MFN China would have little to lose in economic terms by failing to cooperate with the United States and this would undercut the reform effort.[72] Within the NSC and the State Department in general (EAP specifically), human rights were seen through a prism that linked long-term progress in China to MFN and open trade relations. James Bishop, principal deputy to the assistant secretary for human rights during the Bush administration, stated that within the State Department—even within the human rights bureau—there was agreement that commercial relations and MFN should not be denied to China: "If we used more subtle forms of pressure and remained engaged, then the process of economic liberalization would inevitably result in less abusive human rights practices by the Chinese leadership." China had made great progress and would continue to do so.[73]

The Bush administration continued to emphasize new progress with China resulting from the high-level dialogue it had maintained after Tiananmen. Although it had taken tough action when necessary, it supported the opportunity to engage constructively with the Chinese.[74] It was careful, however, not to draw specific conclusions that could box them in. The administration reported "limited positive steps" to Congress, with the caveat that new restrictive measures in China continued to stifle free expression. Relations would remain far from normal until the PRC took significant steps to turn away from repression. The administration wanted to avoid isolating China's regime because it would "only diminish prospects for reform or slow even further the pace of improvements in the important area of human rights." The report concluded it would be premature to link particular U.S. and multilateral policies with internal developments in China.[75]

The relationship got somewhat back on track in late 1990 because the United States needed China's support in the UN for its action in Iraq. When Foreign Minister Qian Qichen came to Washington from November 30–December 1, he sought and received a meeting with President Bush, despite Baker's reluctance to do this without winning greater concessions. This decision signaled that the president had again taken over the agenda for the relationship with an eye toward strategic realities.[76]

By 1991, the president more openly claimed success—that through his efforts the Chinese government had acknowledged the legitimacy of human rights as a subject of bilateral discussion and tangible improvements had been made, including freeing some political prisoners. On proliferation concerns, he declared that the dialogue had helped China move toward the international consensus on nonproliferation in areas of importance to the United States such as the Middle East arms control initiative, the Missile Technology Control Regime (MTCR), and the Non-Proliferation Treaty (NPT). On trade and economic issues the administration stated its commitment to achieving with China the same goals that guided U.S. trade policy with all other countries. Specifically, through engagement it sought to improve U.S. access to China's marketplace, to protect intellectual property, to end fraudulent practices by textile exporters, and to help Beijing make the reforms required for GATT membership.[77]

Despite improvement, the balance in U.S.-China relations and in domestic politics was easily upset. The question of the sale of 150 F-16s to Taiwan in summer 1992 as the presidential election approached demonstrated a return to a domestic political calculation involving Taiwan despite the potential damage it might cause to U.S.-PRC relations. The purpose of the sale was to get the support of pro-Taiwan Republicans and to win Texas in 1992.[78] Chas Freeman alleges that the authorization of the largest sale in U.S. history to Taiwan essentially shredded the 1982 communiqué and undermined Sino-American relations: "It released the Chinese from their undertaking to tolerate arms sales to Taiwan . . . and it began the process that has produced a reemerging crisis in U.S.-China relations."[79] A second former administration official argued that the codicil attached to the 1982 communiqué by President Reagan justified the F-16 sale to Taiwan because the balance of power was shifting across the Taiwan Strait in China's favor.[80]

The F-16 sale also was accompanied by a package of concessions to placate the Chinese presented in late 1992 by Assistant Secretary for East Asia William Clark; these included moves to reestablish military-to-military ties and a joint committee hearing on commerce and trade (a mechanism halted after Tiananmen). During his trip, Clark succeeded in reducing the level of hostility that Beijing was voicing.[81] Despite the obvious domestic considerations for the sale, the strategic importance of China remained central to Bush's foreign policy.

Conclusion

The first Bush administration covered a pivotal time period in Sino-American relations encompassing the collapse of the Soviet empire and the Chinese crackdown that seared a negative image of China into the public's mind. Chas Freeman concluded: "And so the two things coming together meant that the previous policy of setting aside ideological differences in order to pursue practical cooperation between the United States and China effectively came to an end, symbolically, with the ill-fated December 1989 visit of National Security Adviser Brent

Scowcroft to Beijing."[82] Tiananmen Square squashed some of the euphoria over China, and the president's efforts to frame policy in familiar terms became more difficult in the face of rising opposition.

Like Nixon's, the Bush administration case illustrates how the president's beliefs about his effectiveness in foreign policy influenced his perception of his ability to address the situation. Because George Bush had a well-defined belief system and China schemata with well-developed goals and subgoals, his policy remained remarkably stable in the face of numerous challenges. He believed his approach to China was the only viable one, and this was reinforced by his experience there, his confidence in his ability to direct foreign policy, and a foreign policy team that to a great extent shared his outlook and values.[83]

In the Bush administration advisers played an important role of bolstering rather than shifting the president's attitudes. There is no doubt that General Scowcroft shared and affirmed Bush's strategic concerns. Secretary of State Baker stayed out of the day-to-day decisionmaking but did keep an eye on the domestic political side. The cohesiveness in Bush's foreign policy team and the outside pressure they faced helped them develop a bunker mentality. The high level of self- and collective efficacy inside the administration may have made them vulnerable to groupthink symptoms, but in this case there were few corresponding negative outcomes.

Because he faced opposition from both sides of the aisle, Bush proceeded carefully, emphasizing multiple win-win themes—including strategic, economic, and progress themes—that could appeal to a diverse audience. Arguments that emphasized presidential prerogative, the geostrategic/historical relationship, and progress through engagement demonstrated the risks associated with "rash" actions, and also the opportunities associated with a measured approach. Only reluctantly did the administration impose sanctions. It also consistently fought the scope of sanctions that the Congress tried to impose and largely succeeded in its efforts.

Notes

1. Gallup Poll survey released April 6, 1984.
2. Baker, *Politics of Diplomacy*, 101.
3. National Security Strategy Report Fact Sheet, Office of the White House Press Secretary, March 20, 1990, Folder, National Security COAS299, White House Press Office, Subject File, Box 85, Bush Presidential Library.

4. Mulcahy, "The Bush Administration and National Security Policy-making."

5. Baker, *Politics of Diplomacy*, 100; James A. Baker telephone interview by the author, November 7, 2002; Michael B. Smith, oral history interview, August 25, 1993.

6. National Security Directive (NSD) 1, January 30, 1989, pp. 1–4.

7. Brent Scowcroft, telephone interview by the author, September 16, 2002.

8. Bush and Scowcroft, *A World Transformed*, 17–19; R. W. Apple Jr., "New World: Is Bush Prepared to Imagine the Future?"; Elaine Sciolino, "Bush's Washington: Who's Who—Second Article of a Series," A1, A25; Baker interview.

9. Peter W. Rodman, oral history interview, May 22, 1994; Robert H.B. Wade, oral history interview, January 20, 1990.

10. Anne O. Cary, oral history interview, November 30, 1995.

11. Paul A. Russo, oral history interview, February 8, 1991.

12. Elizabeth Ann Swift, oral history interview, December 16, 1992.

13. Scowcroft interview.

14. Press Guidance for the Trip of President Bush to Japan, the PRC, and Republic of Korea, February 22–27, 1989, U.S. China Relations, Bureau of Public Affairs, Department of State, Folder: Presidential Trip to Japan, China, and Korea, February 1989, OA/ID [CF00867], NSC Roman Popandiule [OA/ID CF 0067] Files, NSC Doug Paal, China-US January–February 1990 [1] to Public Liaison James Schaefer, OA/ID 01560, Box 5 of 5, Bush Presidential Library.

15. Department of State, East Asian Bureau, Press Guidance, February 23, 1989, Folder: China [OA/ID 06786], White House Press Office, Marlin Fitzwater Files, CBS [OA6786 through Christmas Card/Part [2] [OA6786], Box 4, Bush Presidential Library. See also EAP Press Guidance, "China Travel Restrictions and Weapons Sales," February 23, 1989 (no. 01011); EAP Press Guidance, "China: Helping Iran Build Missile Factory," March 9, 1989 (no. 01013); EAP Talking Points, "Chinese Missile Proliferation," April 4, 1989 (no. 01019), National Security Archives Collection: China and the United States.

16. R. W. Apple Jr., "Bush Hails Seoul for Building Ties with North Korea." Apparently, Fang Lizhi had been included on the guest list to placate domestic interests rather than reflect any particular administration interest in human rights. See Marlin Fitzwater Background Information and Press Guidance on Invitation to Chinese Dissident to President's Dinner, February 1989, Folder China [OA/ID 06786], White House Press Office, Marlin Fitzwater Files, CBS [OA6786 through Christmas Card/Part [2] [OA6786], Box 4, Bush Presidential Library. Secretary Baker noted that the way to get progress on human rights "is not to do it in a big public way and do it with a great deal of public display and fanfare. The way you do it is to quietly press for it." See Transcript of Interview of Secretary James A. Baker III by Tom Brokaw of NBC, February 24, 1989, Folder: China [OA/ID 06786], White House Press Office, Marlin Fitzwater Files, CBS [OA6786 through Christmas Card/Part [2] [OA6786], Box 4, Bush Presidential Library.

17. Baker, *Politics of Diplomacy*, 102; Bush and Scowcroft, *A World Transformed*, 87–88; Tyler, *A Great Wall,* 346–353.

18. Memo to Carnes Lord, White House, from Department of State Bureau of East Asian and Pacific Affairs (EAP), "Proposed Visit of Chinese Politburo Member Wan Li," February 21, 1989 (no. 01010); Action Memo to Mr. Kimmit from EAP William Clark Jr., "Request for Presidential Aircraft for the Visit of PRC Chairman of the National People's Congress Wan Li," March 24, 1989 (no. 01015); Confidential Dept. of State Incoming Telegram from American Embassy Beijing to Secretary of State (no. 01021); EAP Press Guidance, "Sino-Soviet Summit," May 10, 1989 (no. 01039); Bureau of Intelligence and Research Weekend Edition, "The USSR and China at the Summit: Common Goals, Enduring Differences," May 14, 1989 (no. 01049); Background Paper for the President, "The President's Meeting with Wan Li," May 13, 1989 (no. 01048), National Security Archives Collection: China and the United States.

19. Memorandum of Conversation of President Bush with Chairman Wan Li, May 23, 1989 (no. 01051); Talking Points to James Baker from EAP, "Points to Be Made" (no. 01028); Memo to Carnes Lord in the White House, from Department of State, Bureau of East Asian and Pacific Affairs (EAP), "Proposed Visit of Chinese Politburo Member Wan Li," February 21, 1989 (no. 01010); Action Memo for Mr. Kimmit from EAP William Clark Jr., "Request for Presidential Aircraft for the Visit of PRC Chairman of the National People's Congress Wan Li," March 24, 1989 (no. 01015); Confidential Dept. of State Incoming Telegram from American Embassy Beijing to Secretary of State (no. 01021); EAP Press Guidance, "Sino-Soviet Summit," May 10, 1989 (no. 01039); Background Paper for the President, "The President's Meeting with Wan Li," May 13, 1989 (no. 01048); Bureau of Intelligence and Research Weekend Edition, "The USSR and China at the Summit: Common Goals, Enduring Differences," May 14, 1989 (no. 01049), National Security Archives Collection: China and the United States. See also Baker, *Politics of Diplomacy*, 99; Bush and Scowcroft, *A World Transformed*, 91–97.

20. This information on background was provided in an interview with a Bush administration official, June 5, 2002, Washington, D.C.

21. Secretary's Morning Summaries for June 1 (no. 01053), June 2 (no. 01056), and June 3, 1989 (no. 01058); Cables from American Embassy Beijing to State Department, all on June 3 (01059), (15405), (01061), (15383), (01060); Limited Official Use Cable from Beijing Embassy to Secretary of State, June 3, 1989 (01063), National Security Archives Collection: China and the United States.

22. Scowcroft interview.

23. "The President's News Conference," June 5, 1989; Bush and Scowcroft, *A World Transformed*, 89–102.

24. Marlin Fitzwater, "Statement by Press Secretary Fitzwater on United States Sanctions Against the Chinese Government," June 20, 1989; Baker, *Politics of Diplomacy*, 107.

25. Bill McAllister, "Lawmakers Ask Strong U.S. Action; Punish Authorities, White House Told"; see also Robert Pear, "Crackdown in Beijing;

President Assails Shootings in China"; Thomas Friedman, "Crackdown in Beijing; Administration Ponders Steps on China."

26. Baker, *Politics of Diplomacy*, 108; Harry Harding, *A Fragile Relationship: The United States and China Since 1972*, 233; Thomas Friedman, "Congress, Angry at China, Moves to Impose Sanctions"; Susan F. Rasky, "House Toughening China Curbs."

27. Martin Tolchin, "House, Breaking with Bush, Votes China Sanctions."

28. Scowcroft interview.

29. Author interview on background with State Department official, June 11, 2002.

30. Author interview on background with Bush administration official, June 5, 2002.

31. Author interview on background with State Department official, June 11, 2002; Scowcroft interview.

32. Bush and Scowcroft, *A World Transformed*, 157–158.

33. Baker, *Politics of Diplomacy*, 98; see also Raymond Garthoff, *The Great Transition: American-Soviet Relations and the End of the Cold War*, 640–643; Harding, *A Fragile Relationship*, 173–214; Steven Hurst, *The Foreign Policy of the Bush Administration*, 38–40.

34. See Robert W. Barnett, oral history interview, March 2, 1990.

35. Talking Points on China and Chronology of White House Comments on the Situation in China, June 1989, Folder: China [OA/ID 06786], White House Press Office, Marlin Fitzwater Files, CBS [OA6786 through Christmas Card/Part [2] [OA6786], Box 4, Bush Presidential Library.

36. "The President's News Conference," June 5, 1989; Bush and Scowcroft, *A World Transformed*, 98–102; Thomas Friedman, "Turmoil in China; A Rocky Period Lies Ahead for Washington and Beijing."

37. Baker, *Politics of Diplomacy*, 104.

38. Thomas Friedman, "Crackdown in China; Foley Says U.S. Should Consider Further Sanctions Against China"; Friedman, "Congress, Angry at China."

39. "Statement on the Chinese Government's Suppression of Student Demonstrations," June 3, 1989; Bush and Scowcroft, *A World Transformed*, 89; Confidential Cable from Beijing Embassy to Secretary of State, "Suggested Talking Points for CNN Interview," June 3, 1989 (01064), National Security Archives Collection: China and the United States.

40. Transcript from NBC *Meet the Press,* Folder: Monday, June 5, 1989 [OA 2513], White House Press Office, Fitzwater Guidance Files, Thursday May 25, 1989–June 7, 1989 [2], Box 66, Bush Presidential Library.

41. Baker, *Politics of Diplomacy*, 99–101; Bush and Scowcroft, *A World Transformed*, 91–97.

42. EAP Press Guidance, "Intellectual Property Rights" (no. 01035); "Market Access in China" (01036); "PRC GATT Accession" (01037), all May 10, 1989, National Security Archives Collection: China and the United States. Other press guidance at the time emphasized the increased ties between Taiwan and China.

43. A. M. Rosenthal, "On My Mind; The Absent Americans"; Don Oberdorfer, "Scowcroft Warned China of New Hill Sanctions; U.S. Emissaries Stressed Need for Action by Beijing, Sources Say."

44. Baker, *Politics of Diplomacy*, 68–69; Bush and Scowcroft, *A World Transformed*, 13, 91.

45. Friedman, "Crackdown in Beijing"; Tom Wicker, "In the Nation; Darkness in China." National Security Directive 23 from September 1989 reinforced the message that the Soviet military threat had not diminished. See NSD 23, p. 2.

46. Michael Weisskopf, "Baker Outlines Goals of Mission to Beijing; Resolving Human Rights Differences, Forestalling Isolation, Briefing on Summit Cited"; Don Oberdorfer and David Hoffman, "Scowcroft Warned China of New Hill Sanctions," A1.

47. Lawrence Eagleburger testimony in hearings before the Senate Foreign Relations Committee, February 8, 1990.

48. Scowcroft interview.

49. Talking Points for Use with Congressmen on Satellite Licenses for China, United States Department of State, December 15, 1989, Folder: China-U.S., October–December 1989 [3] [OA/ID CF 00316, NSC Douglas Paal Files, Box 3 of 5; Press Guidance for China Satellites, Folder: Tuesday, December 12, 1989 [UA 3932], Press Office Subject File, Box 85, Bush Presidential Library.

50. Letter with attachments to Senator Max Baucus from the White House, July 17, 1991, Folder: TPRG: China [OA/ID F01855], Box 1 of 5, Council of Economic Advisers Paul Wonnacott TPRG Files, A-M, Bush Presidential Library; Statement of Administration Policy, July 15, 1991, Folder: MFN for China O/A/ID 07687, Box 1 of 5, Paul Korfonta Files, p. 1, White House Office of Cabinet Affairs Collection, Bush Presidential Library; Fact Sheet on Continuation of MFN for China, June 18, 1991, Folder: MFN Status for China [OA/ID 08202], Box 1 of 5, White House Office of Correspondence, Beverly Ward Files, pp. 1–3, Bush Presidential Library.

51. Department of State, East Asian Bureau Press Guidance, no date, Folder: China [OA/ID 06786], White House Press Office, Marlin Fitzwater Files, p. 1, CBS [OA6786 through Christmas Card/Part [2] [OA6786], Box 4, Bush Presidential Library.

52. "The President's News Conference," June 5, 1989.

53. "The President's News Conference," June 27, 1989.

54. Michael Duffy and Dan Goodgame, *Marching in Place: The Status Quo Presidency of George Bush,* 182.

55. Baker, *Politics of Diplomacy*, 102–105; Harding, *A Fragile Relationship*, 225; Hurst, *Foreign Policy of the Bush Administration*, 38–40.

56. Action Memo to the Secretary of State through Mr. Kimmitt from William Clark, no date, National Security Archives postpublication Collection: China and the United States.

57. Ibid.; Memo for the President from Secretary Baker, "Recommendations on Policy Toward China in the Wake of Military Crackdown," no date,

National Security Archives postpublication Collection: China and the United States; Scowcroft interview.

58. James Baker, Testimony before Hearings of the House Foreign Affairs Committee, June 22, 1989; James Baker, Testimony before Hearings of the Senate Foreign Relations Committee, June 20, 1989. On June 25, 1989, David Hoffman reported in the *Washington Post* that Scowcroft and Lilley disagreed with Baker on this issue ("China Executions Push Bush to Focus on Future"). Apparently, both advised caution on sanctions in order to avoid further damage in the bilateral relationship.

59. "Letter to the Speaker of the House of Representatives and the President of the Senate on Trade with China," December 19, 1989; see also Baker, *Politics of Diplomacy*, 114.

60. "Remarks and a Question-and-Answer Session with Newspaper Editors," December 11, 1989; see also Draft Presidential Statement, Folder: China-U.S. October–December 1989 [3] [OA/ID CF 00316], NSC Douglas Paal Files, Box 3 of 5, Bush Presidential Library. Interestingly, the administration never enacted an executive order and instead relied on an administrative order issued from the Department of Justice. When this became public in several stories in the *New York Times* and *Washington Post* beginning on April 5, 1990, it added fuel to Bush's China policy critics who saw it as further evidence of the administration's duplicity. See David Hoffman, "Bush Never Issued Executive Order Protecting Chinese Students in U.S."; Baker, *Politics of Diplomacy*, 113.

61. Bush extended and broadened his previous protections to waive the two-year home-country residence requirement, assure immigration status for the students, authorize employment for them, provide notice of expiration of nonimmigrant status, and provide for deferral. His actions would provide the same protection that Pelosi's H.R. 2712 proposed. See Draft Memorandum of Disapproval attached to Memo from Stephen Rademaker from the NSC to Nicholas Rostow, November 30, 1989, Folder: China-Pelosi—1989 (OA/ID CF 00317], Box 4 of 5, NSC Doug Paal Files, China—Nuclear 1989 OA/ID CF00317-China-US, March–April 1990 [4], OA/ID CF 00317, Bush Presidential Library.

62. Memorandum for Brent Scowcroft from Douglas Paal, "Presidential Points to Be Made January 24 Press Conference China," January 23, 1990, Folder: China-US January–February 1990 [4] OA/ID CF 00316, Box 5 of 5, NSC Douglas Paal Files, China-US January–February 90 [1] to Public Liaison James Schifter OA/ID 01560, Bush Presidential Library.

63. Memorandum to Brent Scowcroft from Douglas Paal, January 3, 1990, "Senate Republican Breakfast—China," Folder: China-US January–February 1990 [4] OA/ID CF 00316, Box 5 of 5, NSC Douglas Paal Files, China-US, January–February 90 [1] to Public Liaison James Schaefer OA/ID 01560, Bush Presidential Library.

64. Tom Kenworthy and Helen Dewar, "As Congress Returns to Work, Democrats Seek Advantage Over Bush"; Thomas Friedman, "Bush Is Set Back by House Override of Veto on China"; Helen Dewar, "Senate Narrowly Votes to Sustain Veto of Chinese Students Bill."

65. Baker, *Politics of Diplomacy*, 106–107; Bush and Scowcroft, *A World Transformed*, 104; Eagleburger Testimony before the Hearings of the Senate Foreign Relations Committee, February 8, 1990; see also *New York Times*, June 14, 1989.

66. Baker, *Politics of Diplomacy*, 110–112; Paula Yost, "Sununu Defends Selling Jetliners to China; Bush Decision Called Move to Encourage Leniency to Demonstrators."

67. Talking Points for the Press, Folder: China-Sensitive 1989 [4] [OA/ID CF 00317], NSC Douglas Paal Files, Box 3 of 5, Bush Presidential Library.

68. Talking Points for Congressional Calls on China (origin Department of State), December 1989, p. 1, Folder: China-U.S., October–December 1989 [3] [OA/ID CF 00316, NSC Douglas Paal Files, Box 3 of 5, Bush Presidential Library.

69. Baker, *Politics of Diplomacy*, 114; Bush and Scowcroft, *A World Transformed*, Hurst, *The Foreign Policy of the Bush Administration*, 42; Oberdorfer, "U.S. Optimistic Dissident Fang Will Be Freed."

70. The administration also knew that it walked a fine line. Treasury officials blocked attempts by the World Bank to resume loans to China in early 1990 based on the knowledge that it could undermine congressional support for the Bank in the context of the post–Tiananmen Square environment. The secretary of the treasury argued that the Bank's lending program should be scaled back in size and reoriented to basic human needs, infrastructure, and support for economic reform, and should not include lending to state-owned entities. These recommendations acknowledged the tenor of Congress that any loans and financial or technical assistance be in accordance with recent human rights legislation. See Memorandum for Secretary Brady from John M. Niehuss, Acting Assistant Secretary of International Affairs, "Restraining a Resumption of Normal World Bank Lending to China," probably December 1989, pp. 2–4, Folder: China-U.S. October–December 1989 [3] [OA/ID CF 00316, NSC Douglas Paal Files, Box 3 of 5, Bush Presidential Library.

71. In 1974, Congress passed the Jackson-Vanik Amendment, now known as Title IV of the Trade Act. Jackson-Vanik forbids the granting of MFN status, now known as normal trade relations (NTR), and the privileges MFN/NTR offers, to any country that had a poor track record of human rights violations and orchestrated emigration barriers.

72. Report to Congress Concerning Extension of Waiver Authority for the PRC, May 24, 1990, Folder: Further Extension of Jackson-Vanik Waiver Authority Waiver to PRC Case no. 14378355 SP290-43, Box 55 (Sp 290-40 13996855-SP 290-46 13611255 [5], WHORM-Subject File–General, Bush Presidential Library.

73. James K. Bishop, Jr., oral history interview, November 15, 1995.

74. Department of State, East Asian Bureau, Press Guidance, no date, Folder: China [OA/ID 06786], White House Press Office, Marlin Fitzwater Files, p. 6, CBS [OA6786 through Christmas Card/Part [2] [OA6786], Box 4, Bush Presidential Library. See also ibid., no date, but after Tiananmen Square, p. 1.

75. Report of the President on China Economic Sanctions Required by

Subsection 902© of P.S. 101-246 and accompanying memorandum for the President from Brent Scowcroft, May 11, 1990, Folder: June 1989, Effects of China's Sanctions Since Military Crackdown, Case no. 14038455 (SP 290-42), Box 55 (Sp 290-40 13996855-SP 290-46 13611255 [5], pp. 1–4, WHORM-Subject File–General, Bush Presidential Library.

76. Author interviews with Bush administration officials, June 5 and 11, 2002.

77. Letter with attachments to Senator Max Baucus from the White House, July 17, 1991, File TPRG: China [OA/ID F01855], Box 1 of 5, Council of Economic Advisers, Paul Wonnacott, TPRG Files, A-M, Bush Presidential Library; Statement of Administration Policy, July 15, 1991, Folder: MFN for China O/A/ID 07687, Box 1 of 5, Paul Korfonta Files, p. 1, White House Office of Cabinet Affairs Collection, Bush Presidential Library.

78. Author interview with Bush administration official, June 11, 2002.

79. Freeman interview; Press Guidance for China/F-16s, Folder: China [OA 6786], White House Press Office, Marlin Fitzwater Subject Files BS [OA6786 through Christmas Card Party [2] [OA 6706], Box 4, Bush Presidential Library.

80. Personal interview with former Beijing embassy official, June 5, 2002.

81. William Clark Jr., oral history interview, January 11, 1994; Freeman interview, April 14, 1995.

82. Freeman interview.

83. George Bush could be categorized as one of John Steinbrunner's theoretical thinkers whose belief patterns are internally consistent and tend to be stable over time and display a high level of commitment (generally found in experts such as national security advisers). As such, he was less likely to rethink his policy goals or to question his initial understanding of a policy situation. See Steinbrunner, *The Cybernetic Theory of Decision.*

7

A Tale of Three Engagements:
Clinton and the Struggle to Balance
Competing Interests

With the end of the Cold War, President William J. Clinton and his advisers were primed for changes in the policy emphasis regarding China. In the post-Tiananmen context, candidate Bill Clinton adopted the congressional democratic leadership's position that George H.W. Bush had coddled the "butchers of Beijing." Once in office, his first move was to link trade rights to progress in human rights as the central element of U.S. policy toward China, noting that if a government does not protect the rights of its citizens and follow the rule of law, then it cannot be trusted in commercial relations.

The Clinton administration's policy approach to engage China on issues like trade and human rights was premised on the link between economic liberalization and democratic enlargement. During his secretary of state confirmation hearing, Warren Christopher argued that the policy would "be to seek to facilitate a broad, peaceful evolution in China from communism to democracy, . . . by encouraging the forces of economic and political liberalization."[1] In a speech in September 1993, National Security Adviser Anthony Lake articulated the engagement policy further. He argued "the spread of democracy will help solve all other American foreign policy problems, in that democracies do not violate human rights, attack their neighbors, adopt restrictive trade policies, engage in terrorism, or generate refugees." The United States could help to steer countries like China down this path, "while providing penalties that raise the costs of repression and aggressive behavior."[2] The assumption was that China would yield on human rights in a showdown over trade benefits because its very prosperity depended on its exports to the United States. The Clinton administration calculated that the United States had the upper hand and leverage in trade dealings with China because it was the world's largest economy.[3]

Clinton's focus in China policy on commercial relations over traditional security issues was a marked shift from his predecessor, but a natural one for a post–Cold War president who viewed foreign policy through a domestic economic prism. Clinton sounded the theme that a new global economy needed to be harnessed to benefit the U.S. population. Markets for U.S. exports would be expanded by coordinating policy among major industrial powers to increase growth and promote economic expansion in the developing world.[4] As part of this engagement, China would become more open to free trade, human rights, and to international norms regarding issues such as weapons proliferation. This policy meant to integrate the values and interests of the United States into one grand engagement strategy.[5]

Unfortunately for the Clinton administration, its early efforts failed to provide a solid basis for stable U.S.-China relations. A close evaluation of engagement policymaking shows how this concept meant different things to competing constituencies. As the early consensus that the administration could pursue its democratic/human rights ideals and simultaneously open up commerce waned, a series of crises with China placed the status quo of the relationship in jeopardy. How Clinton and his advisers reconciled competing interests and responded to growing domestic challenges over MFN (or normal trade relations, NTR) and the Taiwan question (which could upset the basis for the Sino-American relationship) became the core challenges in his first term. Into his second term, Republican voices increasingly challenged Clinton's trade and security positions and called for an aggressive foreign policy targeting China as a threat. Clinton forged ahead with a strategic partnership and permanent normal trade relations (PNTR) despite this contentious environment (and through his personal scandals), but with mixed results.

The Foreign Policy Team and Competing Visions of Engagement

The initial foreign policy team put together by Bill Clinton in his first term was comprised of a familiar group of Democrats-in-waiting. Both Secretary of State Warren Christopher and National Security Adviser

Anthony Lake had held positions in the Carter administration. Both also were committed to organizing an advisory system, modeled after Brent Scowcroft's system in the first Bush administration, that avoided the kind of infighting that had typified the Carter administration. The national security adviser would be a neutral arbiter bringing options to the president, while the secretary of state was the administration's chief foreign policy spokesman. Although the members of the inner circle seemed to get along, the lack of formality in the system caused a decentralization of authority and thus an absence of coordination in China policy.

Organizing the Advisory System

At the highest levels little attention was paid to traditional aspects of U.S.-China relations; this was true partly because the president lacked interest in traditional foreign policy but was encouraged specifically by the organization of his foreign policy system. Clinton's January 21, 1993, presidential decision directive creating the National Economic Council (NEC) to coordinate international economic policy in the White House illustrated the elevation of economic issues over the traditional focus on strategic security. This new arrangement gave the NEC overlapping jurisdiction with the NSC. In practice, this meant that National Economic Adviser Robert Rubin and Secretary of the Treasury Lloyd Bentsen each had a seat on the NSC/Principals Committee, while the national security adviser and his staff were expected to consider trade and other international economic issues in developing security policy. Joint NSC and NEC committees hammered out policy, and depending on the particular issue under consideration, it could be coordinated through an NSC or NEC process.[6] Furthermore, trade policy was placed under the direction of Robert Rubin, Secretary of Commerce Ronald Brown, and the office of the United States Trade Representative (USTR). According to former USTR Charlene Barshefsky, Clinton's knowledge in trade issues gave unprecedented influence to economic advisers such as the USTR in the making of foreign policy, including China policy.[7]

These economic advisers filled a vacuum left by the traditional shapers of Sino-American policy who were not interested in China. For example, Christopher was much less influential than his predecessors because he spent little time personally focused on China and never developed close ties to the president. Similarly, Secretary of Defense Les Aspin did not see Asian policy as a priority. Without high-level attention from the traditional shapers of the U.S.-China relationship, policy authority on China resided deeper in the bureaucracy and was spread among different departments and agencies.[8]

Players and Their Positions

These circumstances set the stage for different aspects of China policy to be fragmented among various players like the State Department, NSC, Defense Department, Commerce Department, Treasury Department, and the NEC. Each group had different policy goals, but three primary agendas were visible from the beginning: human rights and daily operations, economic/commercial, and security interests.[9] The first agenda focused on human rights and included coordinating day-to-day operations such as development of the executive order that linked human rights to trade. These activities were coordinated through the NSC process (with Lake and Christopher's support) by the assistant secretary of state for East Asia and the Pacific, Winston Lord. Lake and Lord, with no input from the commercial side of the administration, set up a hard-line, principled human rights position linking MFN renewal to progress in human rights.[10] Simultaneously, they advocated a non-compromising, prosanctions sister policy on arms proliferation. Reports of Chinese sales of M-11 missile components to Pakistan and reports of a Chinese vessel, the *Yin He,* carrying chemical weapons' components to Iran hardened Lake and Lord's resolve through the summer of 1993. Both agreed that the United States should not accept Chinese assertions that the *Yin He* did not carry chemicals and instead called for it to be searched; on September 4 it was boarded but not found to be carrying chemicals. They also threatened sanctions to curb China from exporting arms to Pakistan and other Middle East destinations (M-11 sanctions were lifted in October when Beijing pledged to stop exporting the missiles to Pakistan).[11]

The economic team, representing the second agenda, had little say in linkage policy or the prosanctions stance early on, in part because these moves did not seem to threaten its broad interests. During this period it pursued its agenda separately by sending a trade delegation to discuss China's entry into the world trade system (the GATT) and U.S. access to the Chinese market.[12] However, the lack of progress on trade through mid-1993 made the economic engagers and domestic business interests nervous. Arguing that trade relations were an important way to improve China's economic conditions and promote its transition from Communism to a market economy, they began to push independently to end MFN linkage, which they felt threatened overall U.S.-China relations.[13]

This position reflected increasing intolerance to risking potential economic gains, which is illustrated by the controversy over a ban on satellite exports to China in response to China's sale of M-11 technology. When the sanctions hurt companies such as Hughes Aircraft who had contracts with China, the Department of Commerce backed a Hughes claim that the export constraints hurt U.S. business rather than Chinese. Hughes claimed the sanctions threatened the jobs of three thousand workers and risked $250 million in revenue, while the State Department argued that exemptions would gut the sanctions. Eventually, White House support for the Commerce Department on this issue in October 1993 was a harbinger for a slow abandonment of the State Department's confrontational approach to China.[14]

Defense officials such as Assistant Secretary of Defense William Perry (who succeeded Les Aspin in February 1994) represented the third agenda—one that sought to develop strong relations with China and to reestablish the military-to-military dialogue interrupted by Tiananmen Square.[15] He was joined by other Pentagon officials willing to engage China on a number of issues, despite State Department and NSC reluctance, because of mutual interests in resolving the emerging crisis over North Korea's nuclear-weapons program and the persistent disagreements on arms proliferation. These efforts also were blocked early on by human rights interests. For example, when the North Korean nuclear issue arose in March 1993 at a meeting in the White House Situation Room, Chas Freeman, former assistant secretary of defense for regional security, reports that Secretary Aspin's suggestion to discuss Perry's idea to confer with the Chinese on the issue was nixed by Anthony Lake on the grounds that China was politically unacceptable. He claims the White House blocked these efforts because it "wanted nothing to do with the Chinese, who were egregious violators of human rights, the so-called butchers of Beijing."[16]

These tensions led to a deteriorating relationship with China and internal pressure for a China policy review in summer 1993.[17] The review, completed by Lord, created the expectation that the United States was ready to break with past problems, but in practice the human rights linkage lingered. In meetings with their Chinese counterparts, Warren Christopher and other State Department officials still argued that progress in China's human rights, trade, and proliferation records all were prerequisites for fundamental progress in the relationship. Assistant Secretary of State for Human Rights John Shattuck pointed out specifically that China's human rights record jeopardized MFN renewal in 1994 because the president and Congress were in full agreement on linkage.[18] Their tone remained consistent with the terms of engagement articulated by Anthony Lake in his September 1993 speech, where he declared that penalties could be used to steer countries toward democracy and liberalization. In his speech, Lake grouped China with other "backlash" states like Iran.[19]

More important, the practical result of Lord's review was that it set guidelines to engage China across a broad range of issues at multiple working levels so that policy coordination became more decentralized than before. In fact, it now guaranteed the broad participation of actors with the competing agendas discussed above. Over a four-month period there were various high-level visits to China, including ones by John Shattuck, Chas Freeman, Warren Christopher, Secretary of Agriculture Mike Espy, Trade Representative Charlene Barshefsky, and Secretary of the Treasury Lloyd Bentsen, which sent conflicting messages to the Chinese.[20]

As multiple players developed direct contacts with their Chinese counterparts, the PRC was encouraged to wait out the administration's threats on human rights. The competing agendas (noted above) came to a head as the debate over MFN approached in 1994. The Taiwan question would pose a second test to the administration's resolve.

Building a New Commercial
Engagement Frame and Sustaining It Through Crises

Diagnosing the Policy Problem

The real policy question for the Clinton administration was developing a shared definition of engagement and specifying the appropriate tactics to use to change China's behavior. As noted, different groups responded with different answers about how to approach China and establish trade relations on acceptable terms. Human rights advocates felt that China's record of human rights abuses meant it could not be trusted in other areas, and thus they favored sanctions. Those who focused on trade relations opposed sanctions and argued for an evolutionary approach that focused on the strategic importance of elevating trade over human rights in the overall Sino-American relationship. The Pentagon security perspective emphasized a position closer to the commercial engagers.

Commercial officials used what leverage they could to weaken the prosanctions position from late 1993 through the first quarter of 1994, in order to avoid a confrontation with China that would undercut long-term trade prospects. For example, Ambassador Stapleton Roy stated publicly that the PRC had made "dramatic" progress in certain areas, specifically by providing for the material needs of its people. His statements reframed the argument, similar to President George H.W. Bush's perspective, to emphasize progressive themes that warranted MFN renewal. As the State Department's human rights crowd accused Roy of disloyalty to the administration, Roy's comments encouraged the "business" side of the administration, namely the Departments of Commerce and Treasury and the NEC, to break ranks and push for MFN independently of human rights. Lloyd Bentsen and Robert Rubin, particularly, pushed for accommodation on the MFN issue to preserve the overall trade relationship. On January 29, Rubin told the Chinese that the administration would end the linkage between trade and human rights if China kept its commitments concerning treatment of political prisoners, prison labor, and other rights issues. Bentsen traveled to China that month carrying the same message, with a directive to promote trade and investment in China.[21]

Early 1994 talks with Vice Premier Qichen Qian found Christopher refuting the Chinese expectation that the United States was wavering in its determination to withdraw MFN.[22] John Shattuck repeated this message during his trip in March and told the Chinese they should not assume the MFN decision would be favorable to them. He indicated Christopher would approach his decision rigorously from a "lawyer's point of view" and "simply would not make a recommendation that he does not believe consistent with 'overall, significant progress' on human rights."[23] Shattuck maintains that his meeting with China's most prominent dissident, Wei Jinsheng, signaled that the United States would not bend on its linkage policy.[24] In response, Li Peng and other Chinese leaders blasted the U.S. human rights policy and accused Shattuck of interfering in China's internal affairs. China remained confident that the minor concessions it proposed (i.e., to provide information on the status of around two hundred political prisoners, including Tibetan ones, and to reach an agreement ending exports on prison-made goods) would secure MFN renewal.[25]

Christopher's failure to gain significant human rights concessions undermined the human rights position and became a catalyst for change inside the administration. Even former supporters such as Lake, Berger, Christopher, and Shattuck were convinced a change in tactics was needed. Berger and Lake scrambled to minimize the damage to the policy by initiating contact with the Chinese. Lake met with Chinese Ambassador Li Daoyu at Richard Nixon's funeral in April 1994 to secure last-minute concessions necessary to justify MFN renewal. And Michael Armacost went to China as a special presidential envoy with the proposal that if the Chinese made minor gestures to cover the executive order, the administration would permanently drop the linkage.

Ultimately, China did respond with enough minor concessions on the mandatory items to give the president room to de-link MFN and seek a compromise with congressional Democrats.[26] Clinton's May 26, 1994, announcement of de-linkage and subsequent support for MFN argued that the effort to link human rights to MFN had run its course. Rather than admit defeat, the president claimed that human rights would now be pushed through new steps with the business community, increased international broadcasting, and in multilateral efforts in the UN Commission on Human Rights.[27] Mickey Kantor characterized the change as recognition that the United States had strategic, economic, and regional concerns beyond human rights. He says Clinton realized the previous policy "was not a logical, rational, or effective policy."[28] For his part, Winston Lord blamed the failure on the tug-of-war inside the administration resulting from its eclectic range of interests.[29]

The MFN reversal in 1994 marked the end of the view backed by Winston Lord, which elevated human rights and asserted there was nothing contradictory between U.S. ideals and commercial interests in China.[30] The convergence of ideas behind "comprehensive engagement" had given each side an opportunity to pursue its interests while still arguing it was part of a coherent policy. Liberal Democrats (and human rights engagers) had seen muscle in the trade threat, while business interests (and commercial engagers) saw language ambiguous enough to end the threat to trade that had existed since Tiananmen Square.[31]

What is clear is that Christopher's failure allowed the commercial agenda to win converts, trump the human rights position, and bring a new diagnosis to the problem, emphasizing immediate gains and eventual progress in human rights. The problem was no longer viewed as dependent upon human rights but instead was centered on prospects for long-term commercial stability. With this shift in focus, authority over China policy also seemed to shift away from the undersecretary level in the State Department to rest at times with Sandy Berger in the NSC, but also to the USTR and NEC as trade issues gained prominence.[32]

What Themes Resonated with Bill Clinton and Why?

By May 1994, the president recognized the incompatibility of his policy goals on trade and human rights and the dangers this posed to his broader policy priorities. Christopher's failure primed the president for change and provided an opportunity for the commercial framers to rediagnose the policy problem and garner the president's involvement.[33]

Clinton's beliefs and priorities. According to former USTR Mickey Kantor, Clinton recognized that U.S. policy up to that point in his administration had not been productive and thus needed to stop drifting. His reference point shifted to acknowledge that the policy of engagement was broader than human rights and actually meant "we could engage on these issues and we could walk and chew gum at the same time."[34] When Clinton was forced to choose between human rights and his promise to put economics at the center of U.S. foreign policy, he pragmatically chose economics.[35]

Clinton's shift was a change in tactics and a reemphasis of other core beliefs. The shift did not require the president to rethink his economic priorities or even his commitment to human rights. He accepted the commercial engagement position that the best way to improve human rights for a country's citizens was to increase rather than limit trade. This belief rested on the assumption that more trade and investment would increase economic growth and build a middle class with both consumerism and democracy in mind.[36] Secretary of the Treasury Lloyd Bentsen added that unilateral trade sanctions were the least practical way to advance human rights because they would hurt the United States more than China by allowing other countries to pick up the slack.[37] Charlene Barshefsky states that the linkage policy had made the United States look ridiculous and agreed that it had caused lost economic opportunities to European competitors. China proved to be "too important a country, too pivotal to take a one-issue view."[38]

Once established, the commercial frame proved difficult to dislodge because it resonated with the president's earliest domestic political goals. In social-psychological terms Clinton had a well-established schema to which to link his commercial priorities. The policy wedding of commercial and domestic themes was natural for a president inclined to see the world in terms of economic interdependence.

The emerging strategic commercial policy theme. Because the emerging commercial rationale emphasized the big picture, including mutual dependence and overall stability in the relationship, commercial engagers began to draw links from it to U.S. security. What emerged was a new economic equation being sold in strategic national security terms. For instance, Ron Brown argued that Chinese trade benefits without conditions were a matter of economic security and vital to U.S. national security. The fact that the 1994 MFN decision coincided a second time with a crisis over North Korea's nuclear program highlighted the necessity for China's cooperation if North Korea was to be persuaded to allow full inspections of its nuclear sites.[39] According to Kantor, the strategy was "using engagement to ensure that you would have some sort of stability in Asia and economic progress—which is part of stability." If the broader commercial policy were ignored, then crises such as the Korean one would continue.[40] Commercial engagers believed that stable relations with China could be rebuilt through the process of high-level and working-level dialogue.

Pentagon officials who sought military-to-military contacts joined them in these efforts. Contacts like the visit of PLA General Xu Huizi and Secretary of Defense Perry's November 1994 visit to China were useful for collaboration on the North Korean nuclear issue and helped establish mutual understanding on a number of security issues.[41] The Pentagon pushed for a broader focus because it felt that trade relations and MFN renewal were important first steps to make its proposed military dialogue possible. At the time, Perry declared "the rationale is that China is fast becoming the world's largest economic power, and that combined with its UN PermFive status, its political clout, its nuclear weapons and a modernizing military, make China a player with which the United States must work together. Our security posture dramatically improves if China cooperates with us."[42] Assistant Defense Secretary Joseph Nye emphasized the need to jointly manage new security threats because the interrelated nature of the system meant that crises in different parts of the world could cause markets to crash in others.[43]

This logic gained precedence among central policymakers across a broad spectrum and became the basis for a new consensus. State Department officials argued that the purpose of continued intensive, high-level engagement was "to provide strategic reassurance to China and to seek its constructive participation in the international community."[44] Kent Wiedemann, the deputy assistant secretary of state for East Asian and Pacific affairs, added that "comprehensive engagement" was essential to continuing China's integration into the international community begun under the previous five administrations.[45] The strategy was to link China into a web of international political and economic ties in order to strengthen political forces there that were already interested in peaceful economic cooperation.

A February 1995 Pentagon study entitled *United States Security Strategy for the East Asia–Pacific Region* showed the hopes and limits of this perspective. While it argued for developing a constructive, strategic partnership fostering the integration of China into global and regional institutions, the report counterbalanced that the United States should retain sufficient military capability to respond if China became a military threat.[46] One senior Defense Department official described this as William Perry's effort to "lead the relationship in a positive direction but also to hedge against the possibility of failure and trouble." The Pentagon did have a fundamental, long-term strategic interest in decent relations with China but did not want to abandon important interests like Taiwan.[47]

Domestic political considerations. As noted, from 1993 through mid-1994 economic engagers used domestic political themes linking U.S. prosperity to opening trade with China. Specifically, they argued that opening China's markets to U.S. firms (increasing exports and lowering trade barriers) would create more jobs in the United States. Deals such as the $1.6 billion contract with McDonnell Douglas to provide China with commercial aircraft were seen as a means to build strong business ties that would eventually improve human rights and provide jobs. This emphasis on trade ties offered a new, if more gradual way to achieve the same human rights objectives.[48] As Clinton began to see that confrontation with China did not serve his domestic political purposes, he came to accept the commercial strategic logic.

The commercial engagement team succeeded in changing the China policy agenda in 1994 in part because they developed a united position on the commercial side and gained the support of the Defense Department. In characterizing this group, former Clinton chief of staff Leon Panetta argued that the NEC helped build a real partnership in the administration. There was "a sense that trade was important for all, [and the] tough questions were human rights and security issues that intervened."[49] Additionally, when the NEC, Commerce Department, and Treasury Department successfully placed blame for failure on Winston Lord's initiatives, their main rival was discredited. Christopher's failure to win major concessions during his March 1994 trip to China provided the opportunity to gain control.[50]

This consensus, however, did not guarantee policy success or generate an open policymaking process involving the president and central policymakers that anticipated, and thus diffused, potential problems with China. In fact, the grandiose assumptions that came with the strategic economic frame seemed to lull the administration into a false sense of confidence, which led them to downplay potential points of tension in the Sino-American relationship and the ability of Congress to block policy. A senior Pentagon official, critical of the commercial position, described them as eager capitalists ready to sell, and nothing could disrupt this (unless it was one of their issues). He adds that the China policy was "wholly tactical and reactive in its approach, and totally deferential, in most respects, to domestic interests, rather than responsive to foreign realities."[51]

The 1994 interim election, which brought pro-Taiwan Republicans to leadership positions in the Congress, and Taiwan's democratization challenged the administration's engagement frame through the remainder of the Clinton administration. Increasingly, Congress pressured Clinton to respond to democratizing forces on Taiwan and the election of Lee Teng-hui as its president. A big controversy erupted when President Lee requested a visa to visit Cornell University for June 1995. The Congress actively pressured the president to grant this request. House approval, by a vote of 396-0, of a nonbinding resolution calling on the administration to allow Lee's private visit and the Senate's similar (97-1) vote on the issue forced the administration to permit Lee to come. The administration acquiesced because political pressure from Congress was veto-proof, and an open fight with Congress risked making the visit more formal.[52] This outcome remained at odds with an administration interested in maintaining the ambiguous cross-strait status quo.[53]

For their part, the Chinese perceived a containment-like pattern in U.S. policies, and the visit of Lee Teng-hui illustrated this pattern, which undermined the foundations of the one-China policy.[54] In retaliation they postponed a series of high-level meetings, including talks on nuclear energy and missile technology control. They also recalled their ambassador from Washington while delaying formal acceptance of James Sasser as the new U.S. ambassador. Mid-level officials from the Chinese Ministry of Foreign Trade and Economic Cooperation (MOFTEC) told U.S. embassy officials that U.S.-Chinese relations would continue to deteriorate unless the United States made a significant gesture of reconciliation.[55] The relationship deteriorated even more with the onslaught of Chinese live-fire exercises in 1995 across the Taiwan Strait and again around the time of Taiwan's March 1996 elections.[56] These crises consolidated domestic political opposition for

MFN renewal and opened the door for Congress to more forcefully challenge the president's prerogative in foreign policy.[57] Handling the crisis effectively was even more critical in this charged domestic atmosphere.

Initially, adherents of the strategic commercial frame, including those in the State Department and NSC, were inclined to downplay the crisis. They sought a peaceful resolution to preserve their top priority for East Asian policy—promotion of economic prosperity. In his February 7, 1996, testimony before the Senate Foreign Relations Subcommittee on East Asia and Pacific Affairs, Winston Lord downplayed the chances for conflict by emphasizing that any "confrontation between the PRC and Taiwan, however limited in scale or scope, would destabilize the military balance in East Asia and constrict the commerce and shipping which is the economic life blood of the region."[58] In March 1996, Peter Tarnoff, the undersecretary of state for international economic affairs, repeated that the State Department did not anticipate a military confrontation because too much was at stake for economic development.[59]

William Perry insisted that the administration had to respond. He did not disagree with the State Department's overall position but refused to hold the entire relationship hostage to a single issue.[60] Perry convinced the president to act, and Clinton sent two carrier task-force groups, but neither actually entered the Taiwan Strait. To avoid escalating the situation domestically or with China, Clinton did not take up the cause of Chinese dissidents, and he continued to waive economic sanctions in response to violations of intellectual property rights, human rights abuses, illegal arms sales, and nuclear proliferation. Perry called Clinton's response a measured show of force meant to minimize the controversy, which was in keeping with Pentagon recommendations.[61]

Supporting Conditions:
Moving Toward Centralization of China Policy in the White House

Ironically, the Taiwan Strait controversy convinced the president and others to become more regularly involved in China policy and to take sanctions off the table once and for all to avoid a domestic controversy as the 1996 MFN vote approached.[62] According to one former State Department official, Lake and Christopher worked to fix the relationship themselves and did not rely on the NEC, which had not anticipated any problems over Taiwan. An interagency review concluded it was time to anchor China policy in the NSC (not the NEC) and to end agencies running off on their own and freelancing on sanctions. Leon Panetta states that it was a lack of both presidential involvement and careful vetting of options in the first place that produced the major problems. The human rights backpedaling and the Taiwan Strait crisis revealed that better policy coordination and an established chain of command were essential.[63]

Outliers such as Charlene Barshefsky, who pushed to sanction the Chinese on intellectual property violations during the Taiwan Strait crisis, were quickly overruled by a broad coalition made up of Anthony Lake, Sandy Berger, Warren Christopher, Ron Brown, and Robert Rubin, who opposed any actions they felt would lead to an all-out trade war and re-ignite cross-strait tensions. This coalition was committed to removing the sanctions issue once and for all so that bilateral relations would not be jeopardized.[64] Ultimately, the United States avoided tit-for-tat sanctions with China over intellectual property rights ($3 billion proposed toward China in May 1996) because China agreed to close factories that were pirating goods, crack down on illicit exports of pirated goods, and open up more of its markets to U.S. firms.[65] The United States also waived the declared sanctions in response to Chinese sales of ring magnets to Pakistan ($10 billion in Export-Import Bank loan guarantees) on national security grounds.[66] Mickey Kantor, who had been critical of Chinese piracy, agreed that at such a critical time he did not want issues like intellectual property to be confused with other questions like human rights and MFN.[67]

Following the Taiwan controversy, both Christopher and Lake repeated the theme of progress in the relationship with domestic and international audiences in mind.[68] Christopher focused on the importance of developing an open and secure China and the need to support Chinese integration into the international community, while suggesting the United States manage differences through engagement.[69] In remarks before the Japan-America Society, Lake put the choices in stark terms for administration critics. He argued that Asia faced a choice between the zero-sum politics of the nineteenth century—a world where great powers are permanent rivals—or a world where great powers act to increase cooperation, avert chaos, and strengthen economic growth while maintaining the balances of power that preserve peace. The second vision, he claimed, benefited U.S. national interests. The administration would work to establish global norms "in areas such as trade, nonproliferation and the environment, and join in combating common threats such as terrorism and international crime. Establishing these rules of the road will help promote the stability that benefits us all." Lake asserted that "our clear understanding of each other's position on Taiwan, together with strong progress in other areas, has restored the positive momentum to our relationship."[70] Table 7.1 outlines the policy process that led to the fragile consensus surrounding the strategic economic framework for China policy.

When Warren Christopher returned to China after the presidential election in November 1996, he worked to establish positive momentum

Table 7.1   Components of Bill Clinton's China Policy Frame (1st Term)

Problem Diagnosis	• Challenge to push China on human rights and to expand commercial relations
Themes that resonated with president and public	
Presidential beliefs	• Domestic economic lens for foreign policy • PRC of peripheral importance but assumes can gain PRC acquiescence; reform should be the priority
Policy themes	• Human rights position advocates focus on sanctions and punishment as means to reform PRC • Commercial position sees threat in linkage and works to highlight threat to president's economic policy goals • Strategic military position advocates dialogue • Strategic economic position evolves
Political considerations	• MFN struggle neutralized at first because of agreement with Democratic leadership for linkage • 1994 interim election puts Republicans in charge of both houses, which continue to challenge administration in the second term
Supporting conditions/tactics	• Decentralized advisory system exacerbated internal disagreements • Coalition-building initially with congressional Democrats and ultimately policymaking process became more White House centered

toward a more stable, positive, and predictable U.S.-PRC relationship going into the second term. The strategy for this momentum included organizing an exchange of state visits in 1997 and 1998, as well as working-level dialogues to highlight cooperation in areas such as global security.[71] On the strategic economic front, Joan Spero, the undersecretary of state for economic, business, and agricultural affairs, noted "one of our strategic goals is to have a strong bilateral relationship with a strong and prosperous China and to support China's participation as a responsible member of the international economic system and international economic institutions." Christopher's November visit was an opportunity to demonstrate how the administration wanted to work with the Chinese to bring them into the global system and World Trade Organization (WTO) membership.[72] The strategic economic language was a poor substitute for the Cold War's strategic basis for a strong relationship in that it did not provide the same kind of bipartisan support at home for Clinton's China policy. Without the common threat that had made China an ally during the Cold War, threat scenarios continued to challenge Clinton's win-win framework.

The China Policy Roller Coaster in the Second Clinton Administration

Despite Clinton's engagement position, fears that China's emergence as an Asian power were a threat to U.S. interests in East Asia seemed to dominate the China policy agenda in the second term. Voices in the Republican Party, in particular, called for an aggressive foreign policy campaign targeting China as a threat that needed to be contained. Evidence of this threat was gathered in Congress through a series of congressional committee investigations that received testimony that members of the PLA high command had funneled cash to Democratic political campaigns, hoping to buy influence in the White House, and that China had gained militarily useful secrets from its access to the U.S. space launch market. The most prominent of these investigations, chaired by Christopher Cox, released an unclassified report in May 1999 that focused on Chinese espionage activities, including information obtained on the U.S. neutron bomb and the W-88 thermonuclear warhead in the 1980s.[73]

The trump card for Clinton's opposition, however, was the announcement in January 1998 by special prosecutor Kenneth Starr that he would expand his investigation of President Clinton to include allegations that Clinton encouraged former White House intern Monica Lewinsky to lie about her sexual relationship with Clinton.[74] One former Clinton administration official declared that these issues were 90 percent politics, noting that many right-wing Republicans on the Hill genuinely hated China but they also "really hated Clinton," and "if there was a way to beat him up over these things they would do it."[75] The administration's China policy was held hostage as they attempted to "beat him up."

A New Foreign Policy Team Attempts to Set the China Agenda

Unlike Clinton's first years in office, the NSC in the second term took a more active role in managing China policy because the important players prioritized the relationship and because the policy became so politically controversial. The replacement of Anthony Lake with Sandy Berger formalized Berger's preeminent position as the president's closest and most influential foreign policy adviser. Unlike Lake, Berger kept control of foreign policy in the White House and prioritized China policy. By choice and design the new secretary of state, Madeleine Albright (formerly the ambassador to the UN in the first administration), and the new secretary of defense, William Cohen, were informed but played less of a role in China policy formulation. Formally, Berger consulted Albright and Cohen regularly, continued Lake's custom to meet for lunch with key advisers, and maintained the practice of regular principals and deputies committee meetings to hash out issues.[76] In practice, the greater discipline he enforced inside the administration kept infighting to a minimum and the administration on message.

In his June 1997 speech before the Council on Foreign Relations, Berger put forth policy themes that would recur throughout the second term. Acknowledging upcoming difficulties in making China policy work and the need to promote the one-China policy, Berger told the audience that U.S. interests lay with a China that was "stable, open and nonaggressive; that embraces political pluralism and international rules of conduct; that works with us to build a secure international order." Wielding this influence effectively required sustained domestic support for a revitalized relationship with China and an approach that recognized this was in the U.S. national interest. Berger insisted the correct path was continued engagement with the Chinese and developing a "strategic dialogue" with them because China was at a crossroads. His speech concluded with a call for Congress to extend MFN treatment for

China, which he claimed, if it were not renewed, would undo everything the United States had tried to accomplish with Beijing.[77]

Over the next four years the administration's efforts to promote a strategic partnership and to get trade relations on track had mixed results. At the time of Berger's speech in 1997, MFN renewal seemed in serious trouble, with House Speaker Newt Gingrich suggesting more stringent conditions for MFN renewal and Minority Leader Richard Gephardt and other Democrats denouncing renewal because of China's labor and human rights record. Berger, however, mobilized his congressional liaison staff, made calls and personal visits himself, and called on the president to persuade Congress that MFN was essential to sustain U.S.-China relations. To this end, groups were invited to the White House to hear the president's message.[78] The angle the administration exploited was why not getting MFN would hurt the United States in terms of trade or other issues. The administration described this task as "educating Congress" about why MFN was important to U.S. interests.[79] On June 25, 1997, the House voted 259-173 to approve MFN— the closest margin since 1990. Even after the vote, however, opposition groups continued to raise concerns in areas such as China's human rights abuses, the proliferation of weapons of mass destruction, and the Los Alamos spy scandal.[80]

Exchanging State Visits, Defending the "Three Noes," and Building Toward a Strategic Partnership

Despite China's increasing concern over U.S. domestic rhetoric, both sides pushed for an exchange of state visits in 1997 and 1998 as a means to build momentum behind their policies. The NSC worked to put together a package of "deliverables" that showed visible progress in areas important to the president prior to Jiang Zemin's proposed visit; in fall 1997 these included nonproliferation, a general security dialogue, economic and commercial interests, and human rights. While little progress was made on specifics, both sides did agree to "build toward a strategic partnership."[81] In his memoir, Clinton argues he went to bed following his meeting with Jiang Zemin "thinking that China would be forced by the imperatives of modern society to become more open, and that in the new century it was more likely that our nations would be partners than adversaries."[82]

Leading up to Clinton's 1998 visit to China, the administration discussed and scrapped the idea to sponsor a human rights resolution at the UN Commission on Human Rights. In return for not pursuing one, the

United States sought the release of Chinese dissident Wang Dan, as well as China's signature on the international covenant on civil and political rights. Albright traveled to the PRC in April 1998 to lay the important groundwork. While there, she restated Taiwan policy in a way that notoriously became known as the "three noes." She stated "we have no change in our China policy. . . . We have a one-China policy—not a 'two China,' not a 'one China and one Taiwan' policy—and we do not support Taiwan independence or their membership in international organizations that are based on statehood."[83] Immediately, this statement was taken by Clinton's critics to be a repudiation of Taipei in favor of Beijing. Adding insult to injury, in return for open press coverage of the president's speeches within China, Clinton agreed to a public statement of the "three noes" in China during his own visit.

Clinton tried to use his June 25–July 3 trip to showcase the positive changes that had taken place in China and to emphasize the importance of establishing a constructive strategic partnership with the enormous, rapidly growing power. However, his trip, which had been designed to upstage the poisonous political debate at home with a dose of pageantry, instead reinvigorated the old debate. Clinton's statements on Taiwan opened him to a new round of heavy attack by Congress and the media for appeasement and "stabbing a friend in the back." Madeleine Albright notes that "personal diplomacy is not enough . . . to reshape a government's basic philosophy." China was "integrating their country more fully into the world economy, yet they didn't feel they could survive without holding themselves apart from the worldwide trend toward more open political systems."[84]

Clinton's resolve to push for China's entry into the WTO in late 1998 was complicated by the Senate Select Committee on Intelligence and Cox Committee hearings questioning Chinese acquisition of U.S. technology and examining accusations that the administration had ignored Department of Energy and intelligence community warnings about the vulnerability of the Los Alamos and Livermore labs. Along with the Wen Ho Lee case, the Chinese spy mania generated in the United States called into question the president's whole China policy, with senators insisting now was not the time for discussing China's WTO accession.[85]

PNTR and Clinton's Legacy

The most tangible success of the administration's engagement strategy was passage of Permanent Normal Trade Relations. In 1999, Clinton and Berger again pressed for a WTO agreement. In a speech on U.S.

China policy on April 7, Clinton explained the bottom line: "If China is willing to play by the global rules of trade, it would be an inexplicable mistake for the United States to say no."[86] Charlene Barshefsky claimed "there was a huge strategic component, that is to say, do you want China outside the international community or inside and constrained by international rules?" Additionally, the rest of the world was supporting WTO accession and normal trade relations with China, and the United States could not prevent this from occurring.[87] Given the congressional opposition and weak business support, however, domestic advisers convinced the president to postpone the agreement until greater domestic support could be guaranteed and positive domestic conditions developed. Release of the Cox Committee report on May 25, 1999, which accused the PRC of stealing U.S. secrets and the Clinton administration of inept stewardship of those secrets, was one delaying event.[88]

By September, the president calculated it was time to make a second attempt to put the U.S.-China relationship back on track. On the margins of the September 1999 Asian Pacific Economic Cooperation (APEC) leaders meeting, Clinton met with President Jiang Zemin to push stalled negotiations on China's accession to the WTO. Once the deal was reached in mid-November, the administration brought out all its guns to gain congressional agreement on PNTR. The full-scale campaign begun in January 2000 and engineered by Chief of Staff John Podesta included the active engagement of cabinet members, with Secretary of Commerce William Daley and White House Deputy Chief of Staff Steve Ricchetti leading congressional lobbying efforts on China policy. Clinton himself wrote to congressional leaders on January 24 about the importance of passing PNTR and gave it a prominent place in his State of the Union address days later. Clinton's team chose a balanced tone that acknowledged the pitfalls of the Chinese government but insisted PNTR was a step in the right direction that enhanced chances for reform and the rule of law in China as it brought tangible economic benefits to the United States (including access to China's market and lowered tariffs on U.S. exports).[89]

On March 8, the same day the administration submitted its PNTR legislation, Clinton framed his arguments with a special address at the Paul Nitze School of Advanced International Studies on the historic, strategic, and security dimensions of the overall relationship with the PRC. These geostrategic themes put the debate in stark terms that made it more than just trade benefits at stake. Clinton argued that China's entry into the WTO was about our "national interest" and "represents the most significant opportunity that we have had to create positive change in China since the 1970s. . . ." The United States could use the WTO to influence China's future choices toward the "right" direction or we could "turn our backs and almost certainly push it in the wrong direction." The WTO agreement by definition pushed China in the "right" direction.[90] The zero-sum language was meant to make engagement through PNTR the obvious choice.

The White House message on China also pragmatically noted that if the United States did not grant PNTR, it would deny U.S. citizens access to China's trade and markets that the rest of the world would enjoy automatically. Rejuvenating old human rights themes, the administration emphasized that WTO accession also was part of a larger trend toward reform and opening, and engaging China in international agreements would eventually make it less authoritarian and more pluralistic. Alternatively, rejecting PNTR strengthened those in China who rejected reform and opening up to international influence.[91] In her memoirs, Albright notes that "by entering the WTO, China committed to free itself from the 'House that Mao Built.' . . . There is no automatic connection between trade and democracy, but people can't help being shaped by their own experiences and observations. The millions of Chinese young people who are now learning to think for themselves economically will almost certainly be more likely than their parents to think for themselves politically."[92]

The White House worked hard to secure congressional approval. Berger increased the number of meetings with the four leaders on the Hill. Meetings with the Republicans were to co-opt the disloyal opposition with Republican involvement. "If you include them, you get tremendous points for this; much more able to sustain the position if they are at the table and they have a chance to be heard," observed Chief of Staff Leon Panetta. In his terms, there were always protrade Republicans to deal with, but the real challenge was overcoming the "labor buzz saw."[93]

The administration also made some compromises to pass PNTR. Although it had sought a clean bill with no conditions tied to extending PNTR, it faced numerous bills from members of Congress who wanted a substitute for yearly NTR discussions that allowed them to weigh in annually on China and Clinton's policy. The administration spent tremendous time adding congressional oversight provisions and more reporting requirements involving human rights to reassure members who otherwise would not have voted for PNTR.[94] The goal was to build a bipartisan majority on both sides and to work with key players who always led the charge on trade issues.

Despite opposition from various unions, human rights organizations, and key Democrats and conservatives in both houses, legislation passed in the House on a vote of 294-136 (Republicans in favor 217-2 and Democrats against by 132-77); Senate passage followed on September 19 by an 83-15 margin (Republicans supporting 45-8 and Democrats 38-7).[95] One former member of the NSC staff notes that if the deal had been made in April 1999, the administration would have left it for the next administration to take to Congress. When the president made the deal in November, however, he had the momentum because the administration's conscious strategy to put the deal "out there" beforehand had invigorated the U.S. business community before it was submitted. The "strategy worked almost too well on the American side because enough of the substance was out there that industry groups were just raring to go and it had momentum; it gave us an incredibly good political arena, which helped convince the Chinese that what would not work in April would work in November."[96]

Administration officials and analysts after the fact agree that Clinton's involvement and White House coordination played the critical role in pushing PNTR passage. At the end of his term, Clinton cited China's PNTR as one of the great achievements of his presidency and an important part of his policy legacy. When he signed the bill, he noted "trade with China will not only extend our nation's unprecedented economic growth, it offers us a chance to help to shape the future of the world's most populous nation, and to reaffirm our own global leadership for peace and prosperity."[97] Table 7.2 chronicles the problem diagnosis and framing process in his second term.

Conclusion

Like the first Bush administration, the Clinton administration was challenged by an energized domestic political context that made presidential control of China policy problematic. Mixed voices and the lack of central coordination exacerbated problems with China and made it difficult for a coherent strategy to develop. Because the administration also had underestimated how difficult it would be to reach a compromise with the Chinese, almost too late it recognized that a breach in the relationship could hurt progress in issues as diverse as nuclear proliferation and the general stability of East Asia.

First, problems over human rights linkage energized a strong commercial faction within the administration to undermine the initial

Table 7.2 Components of Bill Clinton's China Policy Frame (2nd Term)

Problem diagnosis	• Challenge to push China agenda, including strategic partnership and normal trade relations, in context of invigorated domestic opposition
Themes that resonated with president and public	
Presidential beliefs	• Domestic economic lens for foreign policy highlights focus on MFN and PNTR • Economic integration represents possible path to reform
Policy themes	• Administration's united position stresses strategic importance of China and link between economic and strategic interests • Emphasis placed on practical gains for U.S. business, and economic and strategic implications for China as part of the international club
Political considerations	• Domestic investigations and scandal affect timing of policy initiatives including PNTR • Lobbying efforts focus on practical gains and link to overall opportunities to effect change in China
Supporting conditions/tactics	• Greater policy centralization to the NSC helps coordinate the administration's message • Success on PNTR requires active lobbying campaign that reaches across party lines

human rights stance of the NSC and State Department. Commercial engagers' access to the policymaking process and the State Department's failure to win concessions allowed them to challenge the State Department's primacy. Commercial engagers maintained their advantage after 1994 because they represented positions that fit with the president's original policy priorities and the traditional principal foreign policy actors remained uninvolved.

Second, the issue of Taiwan's status in U.S.-China policy (and the concurrent controversy over intellectual property rights) forced a reassessment of the policy. As the crisis evolved, the president and secretary of state came back into the equation. The president responded symbolically (i.e., with two carrier task forces), but not in ways that threatened the overall relationship with China. Slowly Clinton and his traditional foreign policy team recognized that the lack of consistent involvement had contributed to both crises.

In the second term, the problem was not lack of coordination but a reinvigorated Congress that used its joint control over economic and trade issues to influence U.S. policy toward China. Yearly MFN debates and the incessant investigations into Clinton's policies and private life gave them a means to challenge the president's agenda.

From a framing perspective labels such as constructive or comprehensive engagement and strategic partnership failed in the contentious domestic environment. The constructive engagement theme, for example, was a search for a metatheme or a way to describe the policy that, according to one staffer, had an "uplifting quality, a big expansive quality and at the same time was sufficiently detailed to work." "The idea [was] that after the Cold War, America could not retrench. If anything we had to engage in a completely new way and the leadership was vitally important." Polling was done on the language to understand how best to portray and to sell to the relevant public what it needed to know.[98] Mickey Kantor argued that these words marked the emergence of a "Clinton Doctrine"—"not mutually assured destruction and a policy of containment but mutually assured prosperity and a policy of engagement" to apply more pressure to open up markets.[99] Engagement, however was too broad to provide a coherent basis for foreign policy or to insulate the administration from its domestic critics. Early on, the engagement umbrella allowed bureaucratic infighting to flourish inside the administration and ultimately left it vulnerable to criticisms that the president had appeased a likely aggressor.

One critical lesson to take from this case is that Clinton's lack of sustained interest and his decentralized foreign policy system led to an environment of crisis management in U.S.-China relations that lasted for most of his eight years in office. What success the administration did have on China policy in the second term seemed to be tied to Sandy Berger's pragmatism when he focused on results rather than grand theories. In a step-by-step process, Berger orchestrated the hard-fought domestic political battle that got PNTR passed in both houses of Congress. The PNTR victory was significant because it meant that bilateral economic relations with China from that point forward began from a new baseline within the WTO multilateral context. However, Clinton's attempts to establish a strategic partnership did not go far in the hostile domestic climate and were repudiated once George W. Bush entered office.

Notes

1. Quoted in Mann, *About Face,* 276.
2. Anthony Lake, "From Containment to Enlargement."
3. Anthony Lewis, "The Clinton Doctrine"; Thomas Friedman, "Clinton's Foreign Policy: Top Adviser Speaks Up."
4. Zagoria, "Clinton's Asia Policy"; author interview with Mickey Kantor, June 13, 2002, Washington, D.C.
5. Lake, "From Containment to Enlargement"; see also Harry Harding, "Asia Policy to the Brink"; Nancy Tucker, "A Precarious Balance: Clinton and China."
6. James Barnes, Margaret Kriz et al., "A Familiar Look"; my interviews with former Clinton NEC and NSC staff members, conducted in June 2002, supported this information.
7. Author telephone interview with Charlene Barshefsky, September 18, 2002; author telephone interview with Winston Lord, March 21, 2003.
8. Freeman interview.
9. Nancy Tucker describes the three groups as the principled engagers, commercial engagers, and security engagers (see, "A Precarious Balance").
10. Daniel Williams and R. Jeffrey Smith, "Clinton to Extend China Trade Status"; author interview with senior Pentagon official from the Clinton administration, June 2002; Lord interview.
11. Tyler, *A Great Wall,* 395–399, 413; Joseph Fewsmith, "America and China: Back from the Brink"; author interview with senior Pentagon official from the Clinton administration, June 2002; ASD Freeman's China Trip Contingency Press Guidance, October 1993 (Doc. no. 01622); Ambassador Freeman's Main Talking Points, October 1993 (Doc. no. 01623); Department of Defense, Office of the Secretary, Talking Points on the *Yin He,* October 1993 (Doc. no. 01625), National Security Archives Collection: China and the United States.
12. Daniel Southerland, "Clinton Sending First Trade Delegation to China."
13. Steven Greenhouse, "Renewal Backed for China Trade"; see Jim Rohwer, "The Titan Stirs"; Steven Greenhouse, "New Tally of World's Economies Catapults China into Third Place."
14. Tyler, *A Great Wall,* 395–399; Mann, *About Face,* 287–288; Freeman interview.
15. Department of Defense Bottom-Up Review Talking Points, October 1993 (Doc. no. 01621); CRS Issue Brief—Chinese Missile and Nuclear Proliferation: Issues for Congress, April 8, 1994 (Doc. no. 01701), National Security Archives Collection: China and the United States.

16. Freeman interview; author interview with senior Pentagon official from the Clinton administration, June 2002; Douglas Jehl, "U.S. Agrees to Discuss Arms Directly with North Korea." ASD Freeman's China Trip Contingency Press Guidance, October 1993 (Doc. no. 01622); Ambassador Freeman's Main Talking Points, October 1993 (Doc. no. 01623); Department of Defense, Office of the Secretary, Talking Points on the *Yin He,* October 1993 (Doc. no. 01625), National Security Archives Collection: China and the United States.

17. Fewsmith, "America and China," 252. The policy review signed in October established a newly formed interagency China Policy Senior Steering Group, chaired by Winston Lord, to coordinate the new policy. See confidential memo from Acting EAP Peter Tomsen on "China Policy Meeting," October 20, 1993 (Doc. no. 01630), National Security Archives Collection: China and the United States.

18. Memo to Peter Tarnoff from EAP Winston Lord, November 1, 1993 (Doc. no. 01635); Memo to Secretary Christopher from Winston Lord, November 2, 1993 (Doc. no. 01642); Memo to Secretary Christopher from John Shattuck, "Status Report on China MFN Conditions," November 1993 (Doc. no. 01634); Memo to President Clinton from Warren Christopher, November 15, 1993 (Doc. no. 01644); Briefing Memo to Secretary Christopher from Winston Lord, November 14, 1993 (Doc. no. 01639), National Security Archives Collection: China and the United States.

19. Lake, "From Containment to Enlargement"; see also Remarks by Anthony Lake before the Japan-America Society.

20. Daniel Williams and R. Jeffrey Smith, "U.S. to Renew Contact with Chinese Military"; CRS Issue Brief, "China-U.S. Relations," January 11, 1994 (Doc. no. 01669), National Security Archives Collection: China and the United States.

21. Quoted in Mann, *About Face,* 294; see also Clay Chandler and Daniel Williams, "Bentsen to Push China on Economic Reforms"; Peter Behr, "Offering China a Carrot on Trade"; Thomas Friedman, "Trade vs. Human Rights"; Patrick Tyler, "Rights in China Improve, Envoy Says."

22. Department of State, China: MFN, Human Rights Talking Points, January 1994 (Doc. no. 01662); Memo to Secretary Christopher from Winston Lord, January 1994 (Doc. no. 01666); Memo from Peter Tomsen (EAP) on Don Keyser's Initial Readout of the Secretary's Bilateral with PRC Vice Premier Qian, November 24, 1994 (Doc. no. 01673), National Security Archives Collection: China and the United States.

23. Memo of Overview of Issues to Be Discussed for Assistant Secretary Shattuck's China Trip, January 18, 1994 (Doc. no. 01671), National Security Archives Collection: China and the United States.

24. John Shattuck telephone interview by the author, September 26, 2002; E. J. Dione Jr., "Goodbye to Human Rights?"

25. See Warren Christopher, *In the Stream of History: Shaping Foreign Policy for a New Era*, 155: Briefing Memo to Secretary Christopher from Winston Lord, March 1994 (Doc. no. 01683), National Security Archives

Collection: China and the United States; Joseph Fewsmith, "America and China," 250–255.

26. Christopher, *In the Stream of History*, 153–156; Douglas Jehl, "Clinton Makes No Progress with Beijing."

27. China MFN Fact Sheet from the White House Staff, May 28, 1994 (Doc. no. 01708), National Security Archives Collection: China and the United States; Mann, *About Face,* 311.

28. Kantor interview.

29. Daniel Williams and Clay Chandler, "U.S. Aide Sees Relations with Asia in Peril."

30. Daniel Williams and Clay Chandler, "The Hollowing of a Threat; Trade Is Squeezing Rights Out of China Policy."

31. Christopher, *In the Stream of History*, 154–156.

32. Author interview with former Clinton State Department official, June 2002; Barshefsky interview; Lord interview; see also Christopher, *In the Stream of History*, 155–156; Briefing Memo to Secretary Christopher from Winston Lord, March 1994 (Doc. no. 01683), National Security Archives Collection: China and the United States; Elaine Sciolino, "U.S. to Try a Conciliatory Tact with China."

33. Shattuck interview; Elaine Sciolino, "Clinton Is Stern with Indonesia on Rights But Gleeful on Trade."

34. Kantor interview.

35. Dione, "Goodbye to Human Rights?"; Thomas Friedman, Elaine Sciolino, and Patrick Tyler, "Clinton and China: How Promise Self-Destructed."

36. Sciolino, "Clinton Is Stern with Indonesia on Rights."

37. Dione, "Goodbye to Human Rights?"; Friedman and Sciolino, "Clinton and China."

38. Barshefsky interview.

39. Secretary of Commerce Ron Brown's Remarks to the American Chamber of Commerce Breakfast in Beijing, August 28, 1994 (Doc. no. 01763); Department of State Briefing Memorandum from EAP Peter Tomsen to the Acting Secretary, August 24, 1994 (Doc. no. 01762); Department of State Information Memorandum from EAP Thomas Hubbard to the Secretary, September 2, 1994 (Doc. no. 01772), National Security Archives Collection: China and the United States. See also Michael Gordon, "U.S. Aide Admits North Korea Nuclear Policy May Not Work"; Thomas Friedman, Elaine Sciolino, and Patrick Tyler, "How President Clinton Agonized over His Crucial China Policy."

40. Kantor interview; China MFN Fact Sheet from the White House Staff, May 28, 1994 (Doc. no. 01708), National Security Archives Collection: China and the United States; Mann, *About Face,* 311.

41. Confidential Department of Defense Cable, "Press Guidance for Xu Huizi Visit," August 3, 1994 (Doc. no. 01753); Confidential Cable from Secretary of Defense to the Beijing Embassy on Plenary Session with PLA General Xu Huizi, August 19, 1994 (Doc. no. 01758); Cable from Office of

Secretary of Defense to Beijing Embassy on Secretary Perry's Discussion with Xu Huizi, August 19, 1994 (Doc. no. 01759); Briefing Book for Secretary Perry's Visit to China, October 16–19, 1994 (Doc. no. 01778), National Security Archives Collection: China and the United States. Author interview with senior Pentagon official from the Clinton administration, June 2002.

42. Memo to Branch Secretaries from the Secretary of Defense, "U.S.-China Military Relationship," August 1994 (Doc. no. 01751), National Security Archives Collection: China and the United States.

43. Assistant Secretary of Defense Explanation of Pentagon Regional Security Strategies After the Cold War, no date, National Security Archives postpublication Collection: China and the United States; "American Optimistic in Beijing."

44. Secret Briefing Memorandum for Warren Christopher Meeting with Foreign Minister Qian Qichen at the United Nations, April 1995 (Doc. no. 01828), National Security Archives Collection: China and the United States.

45. Testimony by Kent Wiedemann, Deputy Assistant Secretary of State for East Asian and Pacific Affairs, before the Senate Foreign Relations Committee Subcommittee on East Asian and Pacific Affairs, July 25, 1995 (Doc. no. 01895), National Security Archives Collection: China and the United States.

46. *United States Security Strategy for the East Asia–Pacific Region*, Department of Defense, Office of International Security Affairs (Washington, D.C., Office of the Secretary of Defense), February 1995 (Doc. no. 01817); Briefing Book for Admiral Mack's April 1995 trip to China, April 1995 (Doc. no. 01831), National Security Archives Collection: China and the United States.

47. Author interview with senior Pentagon official from the Clinton administration, June 2002; Talking Points for Meeting with LTG She-Ung to Discuss Sino-American Military Activities in 1996, November 1995, National Security Archives postpublication Collection: China and the United States.

48. Donald Schaefer, "U.S. Foreign Policies of Presidents Bush and Clinton: The Influence of China's Most Favored Nation"; David Sanger, "Jobs Figuring Large in Diplomacy."

49. Leon Panetta telephone interview with the author, October 11, 2002.

50. Elaine Sciolino, "Winston Lord: Where the Buck Stops on China and Human Rights"; Thomas Friedman, "U.S. May Ease Rights Goals with Beijing"; Thomas Friedman, "Deal with China Urged by Bentsen."

51. Author interview with senior Pentagon official from the Clinton administration, June 2002.

52. Jaw-ling Joane Change, "How Clinton Bashed Taiwan—and Why"; James Mann, "How Taipei Outwitted U.S. Policy"; Mann, *About Face*, 322; Sean Patrick Murphy, "A Sweet and Sour Relationship: Interview with Winston Lord"; Freeman interview; author interview with senior Pentagon official from the Clinton administration, June 2002.

53. On this score, the administration had long delayed a review of policy toward Taiwan; when it was completed, they made only cosmetic changes largely because of the congressional situation. See Department of State,

"Taiwan Policy—New Practices," Department of State Policy Paper for Peter Tarnoff Visit to China, August 1995 (Doc. no. 01908); Department of State "Taiwan Policy—Elements Which Will Not Change," Department of State Taiwan Policy Statement for Peter Tarnoff Visit to China, August 1995 (Doc. no. 01907), National Security Archives Collection: China and the United States.

54. Thomas Lippman, "U.S. Sees Engagement in Current Policy, But China Feels Containment"; Patrick Tyler, "China Is Insisting Clinton Reaffirm One-China Policy."

55. Confidential Cable from American Embassy to Secretary of State, July 6, 1995 (Doc. no. 01871), and Confidential Cable from Beijing Embassy to Secretary of State, July 3, 1995 (Doc. no. 01865), National Security Archives Collection: China and the United States.

56. Mann, *About Face*, 343–345; Alexander Sergounin, "An Age of Uncertainty: Building a Post–Cold War U.S. Security Strategy for East and Southeast Asia." See also Seth Faison, "Clinton Likely to Visit China in 1997 If He Is Re-elected."

57. Tucker, "A Precarious Balance," 245–246; see also Elizabeth Drew, *On the Edge: The Clinton Presidency*; Harding, "Asia Policy to the Brink," 68–73.

58. Winston Lord Testimony on Taiwan, Hearing of the East Asian and Pacific Subcommittee of the Senate Foreign Relations, February 7, 1996.

59. Peter Tarnoff, "Press Conference in Kuala Lampur."

60. R. Jeffrey Smith and Ann Devroy, "U.S. to Seek Closer Ties with China; More High-level Talks Contemplated Between Top Officials This Spring." See also Secretary of Defense William J. Perry, Address before the National Defense University, February 13, 1996 (Doc. no. 01936), National Security Archives Collection: China and the United States; Steven Erlanger, "U.S. Set to Impose Limited Sanctions on China."

61. Paul Blustein and R. Jeffrey Smith, "Economic, Political Concerns Put Clinton on the Spot in China Policy"; Michael Dobbs and R. Jeffrey Smith, "Second Carrier Group Sends a Clear Signal."

62. William Perry, Address before the National Defense University (Doc. no. 01936), National Security Archives Collection: China and the United States; Erlanger, "U.S. Set to Impose Limited Sanctions on China."

63. Panetta interview; Alison Mitchell, "Despite Tensions, Clinton Urges Renewal of China's Trade Status," and "The Clinton Record: Foreign Policy; Clinton's Three Big Objectives Include Peace Through Trade"; Warren Christopher, "Transcript of Secretary Warren Christopher's Interview with Elizabeth Farnworth," May 17, 1996; Warren Christopher, "American Interests and the U.S.-China Relationship," May 17, 1996; Jim Mann and Doyle McManus, "Official Says U.S. Taking Softer Approach to China"; author interview with Clinton State Department official, June 2002; Kantor interview; Steven Erlanger and David Sanger, "On World Stage, Many Lessons for Clinton."

64. Ben Wildavsky "Beyond MFN," and "Under the Gun (at the National

Economic Council)." Blustein and Smith, "Economic, Political Concerns Put Clinton on the Spot in China Policy."

65. Interestingly, Charlene Barshefsky argued that it was important to stand firm on intellectual property because with the Cold War over, "trade agreements must stand or fall on their merits. They no longer have a security component. If we do not get reciprocity we will not get freer trade." She felt U.S. negotiators must demand full reciprocity or see Congress put a stop to freer trade (Barshefsky interview). See also Paul Lewis, "Is the U.S. Souring on Free Trade?"; Keith Richburg, "U.S. Withdraws Its Threat of Sanctions Against China"; David Sanger and Steven Erlanger, "U.S. Warns China over Violations of Trade Accord"; see also Blustein and Smith, "Economic, Political Concerns Put Clinton on the Spot in China Policy"; Wildavsky, "Beyond MFN" and "Under the Gun."

66. Steven Erlanger, "U.S. Studying Limited Penalties for Chinese Sales"; Kantor interview.

67. Peter Behr, "U.S. Sidesteps Piracy Trade Issue with China Until After Rights Deadline"; Kantor interview.

68. Author interview with Clinton State Department official, June 2002.

69. Christopher, *In the Stream of History*, 429.

70. Remarks by Anthony Lake before the Japan-America Society, Washington, D.C., October 23, 1996; author interview with former assistant to President Clinton, June 2002.

71. Talking points for Warren Christopher's November 19 trip to China (no date), and Department of State reporting cable on Secretary's meeting with Vice Premier Qian Qichen, November 20, in Beijing, National Security Archives postpublication Collection: China and the United States.

72. Memo from Undersecretary Spero to the Secretary, October 17, 1996, National Security Archives postpublication Collection: China and the United States.

73. See Tyler, *A Great Wall,* 422.

74. Robert Suettinger, *Beyond Tiananmen: The Politics of U.S.-China Relations 1989–2000*, 339.

75. Author interview with Clinton administration official involved in China policymaking, June 2002, Washington, D.C.

76. Suettinger, *Beyond Tiananmen,* 306. Author interviews in June 2002 with former Clinton administration officials from the NSC, State Department, and Defense Department confirm the increased centralization of China policy to the White House.

77. Remarks by Samuel R. Berger, "Building a New Consensus on China."

78. Author interviews with former NEC, NSC, and White House officials who worked on China policy in the Clinton administration.

79. Smith and Devroy, "U.S. to Seek Closer Ties with China."

80. Suettinger, *Beyond Tiananmen*, 307–330.

81. Ibid., 320–322; see also Madeleine Albright, *Madam Secretary: A Memoir,* 430–431.

82. William J. Clinton, *My Life,* 768.

83. Albright quote from Suettinger, *Beyond Tiananmen,* 342. Various former Clinton administration officials have explained that the "three noes" did not constitute a change in U.S. policy. The mistake they have acknowledged is that articulation of the three noes in China itself gave it greater significance, which sparked a vicious domestic response.

84. Albright, *Madam Secretary,* 431.

85. Suettinger, *Beyond Tiananmen,* 358–362.

86. William J. Clinton, "Speech on U.S. Policy Toward China," April 7, 1999.

87. Barshefsky interview.

88. Suettinger, *Beyond Tiananmen,* 380–384; author telephone interview with former Clinton NSC staffer, July 9, 2002.

89. Granting PNTR involved preparing legislation declaring the Jackson-Vanik amendment (Title IV of the 1974 Trade Act) no longer applicable to China and recommending that nondiscriminatory trade treatment be extended to all Chinese products.

90. Office of the Press Secretary, "Remarks by the President on China," March 8, 2000; Background paper on WTO and PNTR for Ambassador Holbrooke Visit to PRC, March 16–20, 2000, no date, National Security Archives postpublication Collection: China and the United States.

91. These themes recur in numerous speeches given in early 2000. A list of comments, speeches, and documents can be found at http://usinfo.state.gov/regional/ca/uschina/pntrpres.htm.

92. Albright, *Madam Secretary,* 435.

93. Panetta interview. This sentiment was corroborated by author interviews with other former NEC, NSC, and White House officials who worked on China policy.

94. Author telephone interview with member of the Clinton administration's NSC staff, July 9, 2002; State Department PNTR Background Paper, no date, and Background Paper on WTO and PNTR for Ambassador Holbrooke Visit, no date, National Security Archives postpublication Collection: China and the United States.

95. See Overview and Action Summary of H.R. 4444, available at http://thomas.loc.gov.

96. Author telephone interview with Clinton administration NSC staffer, July 9, 2002.

97. Office of the Press Secretary, "Remarks by the President . . . at Signing of China Permanent Normal Trade Relations," October 10, 2000. China's accession on November 11, 2001, was followed by Taiwan's. President George W. Bush declared nondiscriminatory treatment would be offered permanently to products from the PRC effective January 1, 2002.

98. Author interview with former assistant to President Clinton, June 2002.

99. David Sanger, "In Manila, Asians Pore Over Washington's Inner Truths."

8

From Strategic Competitor to Uneasy Ally: G. W. Bush and the Fragile U.S.-China Relationship

In the 2000 presidential campaign G. W. Bush and his central foreign policy advisers outlined a policy that closely followed in Ronald Reagan's footsteps. Bush's message emphasized strengthening U.S. power (including alliances), building a strong military, and confronting challenges posed by major powers such as Russia and China. Bush adopted the language of strategic competition with China, which provided a rubric for a hard-line policy regarding the PRC based on a set of operating assumptions in direct contrast to Bill Clinton's. In the Bush administration's view China was a rising hostile power with a grudge against the West, and the challenge was to manage this threat. The initial East Asian policy emphasized consolidating relations with key allies such as Japan and Taiwan in the face of threats posed by China and North Korea and promoting national and theater missile defense systems.[1]

The crisis generated by the collision of an EP-3 surveillance plane with a Chinese F-8 fighter on April 1, 2001, and China's resulting detainment of twenty-four U.S. servicemen immediately moved China up the foreign policy agenda. It was the first foreign policy test of the administration and became an important marker because it led to a reassessment of the administration's initial policy approach. By the end of the eleven-day confrontation, Bush's tone had softened avoiding the language of China as a strategic competitor and instead using more constructive terms to describe the U.S.-China relationship. Contradicting this trend, however, the president's pledge to "do whatever it takes" to protect Taiwan, including unprecedented sales of arms, added a complicating element to his new commitment to the spirit of the one-China policy.

This chapter explores decisionmaking on China during the EP-3 incident and beyond—particularly Bush's Taiwan policy and his approach to six-party talks with North Korea—to understand continuity and change in his policy toward China. We soon see that stability (and instability) in the relationship were fueled by an internal battle between two strains of thought, one pragmatic and one hard-line, that vied for dominance of U.S. policy toward China and East Asia.

The Central Players and Their Predispositions

Organizing the Advisory System

Formally, George W. Bush's foreign policy system was hierarchically organized and centralized under White House control with both Vice President Dick Cheney and National Security Adviser Condoleezza Rice scripted to play central foreign policy coordinating roles. National Security Presidential Directive-1 (NSPD-1) specifically designated that the vice president would preside over NSC meetings in the president's absence and the national security adviser would conduct most meetings (i.e., determine the agenda, ensure that necessary papers were prepared, and so on). By design the vice president and national security adviser would serve as power brokers in a system designed to be collegial.[2] On the political side of the White House, Karl Rove, Karen Hughes, and Andy Card were positioned to become central players who added a political litmus test to policy decisions. Bush's chairman-of-the-board leadership style and lack of interest in foreign policy meant that he relied heavily on these trusted advisers to coordinate his policy.

In practice, there were two tiers of advisers and deep ideological cleavages among them in the first term. Former Secretary of the Treasury Paul O'Neil describes a general "in" group made up of ideological hawks such as Vice President Cheney and Secretary of Defense Donald Rumsfeld and a pragmatic "out" group represented by Secretary of State Colin Powell. Commenting on Iraq policymaking, O'Neil concludes that the president relied on the "in" group made up of ideologues, with no one serving as an honest broker bringing broad options to the president.[3] O'Neil asserts that the first NSC meeting was a scripted one in which the discussion on Iraq proceeded when Rice "orchestrated," Director of Central Intelligence George Tenet presented, Cheney and Rumsfeld said little (but were aware of events to come), and Powell was surprised by events. O'Neil was convinced that the presence of pragmatists like Powell inside the administration was mostly for "cover" and not to contribute to the policy debate.[4]

Players and Their Positions on East Asia Policy

Competing groups representing different policy approaches to international relations, and China specifically, formed along the lines noted above. The more hawkish position within the administration that some have labeled the "Americanist" camp argued that China with its economic power would seek to expand its territory and soon challenge U.S. interests.[5] Major proponents of the hard-line position, such as Vice President Dick Cheney and Secretary of Defense Donald Rumsfeld, prioritized building missile defense to establish U.S. security unilaterally rather than rely on negotiations they felt only appeased a likely aggressor such as China. For example, as the administration pursued its missile defense plans in spring 2001, no serious attempt was made to placate the Chinese. In fact, Deputy Defense Secretary Paul D. Wolfowitz and Deputy Secretary of State Richard L. Armitage visited countries bordering China (but not the PRC itself)—including Japan, Russia, and India—to enlist their backing for a missile shield.[6] For Rumsfeld and Wolfowitz, in particular, China, like Iraq, was arming to deter the United States and needed to be prevented from taking that path.[7] Foreshadowing this thinking in an article in 1997, Wolfowitz compared China's ambitions to Imperial Germany before World War I when it felt it had been denied a "place in the sun," mistreated by other powers, and was "determined to achieve its rightful place by nationalistic assertiveness."[8]

The hawkish perspective stressed the primary importance of Japan and Taiwan to Asian security cooperation and argued that U.S. interests lay with major democratic partners in Asia rather than with a hostile China. This meant existing alliances needed to be strengthened and a firm stance to defend Taiwan established.[9] In spring 2001, Bush's initial recommended arms sale to Taiwan, which exceeded both the monetary and technological levels of previous sales, reflected this policy inclination.[10]

The hawks were particularly close because of long-standing connections in previous administrations and the close working relationship developed during the Bush presidential campaign. In early 1999,

Wolfowitz, with Rice, served as a central foreign policy adviser on the Bush campaign and helped put together a formal team that included Richard Armitage and Richard Perle. Dick Cheney had developed close ties to Bush senior when he served as secretary of defense; he hired Paul Wolfowitz as one of his senior policy officials when he was secretary of defense and remained involved in discussions about what positions should be taken on foreign policy throughout the campaign. When Cheney agreed to be Bush's running mate, it placed a man known for his conservative foreign policy and defense views and his extensive knowledge of the inner workings of government in the center of the Bush White House structure. Donald Rumsfeld, who had long-term ties to Cheney going back to the Ford administration, developed a relationship with Rice and Wolfowitz when they served on the 1998 commission he chaired on missile defense.[11]

In contrast to the "Americanist" position, Secretary of State Colin Powell pragmatically recognized the U.S. shared interests with China and supported a multilateral approach to foreign policy. Testifying before Congress on January 17, 2001, Powell stated, "Strategic partner China is not, but neither is China our inevitable and implacable foe. China is a competitor, a potential regional rival, but it is also a trading partner willing to cooperate in areas where our strategic interests overlap. China is all of these things, but China is not an enemy, and our challenge is to keep it that way."[12]

Powell also never established a close relationship with the president. During the campaign, he was not privy to internal foreign policy discussions and instead served an external role to help deal with the public and to win political support for Bush among minorities. Long-term tensions between Powell on one side and Cheney and Wolfowitz on the other, when Powell had served as chairman of the Joint Chiefs of Staff (JCS) to Cheney's secretary of defense, kept him outside the inner circle of the new administration. Richard Armitage, who became Powell's number two man at the State Department, became tainted by his association with Powell.

For her part, National Security Adviser Condoleezza Rice benefited from the backing of Brent Scowcroft who brought her to the attention of both Bushes. George W. Bush and Rice were nearly the same age and developed a close relationship based on a shared interest in sports. When they hit it off, Rice was put in charge of foreign policy during the campaign, became Bush's foreign policy tutor, and was the obvious choice for national security adviser.[13] Once in office, Rice stayed close to the president, traveled with him, and spent time at Camp David on week-ends. Rice has observed that her relationship with Bush developed to the point that the president influenced her as much as she influenced him.[14]

In terms of her policy approach, Rice was no expert on Asia, but she shared many of the pragmatic views of her former mentor Brent Scowcroft, which included a commitment to avoid conflict with China over Taiwan while still recognizing China as a potential future challenge to the United States. Rice considered China neither friend nor enemy but instead viewed the country as a great power in the traditional sense. Under this rubric the United States could sustain a broad-based policy that encouraged economic liberalization, but the two powers could compete, if necessary, on security issues. Rice's position, however, remained somewhat unpredictable because while she desired regime change in China, she recognized that the immediate challenge was to proceed carefully so as not to provoke the Chinese government to rash actions. She wanted to resolve any problems with the PRC early and to avoid controversy during its 2002 Party Congress.[15]

These worldview and policy differences set the stage for two distinct factions to emerge in the administration. As we will see, the EP-3 crisis highlighted the danger of confrontation with China and provided an early opportunity for the State Department to set the administration's general policy direction. Later policy discussions over Taiwan and North Korea, however, demonstrated how differing agendas continued to send mixed messages on priorities in East Asia.

The EP-3 Crisis and the "Best" Relationship in Thirty Years

In April 2001, when a U.S. EP-3 and Chinese F-8 collided—killing the Chinese pilot and forcing the U.S. plane to land on Chinese territory on Hainan Island—the resulting detention of U.S. servicemen by the PRC led to an immediate Sino-American confrontation, which centered on China's demand for an apology and the U.S. demand to release its servicemen and return the plane with no apology. A solution needed to be found whereby each side could save face and neither admitted fault. Ultimately, the U.S. letter (drafted by the State Department) compromised and stated the United States was "very sorry" for the loss of the Chinese pilot and for landing without clearance on Hainan Island. Powell's challenge had been to negotiate a solution that placated Chinese demands but did not undermine his position with the president or strengthen those opposed to negotiation.

On the U.S. side, behind-the-scenes decisionmaking for this crisis was handled directly by Richard Armitage, with a direct line to Secretary Powell, and was staffed by career Foreign Service officers from the China desk in the State Department's Bureau of East Asian and Pacific Affairs (EAP). Because James Kelly, the soon-to-be assistant secretary for EAP, and other appointees remained unconfirmed on the sidelines, fewer bureaucratic layers separated State Department principals from Foreign Service officers knowledgeable about China. This direct line between the undersecretary and experts on China facilitated quick handling of the crisis.

The tricky part was that Chinese officials were difficult to make contact with and responded to U.S. overtures more slowly than Washington officials desired. Over the eleven days of the crisis, the group in Washington (with Armitage popping in to monitor progress periodically) and Ambassador Joseph Pruehr and the embassy staff in Beijing tracked the situation around the clock from both ends to keep it from spinning out of control. Although Ambassador Pruehr was a Clinton holdover, his background as a naval officer and former head of the Pacific Command gave him the legitimacy to negotiate with the Chinese and the necessary credibility among U.S. hard-liners.

The real challenge Powell and engagers faced was how to contain the hostile domestic debate in Congress and public speculation about war and economic sanctions in retaliation for China's actions. Ultimately, the debate was kept under control because the crisis was handled in one place (the State Department), and the White House made clear its support for State Department handling of the situation. Donald Rumsfeld and other hawks were cut out and unprepared to fuel the debate. The Defense Department was further hindered because it did not have key appointees in place who might have been involved otherwise and because the Pentagon mistrusted, and thus did not utilize, the professional staff it could have called upon.[16] Reagan's former secretary of defense, Frank Carlucci, called State Department handling of the crisis part of a strategy to handle the issue through diplomatic channels rather than military ones.[17]

Concerned about the long-term policy implications of this and future confrontations, as well as the future of the business relationship with China, both the national security adviser and secretary of state convinced the president of the importance of establishing a more stable and enduring relationship with the PRC.[18] The public announcement of the resolution to the EP-3 incident provides evidence for the administration's fragile convergence around Colin Powell's pragmatic position.

Immediately following the crisis, Powell remained the primary spokesman for China policy, and both Dick Cheney and Condi Rice served supporting roles to help shape a common positive message in a coordinated public relations strategy.

During this time Taiwan arms sales loomed, threatening to complicate the picture and derail the fragile consensus on China. Specifically, Bush's remark to "do whatever it takes" to help Taiwan's defense—including the proposed sale of Kidd class missile destroyers and diesel submarines (items denied by earlier administrations)—sent the State Department scrambling to tone down the president. Although ultimately Bush's arms sales did not include the controversial Aegis radar most opposed by the Chinese, the sale represented part of the Pentagon's long-term effort to promote U.S.-Taiwan defense cooperation regardless of its impact on relations with the PRC. New procedures put in place in 2001 attempted to make arms sales more routine by conducting talks on a regular basis rather than once a year; this generated a harsh Chinese response. These procedures, in effect, downgraded the arms sales but did not change Bush's policy or his commitment to Taiwan.[19]

In summer 2001, high-level contacts between the United States and China resumed and accelerated to new levels, with a tangible working relationship developing after September 11. Rhetorically, the administration began to argue that a China positively engaged in the world was conducive to both the stability and security of East Asia and U.S. security interests.[20] This message was reinforced even more after the events of September 11. For example, during the president's visit to Shanghai in October 2001, previous sticking points in the relationship, such as human rights, arms proliferation, and Taiwan, received less attention. The U.S. failure to back Taiwanese President Chen Shui-bian's efforts to be invited to the APEC meetings demonstrated the administration was not willing to let the symbolic issue of Taiwan's status interfere with its more general foreign policy agenda, which sought to rally China's support for the war on terror.[21]

Commenting before Bush's February 2002 Asian trip, Rice justified the policy based on the familiar one-China consensus developed over the previous six administrations vis-à-vis Taiwan and the PRC: "The United States doesn't want to see any unilateral change in the status quo. This is an issue that people on both sides of the Straits need to resolve peacefully. But the United States has certain obligations under the Taiwan Relations Act to help Taiwan defend itself. Those are the cornerstones of American policy toward Taiwan."[22]

External events such as the EP-3 incident provided the impetus to change the dominant policy frame from a hostile China to a China to be dealt with pragmatically, given the pressing threats and shared interests on various other issues. By 2003–2004, Bush administration officials commonly claimed the relationship was the best it had been in thirty years and credited this to the frequent and candid nature of discussions with the Chinese. This characterization, however, was an exaggeration that simplified reality. It masked fundamental disagreements between the United States and China and papered over deep-seated differences within the administration over Taiwan arms sales and how to handle North Korea, which, if mismanaged, risked causing new confrontations with China.

Evaluating China Policy by Assessing Bush's Taiwan Policy and Approach to Six-Party Talks

Diagnosing the China Policy Problem

The fundamental disagreement in the Bush administration rested on the degree to which China could be trusted and how to balance the need for China's cooperation in areas of strategic common interest such as North Korea without undermining the long-term commitment to Taiwan. Two distinct groups—pragmatic engagers and hard-liners—vied for bureaucratic dominance of the East Asian policy agenda.

Pragmatic engagers. For policy advisers such as Colin Powell, it was important to maintain the cross-strait status quo to prevent confrontation and to emphasize that dealing constructively with China promoted U.S. interests for regional security and stability across the Taiwan Strait and on the Korean Peninsula. Given the broad ties with China, Powell emphasized a broad agenda focusing on cooperation in counterterrorism; promoting economic prosperity and security (by pressing economic/financial reform for mutual prosperity) while managing the trade relationship; promoting democracy and human rights; and urging adherence to international and bilateral nonproliferation and arms control arrangements.[23] The breadth of this list shows areas of agreement and disagreement but also a shared commitment for pragmatic discussions to address differences as well as common interests.

On Taiwan policy, the State Department preferred to manage arms sales quietly and limit military relations in order to avoid any confrontation with China. The department had succeeded in getting the president to tone down his pro-Taiwan rhetoric in 2001, and the post–September 11 policy environment emphasized great-power cooperation over disagreements. Presidential elections in Taiwan during spring 2004, however, brought Taiwan to the policy forefront. As the administration called for China's patience in response to Taiwan's unpredictable domestic situation, it worked to keep President Chen Shui-bian's proindependence language under control.[24] Internally, one official noted that China had "played the adult," not Taiwan, and this hurt Taiwan's position inside the administration.[25]

On North Korea, Powell's first instinct was to continue Clinton's efforts to solve the North Korean nuclear issue through bilateral negotiations. When he was blocked handily in early 2001, by hard-liners who felt negotiation was not an option, two years of stalemate proceeded. Only when North Korea announced it had nuclear weapons, in April 2003, and that it might be willing to sell them, did the administration reluctantly enter multiparty talks at Powell's urging. Promoting six-party talks to solve the North Korea nuclear problem was a policy area where the State Department adopted a more accommodating stance (i.e., a willingness to work with China and others to manage the crisis); it represented the kind of issue that showed U.S.-China common interests.

The first two rounds of talks (the first in August 2003 and the second in February 2004) proceeded with Assistant Secretary James Kelly and State Department negotiators kept on a tight leash. The administration held firm to its position that no progress could be made until North Korea came clean on its highly enriched uranium program and agreed to complete dismantlement. Bush's offer to provide a written security guarantee in exchange for verifiable nuclear disarmament was never taken seriously by the North Korean regime, which demanded energy aid and other concessions before making any admissions or concessions.[26] During the third round in June 2004, the State Department offered a more flexible position that allowed it to negotiate before receiving the North Korean promise to dismantle its nuclear program.

Hawks and hard-liners. The State Department's position on Taiwan and North Korea was complicated by advocates for a harder line who continued to emphasize China's growing military threat to U.S. interests. The September 30, 2001, *Quadrennial Defense Review Report*, for example, emphasized the potential for regional powers (namely China) to develop capabilities to threaten stability in regions critical to U.S. interests. East Asia represented a particularly challenging area where "the possibility exists that a military competitor with a formidable resource base will emerge in the region."[27] Various other Pentagon reports, such as its annual report on China's military, concluded that Chinese political leaders and PLA commanders had developed credible military options to prevent Taiwan from achieving independence. The 2004 report concluded that "the PLA's offensive capabilities improve each year and provide Beijing with an increasing number of credible options to intimidate and actually attack Taiwan."[28] The Pentagon position called for a consistent strategic harmonization between the United States and Taiwan, which made Taiwan part of the U.S. force structure and created a de facto military alliance.[29] Specifically, the United States needed to restore the military balance across the Taiwan Strait before China acted preemptively. In conjunction with the pro-Taiwan stance, conservatives questioned the need for military exchanges with China, arguing that these provided the PLA with an opportunity to gather intelligence about the U.S. military while not sharing useful and reciprocal information with the United States. Rumsfeld successfully resisted the White House call to resume military exchanges, temporarily stopped following the EP-3 incident, until his meeting with Chinese General Cao Gangchuan in October 2003.[30]

Skepticism on China also enhanced conservative mistrust of the six-party talks on North Korea's nuclear issue. Regarding North Korea, hard-liners led by Cheney, Rumsfeld, and John Bolton, the undersecretary of state for arms control and international security, insisted on regime change while engagers led by Powell and Jim Kelly believed dialogue had a chance of succeeding. Hard-liners repeatedly undermined the talks by weakening the language of the proposed security guarantee and the leeway given to Assistant Secretary of State Kelly in his negotiating, which prevented him from engaging in substantial back-and-forth dialogue.[31]

Explaining Shifting Perceptions of China's Threat

The different problem diagnoses noted above set the stage for competing policies pursued in separate policy tracks. Bush's lack of consistent involvement meant that he played little part in the process and did little to broker the differences.

Presidential beliefs and priorities. Early on, Bush seemed psychologically predisposed to see the world in terms of threats and to see China as fundamentally hostile to U.S. goals. In a telling campaign statement in

January 2000, Governor Bush declared, "When I was coming up, it was a dangerous world and we knew exactly who the 'they' were. It was us versus them, and it was clear who 'them' was. Today, we're not so sure who the 'they' are, but we know they're there."[32] By the time President Bush entered office in 2001, China loomed as the "them" that needed to be contained.[33]

The EP-3 incident, however, helped bring to the fore pragmatists who emphasized real costs to U.S. interests if the situation was not stabilized. A lot was at stake, including U.S. business interests that had always been a priority of the president's supporters and a priority he shared with his father. Additionally, when September 11 happened, it provided Bush with a new "them" and China became a "friend" in the strategic struggle against terrorism.[34] In simplistic terms, for President Bush China shifted quickly from a them to an us position in the post–September 11 environment, as arguments focusing on shared mutual interests and cooperation gained precedence. As long as Taiwan's interests simultaneously were served, there was much common ground with China and no need to make trade-offs. Thus in late 2003, when the president warned Taiwan President Chen Shui-bian not to move Taiwan toward independence, he reaffirmed the one-China policy and made it clear he was opposed to any unilateral decision by either side to change the status quo.[35]

On North Korea, what the president said he wanted and what his negotiators were allowed to carry out were often at odds. For example, although Bush stated he wanted a negotiated solution, the State Department special envoy was allowed no room to negotiate. The very directions he received guaranteed a North Korean refusal of the U.S. position. As pressure mounted from South Korea and Japan for the administration to show some flexibility in its stance, Bush shifted away from his confrontational tone. In June 2004, as the third round of negotiations began, it seemed the president could embrace the six-party process as a means to test North Korea's intentions and engage China's cooperation. The lack of progress, however, renewed questions as to the administration's commitment to substantive six-party talks. The president's position appeared ambiguous at best and vulnerable to shifting policy arguments.

Competing policy themes and logic. Underlying the president's indecisiveness and the pragmatic and hard-line positions noted above were different assumptions about the geopolitical landscape in East Asia. Hard-line assumptions based on a zero-sum analysis ignored countervailing conditions, such as increasing East Asian economic interdependence and China's dependence on the U.S. market, which the pragmatists acknowledged. The Pentagon assessment was based on the growing belief that the Chinese were developing the capability for a rapid intense strike that would create confusion and undercut Taiwan's government before the United States could respond. A 2004 Pentagon report predicted the balance of power across the strait would shift in China's favor by 2005 if Taiwan did not embrace military modernization; it pointed to the PLA's new weapons purchased from Russia and the positioning of hundreds of missiles across from Taiwan.[36] In response, military cooperation and training between Taiwan and the United States were increased, including establishing a secure communications link between the Seventh Fleet in Honolulu and Taiwan and sharing communication codes between the two militaries in order to facilitate communication for joint operations in a future crisis.[37]

The risk, as pragmatists have noted, was that these expanding ties might anger China, triggering a sharp response, and compromise many areas of cooperative relations. Consistently, the State Department position acknowledged the need to assist Taiwan but recommended that relations with the island should be kept low key so that the United States avoided unnecessary and potentially destabilizing political confrontations with the PRC.[38] In a hearing before the Senate Foreign Relations Committee on April 21, 2004, Assistant Secretary James Kelly responded to hard-line accusations by reiterating that the United States would continue to sell appropriate defensive military equipment to Taiwan in accordance with the TRA, which would maintain the capacity to resist any coercion against Taiwan. He also noted, however, that any unilateral moves toward independence would "avail Taiwan of nothing it does not already enjoy in terms of freedom, autonomy, prosperity and security" and, in fact, could trigger a military response by China that could destroy what Taiwan had built.[39]

The cleavage between the hard-line position and the engagement position was even more overt in the case of North Korea policy. Until the third round of negotiations in June 2004, hard-liners kept the U.S. negotiating position hamstrung so that no progress could be made. The negotiations also were hurt as they proceeded when they were attacked concurrently via leaks to the *Washington Times* and "charges" against U.S. negotiators, such as special envoy Joseph Detrani and Jack Pritchard before him, by hard-liners that they were "soft" on North Korea. For example, in May 2004, Detrani was accused of exceeding his instructions by telling North Koreans that construction of a light-water reactor was possible if it gave up its nuclear program and rejoined the international nuclear control agreements. Critics charged the State Department was providing inducements to the North Koreans for compliance and "giving in" to them. In response, the State Department spokesman reiterated that the goal was "complete, verifiable, and irreversible dismantlement," or CVID.[40]

In both Taiwan and North Korean policy, the critics of the State Department accused those who negotiated and dealt with China of being "pro-China officials." This group was accused of trying to shift the administration's policy to favor Beijing's position that Taiwan is part of China and that the United States should not support a free, independent Taiwan. Similarly, the State Department repeatedly was accused of giving in to the North Koreans. These accusations, however, were political attempts by hard-liners to define the problem in zero-sum terms, which placed pressure on the State Department's status quo position of engagement with China favored in the administration.

Domestic considerations and the 2004 election. Attitudes in Congress and among the public toward China vis-à-vis Taiwan remained volatile and complicated through Bush's first administration. The strong support for Taiwan on the Hill led to a constant dance between the executive and legislative branches, which had different reference points for their policy. Although Bush was more supportive of Taiwan than any president since Ronald Reagan, he also came to see the need for stable relations with China. He faced the same congressional pressure to take a tougher stance on China vis-à-vis Taiwan. In one example, a House measure passed in May 2004 (opposed by the State Department) called on Pentagon officials to set up high-level military exchanges between the U.S. and Taiwanese militaries. In sympathy, the *Washington Times* called the current policy ban of exchanges between senior Taiwan and U.S. military officers a "remnant of the Clinton administration's pro-Beijing policies" that focused exclusively on military exchanges with the PRC.[41]

Bush also faced significant domestic cross-pressures in regard to the growing economic interdependence with China. Due to congressional pressure and given election-year dynamics, news about China in 2003 and 2004 was dominated by negative stories focusing on unfair Chinese trade practices and the blossoming trade deficit with China. In this environment new constituencies developed advocating for a harder line regarding China's economic policy and the appropriate U.S. response. (These pressures emerged to challenge the previous assumption that economic interdependence always created a win-win scenario.)

The administration faced more criticism from Democratic presidential candidates linking Bush's policies to the outsourcing of tens of thousands of U.S. manufacturing jobs. In spring 2004, Bush was urged to accept two petitions to bring WTO cases against China. The first, an AFL-CIO petition on labor, was rejected, and the administration indicated it would not accept a second—a petition on Chinese currency.[42] Rather than appearing to give in to organized labor, the Bush administration used the benefit from a successful visit of Vice Premier Wu Yi and concessions on intellectual property issues at the April 2004 Joint Commission on Commerce and Trade (JCCT) to reassure the U.S. business community that it had enough contacts with Chinese officials to raise these issues in other forums, rather than pushing for an indirect solution through a WTO case against China.[43] The administration felt it had a sufficiently positive outcome from the JCCT to use as evidence in conflicts with Congress and democratic opponents for China's progress on its obligations.

The administration's flexibility on North Korea in June 2004 provided the clearest link to its calculations on domestic political realities and the 2004 presidential election. The evidence shows that it became more flexible toward North Korea because it feared a failure in June would trigger reviews of the utility of the negotiating process before the November election. Observers claimed that a key element favoring the State Department was that White House domestic advisers felt if the Korean stalemate continued, its chances of becoming a domestic liability would increase because the Kerry campaign had articulated a careful plan to resolve it. Assistant Secretary Kelly's hearings on North Korea policy before the Senate Foreign Relations Committee on July 15, 2004, revealed the pressure Democrats had brought to bear on the administration's policy. In the hearing, Democrats accused the administration of allowing a North Korea nuclear breakout by failing to negotiate for three years. On the other side, Kelly faced critics of engagement such as Senator Sam Brownback (R-Kansas), who questioned the utility of negotiations and brought up North Korea's poor human rights record.[44]

In light of Bush's lack of involvement and the presence of competing policy factions, infighting and mixed messages dominated policy discussions. Additional organizational factors reinforced this pattern.

Bureaucratic Factors and Conditions That Explain Bush's Maneuvers

Under Bush, U.S. China policy evolved as a function of bureaucratic disagreement, with the State Department influencing the overall tone but not necessarily how the policy was implemented. The Pentagon's clear policy position (noted above), its central importance to policy implementation in these areas, its size, and extensive resources gave it great ability to block new policy initiatives. More than once the Pentagon's focus on contingency planning pushed the State Department's policy envelope. The Pentagon's quiet efforts to restructure Taiwan's military and improve its ability to defend itself against China challenged the State Department's long-standing policy to limit military relations with Taiwan and avoid confrontation with China. For example, as of July 12, 2004, the National Defense University (NDU) had been authorized by Rumsfeld to conduct nine war-game scenarios focusing on cross-strait relations. The July 2004 game, code named "Dragon's Thunder," was based on China's growing military threat.[45]

Competing agendas flourished, in part, because the national security adviser failed to broker differences between the pragmatic and hard-line factions, for example, the competing interests between Powell and Rumsfeld and also Powell and Cheney. The two tracks on China/Taiwan policy and infighting over negotiations with North Korea highlighted this problem. Rice's ability to broker these differences was made more difficult because both Rumsfeld and Cheney had greater experience and an independent power base that she lacked. Cheney, in particular, emerged as the sole power broker. His agreement to the State Department–generated consensus on the EP-3 incident was essential to undercut hard-line disgruntled voices. Similarly, his opposition to talks with North Korea kept the negotiations hamstrung in the first administration, halting meaningful negotiations and limiting what could be offered in the talks. He remained mistrustful of Pyongyang and pointed to North Korea's history of irresponsibility and deceit that had undermined previous negotiations.[46]

When Rice weighed in on policy debates, there was less internal sniping and progress was possible. Until she authorized a repackaging of the State Department's negotiating position with North Korea (i.e., that the United States would talk with North Korea before demanding it dismantle its program and confess to having a highly enriched uranium program), no flexibility had seemed possible. The new position was acceptable to hard-liners because it tested North Korea's true intentions. State Department sources claimed the opening position was laid out in terms more explicit about what was expected from North Korea and by other parties.[47] Table 8.1 details the strategic framing of China policy in the Bush administration.

Table 8.1   Components of George W. Bush's China Policy Frame

Problem diagnosis	• Fundamental disagreement about the degree to which China could be trusted, and how to balance the need for China's cooperation in areas of strategic common interest such as North Korea without undermining the long-term commitment to Taiwan
	• EP-3 crisis reinforces need to engage PRC to promote peace and stability in East Asia
Themes that resonated with president and public	
Presidential beliefs	• Predisposition to see China as a potential threat and give priority to Taiwan as an old friend
	• September 11 triggers new, broader threat perceptions that put China into pragmatic context
Policy themes	• Competing strains of thought between the *hawks and hard-liners* who focus on the need to recognize China as a potential hostile power (i.e., reorient policy away from China to long-term allies such as Japan and Taiwan) and the *pragmatic engagers* who see the need to avoid confrontation with China and to manage China in pragmatic ways within a multilateral framework
	• Pragmatic position is reinforced by strategic context after September 11
Political considerations	• Anti-Chinese rhetoric linked to increased losses of domestic U.S. jobs as 2004 election approaches
Supporting conditions/tactics	• Highly centralized administration values consensus-driven policies but ineffectively manages bureaucratic conflict, which in turn hinders coherent foreign policy development

Conclusion

As a novice in foreign policy President George W. Bush entered office uninterested in foreign policy and uninvolved in day-to-day decisionmaking. His "chairman of the board" leadership style created a White House often unable to broker the relationship between competing advisers, who had deep-seated differences that led to overt policy disagreements.

The EP-3 incident and the war on terror in response to September 11 provided an external impetus (focusing event) that reinforced the strategic rationale for closer ties to China. This context also reinforced a tilt toward Secretary of State Colin Powell's position. President Bush, much like Ronald Reagan earlier, emphasized new priorities based on the geostrategic equation and pragmatic recognition of the costs of disrupting close economic interdependence between the two economies. The "new," but fragile relationship was reflected in the return to a broad range of relations, including finalizing China's entry into the WTO, high-level contacts such as Bush's trip to Shanghai for the APEC talks, and the resumption of military-to-military exchanges.[48]

China scholar David Lampton argues that President Bush presided over a U.S.-China relationship closer than ever before; the new relationship rested on the war on terror, the binding forces of globalization, Chinese preoccupation with domestic challenges, and Beijing's growing economic and international influence.[49] In contrast, Robert Sutter claims that despite mutual interest in cooperative relations, differences over Taiwan and other issues simmer below the surface. He notes that public statements lauding China's importance in the war on terror mask the real U.S. policy to downplay China, as relations with key allies such as Japan are nurtured.[50] The fact that these authors have different analyses shows that what you see depends on where you are looking. In this chapter we have seen the two China policy agendas that existed in the first term of the Bush administration. For example, while the administration's rhetoric emphasized the status quo on Taiwan, in practice the Defense Department carried out an independent policy that increasingly lined up U.S. policy with proindependence forces on Taiwan. Similarly, attempts to move negotiations forward with North Korea were summarily blocked by the Cheney-Rumsfeld faction.

Ambiguities over policy toward China allowed different agendas to coexist. Hard-liners such as Cheney or Rumsfeld could pragmatically engage on China while hedging in other areas such as Taiwan. Even though Bush seemed to adhere to the quantity and quality clause of the 1982 communiqué (the document stating that Taiwan arms sales must be in proportion to the Chinese threat), there was latitude to respond to Taiwan and to engage China.[51] The engagement premise that developed in Bush's first term encompassed the pragmatic recognition that the

Sino-American relationship remained contradictory, but too much was at stake to leave it to flounder unattended.[52]

The open question for the second Bush term is the extent to which pragmatism or ideology will dominate the making of U.S. policy toward China. The changes the president had made in his foreign policy team by the end of 2004 generally signaled the continuing dominance of the neoconservative agenda in foreign policy. The resignations of Colin Powell and Richard Armitage, along with the appointment of Condoleezza Rice as secretary of state (as well as changes made down the line to the deputy assistant secretary level in the State Department), signal the administration's efforts to curtail State Department independence and to bring it into line with the White House.

Much will depend on Condoleezza Rice's priorities as secretary of state and whether she is able or desires to establish herself as an independent force in the administration able to counter the Cheney/ Rumsfeld position. In terms of operating style, Rice is more likely to rely on those she trusts, rather than career department officials who were elevated to prominent positions by Colin Powell. In this regard, she is likely to follow the James Baker model more than Powell's in how she utilizes State Department personnel. While this may be a harbinger for a hard-line shift in China policy, it is important to remember that Rice has been a pragmatist on China policy, and when she has participated in that policy, she has opted for cooperation over confrontation, toed the line on past administrations' one-China policy, and pushed for some flexibility for negotiators in the six-party talks over North Korea.

How U.S.-China relations will develop is an open question. Because the events of September 11 seem to have convinced many in the administration that the United States is now involved in a struggle between modernity and fundamentalism, how China policy is framed will be crucial. As long as China remains a part of the solution (i.e., is perceived to cooperate in the war on terror), there is a good chance positive relations will be maintained. However, if more conservative elements of the administration gain control of the East Asian policy agenda, and Chinese intransigence on issues such as arms proliferation is perceived as a hostile act, then a China-as-threat scenario may come to dominate the administration's agenda. While confrontations over Taiwan, arms proliferation, trade disputes, human rights, or other issues are likely, who handles the problem and how it is framed will continue to shape prospects for stability or instability in the U.S.-China relationship.

Notes

1. See David Bachman, "The United States and China: Rhetoric and Reality."

2. National Security Presidential Directive-1 (NSPD-1), February 13, 2001.

3. Ron Suskind, *The Price of Loyalty: George W. Bush, the White House, and the Education of Paul O'Neil,* 120, 127–129.

4. Ibid., 72–76, 130; Richard Clarke, in *Against All Enemies: Inside America's War on Terror,* confirms that these cleavages were deep within the Bush administration. In circumstances like those surrounding the decision to invade Iraq—where potential naysayers were quieted or cut out of central decisionmaking venues and central decisionmakers made up their minds early—it is no surprise the Bush administration developed many of the symptoms of groupthink, which led to the Iraq policy fiasco. Ivo H. Daalder and James M. Lindsay in *America Unbound: The Bush Revolution in Foreign Policy* (Washington, DC: Brookings Institution, 2003) distinguish two groups within the "hawks"—the "nationalists" such as Vice President Cheney and Secretary of Defense Rumsfeld who represent an aggressive realist stance, and the "neo-conservatives" represented by Paul Wolfowitz and Douglas Feith who focus on democracy promotion and a broader rebuilding or "nation-building" agenda for Iraq. On Iraq policy, the authors note that the two groups shared the same goal of regime change in Iraq—if for different reasons.

5. Lanxin Xiang, "Washington's Misguided China Policy," 12; see John Dumbrell, "Unilateralism and 'America First'? President George W. Bush's Foreign Policy." Some of Bush's senior advisers had spent the previous eight years refining their conception of a new world order—one comprising a unipolar system with a vision rooted in neoconservative ideology and a pessimistic reading of history.

6. "George W.'s World View," *New Perspectives Quarterly.*

7. Suskind, *The Price of Loyalty,* 77.

8. See Paul Wolfowitz, "Bridging Centuries," 7.

9. Andrew Scobell, "Crouching Korea, Hidden China: Bush Administration Policy Toward Pyongyang and Beijing," 348. See also Richard Armitage, "A Republican View: Managing Relations with Russia, China, India—An Interview with Ambassador Richard Armitage"; Ralph A. Cossa, "The Bush Administration's 'Alliance-based' East Asian Policy."

10. The final sale included four Kidd class destroyers, twelve antisubmarine P-3 Orion aircraft, eight diesel submarines, helicopters, missiles, and other equipment; excluded were the Aegis radar system that could track up to 100 incoming missiles and aircraft and the Patriot 3 antimissile defense system. See Bruce J. Dickson, "New Presidents Adjust Old Policies: U.S.-Taiwan Relations Under Chen and Bush," 649–650.

11. James Mann, *Rise of the Vulcans: The History of Bush's War Cabinet,* 248–253.

12. Colin L. Powell, confirmation hearing before the Senate Foreign Relations Committee.

13. Mann, *Rise of the Vulcans*, 249–255.

14. Elisabeth Busmiller, "Bush's Tutor and Disciple, Condoleezza Rice."

15. Mann, *Rise of the Vulcans*, 281; Jacob Heilbrunn, "Condoleezza Rice: George W.'s Realist"; Scobell, "Crouching Korea, Hidden China," 349. To evaluate her realism in her own terms see Condoleezza Rice, "Promoting the National Interest," 56.

16. This recounting of U.S. handling of the EP-3 incident is based on author interviews with various Bush administration officials knowledgeable about the event.

17. Carlucci's comments were made during an April 12, 2001, "Forum on the Role of the National Security Adviser," cosponsored by the Woodrow Wilson International Center for Scholars and the James A. Baker III Institute for Public Policy of Rice University.

18. Bachman, "The United States and China," 261; David Shambaugh, "Sino-American Relations Since September 11: Can the New Stability Last?"; Robert Kagan and William Kristol, "The 'Adults' Make a Mess"; Michael Gordon, "Rumsfeld Limiting Military Contacts with the Chinese."

19. Bill Gertz, "Taiwan Shoring Up Defenses with U.S. Assistance."

20. See Bachman, "The United States and China," 261; Shambaugh, "Sino-American Relations Since September 11"; Kagan and Kristol, "The 'Adults' Make a Mess"; Gordon, "Rumsfeld Limiting Military Contacts with the Chinese."

21. Dickson, "New Presidents Adjust Old Policies," 653–654; Shambaugh, "Sino-American Relations Since September 11."

22. Transcript of Condoleezza Rice briefing to Press, February 14, 2002, on eve of presidential visit to Asia, "Bush to Focus on Terror, Security, Economy in Asia Trip."

23. These areas of promoting cooperation are outlined in the State Department's yearly Bureau and Post review process that measures the success and failure of U.S. government policy efforts regarding China.

24. Edward Cody, "Chen's Inaugural Address Skirts Independence Vow."

25. Author interview with Bush administration official.

26. Joshua Kurlantzick, "Look Away, A Do-nothing Korea Policy."

27. Department of Defense, *Quadrennial Defense Review Report*, 4.

28. Maxim Kniazkov, "China Developing 'Credible Military Options' to Confront Taiwan, US Warns."

29. Gertz, "Taiwan Shoring Up Defenses with U.S. Assistance."

30. Bill Gertz, "Rumsfeld Confers at Pentagon with His Chinese Counterpart."

31. Kurlantzick, "Look Away, A Do-nothing Korea Policy."

32. George W. Bush quoted in Frank Bruni, "The 2000 Campaign: The Syntax."

33. See Thomas Carothers, "Promoting Democracy and Fighting Terror."

34. Stanley Renshon, "The World According to George W. Bush"; Fred I.

Greenstein, "The Contemporary Presidency: The Changing Leadership of George W. Bush: A Pre– and Post–9/11 Comparison." Presidential scholars such as Fred Greenstein give the president high marks in emotional intelligence following September 11 for radiating a sense of self-assurance, a firm grasp of policy specifics, good face-to-face political skills, a clear sense of direction, an ability to organize a skilled national security team, and for becoming an effective public communicator. This event seemed to be a defining one for Bush that reinforced his earlier predisposition to see the world in black-and-white terms.

35. Philip Pan, "Taiwan's President Unfazed by U.S. Warning"; John Pomfret, "China Lauds Bush for Comments on Taiwan."

36. See John Pomfret and Philip Pan, "U.S. Hits Obstacles in Helping Taiwan Guard Against China." Ironically, Taiwan's legislature was stalemated on purchasing the weapons systems authorized by President Bush and in fact complained that the United States pressured Taiwan to purchase weaponry it deemed unnecessary at often inflated prices, which benefited the U.S. military manufacturing industry. See Bradley Graham, "Pentagon Announces Plans to Sell Radars to Taiwan."

37. Dickson, "New Presidents Adjust Old Policies."

38. Bill Gertz and Rowan Scarborough, "Nation; Inside the Ring," May 28, 2004; Bill Gertz and Rowan Scarborough, "Nation, Inside the Ring," December 5, 2003.

39. Bill Gertz, "U.S. to Continue Sale of Defensive Arms to Taiwan"; Graham, "Pentagon Announces Plans to Sell Radars to Taiwan."

40. Bill Gertz, "State Confirms N. Korea Light-Water Reactor Talk."

41. Gertz and Scarborough, "Nation; Inside the Ring," May 28, 2004.

42. In September 2004, the China Currency Coalition filed its 301 petition on China's currency manipulation despite strong rejections by USTR and the Treasury Department. The petition claimed that every day the administration failed to address the Chinese currency issue meant more lost U.S. manufacturing jobs and businesses. The timing for the petition was an obvious attempt to place pressure on President Bush in an election year. These issues pointed to a potential vulnerability for George Bush and an opportunity for John Kerry to capitalize. After the November election, the petition was rejected.

43. Paul Blustein, "U.S. Pushes China Hard on Trade."

44. Assistant Secretary James Kelly, Hearing of the Senate Foreign Relations Committee on latest round of six-way talks on nuclear weapons in North Korea, July 15, 2004.

45. Sofia Wu, "MND Mum on U.S. Crisis-Simulation Drill Reports."

46. See Glenn Kessler, "Cheney Urges Increase in Freedoms for Chinese"; Glenn Kessler and Edward Cody, "Cheney Warns China About Hong Kong"; Glenn Kessler, "Cheney to Reassert U.S. Position on Taiwan's Status."

47. This discussion is based on Bush administration sources and other Washington observers knowledgeable about the internal dynamics of Bush's North Korea policy discussions.

48. See Bachman, "The United States and China," 261; Shambaugh, "Sino-American Relations Since September 11"; Gordon, "Rumsfeld Limiting

Military Contacts with the Chinese"; Dickson, "New Presidents Adjust Old Policies"; David Sanger, "U.S. Would Defend Taiwan, Bush Says."

49. David Lampton, "The Stealth Normalization of U.S.-China Relations."

50. Robert Sutter, "Bush Administration Policy Toward Beijing and Taipei."

51. Dana Milbank and Mike Allen, "Bush to Drop Annual Review of Weapons Sales to Taiwan."

52. Lou Dobbs, "Our New Diplomatic Partner."

9

Recurring Patterns in U.S. China Decisionmaking

In the last thirty-five years U.S.-PRC relations have developed into a complex relationship much deeper and broader than most observers would have anticipated in 1969. Since Richard Nixon left office, both Republican and Democratic presidents have concluded that a stable, broad-based relationship with China is in the best interest of the United States. Simultaneously, over the last fifteen years the domestic political environment has made it difficult for presidents to maintain such a relationship. Chronicling and explaining the how and why of the fluctuations in the relationship has been a central purpose of this study. As such, it has utilized a foreign policy decisionmaking perspective (specifically strategic framing) as the conceptual approach to explain how the policy process proceeded across these administrations and how this influenced the policy choices made in each of them.

To understand the broader conceptual and empirical "lessons" to be derived from this study, we need to compare continuity and change across each administration's China policy, specifically in response to the Tiananmen Square massacre and the end of the Cold War.

The Cold War Context and U.S.-China Relations

When the Nixon administration successfully used the symbolic context of the Cold War to shift the terms of debate from China as an enemy to be contained (or overthrown) to China as a friend in the larger struggle with the Soviets, it laid the groundwork for a dramatic policy change. The administration took advantage of changed strategic circumstances and created its own focusing events (Nixon's historic trip) to frame its efforts. The administration's efforts cast the policy change in positive terms of gains rather than losses, while leaving controversial issues such as Taiwan ambiguous and unresolved.

The Nixon administration took advantage of a "historic" opportunity for change based on the shifting strategic context involving China and domestic political changes that made the U.S. public weary of war. Its equation for stability and peace in East Asia evolved gradually enough to appeal to a broad cross section of conservatives who feared that détente weakened the U.S. position and to liberals who saw it as an opportunity for peace in East Asia. The ambiguity of the Shanghai Communiqué on the question of Taiwan was an important calculation about how the relationship must be finessed given the domestic political context in the United States. On the other hand, decisionmakers within the Carter and Reagan administrations pushing engagement with China had a different starting point for their policy initiatives. The task for supporters of engagement was to maintain Nixon's frame rather than changing the terms of debate. Each administration had a strong advocate—Brzezinski for Carter and Haig for Reagan—for Kissinger's geostrategic approach and for the central importance of China in global politics.

Because normalizing relations entailed ending diplomatic relations with Taiwan and abrogating the mutual defense treaty, policy trade-offs came into the open over the Taiwan question and challenged Nixon's geostrategic frame in 1978. In response, advocates for normalization emphasized a hierarchy of values that gave central importance to China in U.S. strategic interests vis-à-vis the Soviets. Once again, supporting frames that painted a hostile international context (e.g., Soviet intransigence in détente and the invasion of Afghanistan) provided evidence to advocates for normalization. Despite these favorable conditions, however, domestic political conditions limited how far each president could go. The Taiwan lobby convinced its sympathizers in Congress to force stronger statements of support for Taiwan in the form of defense guarantees and informal relations through the Taiwan Relations Act (TRA). Ultimately, the presence of the U.S.-PRC joint communiqué and the TRA allowed both the supporters of normalization and Taiwan's supporters to declare a victory. Again, the ambiguity of Taiwan's status allowed different sides of the debate to emphasize things differently and to move forward.

In 1981, President Reagan himself seemed poised to negate Nixon's geostrategic engagement frame because of Taiwan's status. While there were many pro-Taiwan advocates in the administration, Congress, and the public who lauded Reagan's early hard-line rhetoric, when he learned the extensive policy and political costs of changing the direction of East Asian policy, he shifted his stance. Once the Sino-American relationship was framed vis-à-vis the Soviets and the Taiwan question appeared resolved, Reagan and hard-liners in his administration recognized the tangible military, economic, and political benefits in the new relationship. Taiwan's position and its continued close economic and cultural ties with the United States despite normalization made people believe it was possible to quietly support Taiwan and openly court China. Table 9.1 presents the important components of the strategic framing process for the Nixon, Carter, and Reagan administrations in comparative perspective.

The Post-Tiananmen, Post–Cold War Context of U.S.-China Relations

Following the "golden age" in Sino-American relations during the late 1980s, post–Cold War presidents had to adjust to a changed international and domestic context. In 1989, reforms in the Soviet Union and China were interpreted as harbingers of an end to international conflict and the triumph of democratic liberal systems. However, that year brought instead a double blow to U.S.-China relations. First, as the Soviet Union crumbled, the most important unifying component of Nixon's engagement frame—the Communist threat—was undercut. Second, the Tiananmen Square massacre quashed optimistic assumptions about the nature of reform in China and was particularly jarring in the U.S. domestic political context because it directly challenged the rosy U.S. view of China as a friend developing like "us." In these circumstances, Tiananmen Square became the kind of focusing event that produced a radical shift in terms of the domestic debate on U.S. policy toward the PRC. Gallup opinion polls from the time chronicle the dramatic change in U.S. attitudes from a 72 percent favorable rating for China in February 1989 to 31 percent in August, when China did not meet public expectations (see Appendix B). This event, in particular, energized a variety of engagement opponents and provided the context to challenge the basis of engagement policy to this day.

In the immediate post–Cold War, post–Tiananmen Square period,

Table 9.1 Strategic Engagement Frames in the Cold War Context

	Nixon	Carter	Reagan
Problem diagnosis	• China was a useful, but untapped tool in the struggle with the USSR; need to redefine China from threat to essential ally	• Competing priorities on arms control led one faction to see China as a threat to détente and the other to see it as a source of leverage against the Soviets	• Competition between prioritizing strategic importance of Sino-American relationship and broader pan-Asian focus emphasizing relations with allies such as Japan and Taiwan
Themes that resonated with president and public			
Presidential beliefs	• PRC a priority and seen as useful counter to USSR • Personal confidence in his foreign policy expertise solidified his efforts	• China and East Asia a secondary priority • Personal priority was arms control with Soviets	• Taiwan seen as East Asian priority and initially hostile toward China • Strong anti-Soviet stance/anti-Communist perspective made China palatable
Policy themes	• China as strategic opportunity and anti-Soviet • Peace and stability in East Asia	• Brzezinski argues Soviets cannot be trusted and normalization needed to be early priority • Vance asserts PRC normalization a threat to arms control values	• Haig sees opportunity for strategic association with PRC vis-à-vis the Soviets; prioritizes China relationship over Taiwan

(continues)

Political considerations	• Need to tread carefully between opposition from political left (critics of Vietnam policy) and right (traditional China lobby) • Spring "opening" to China to undercut opposition	• Full foreign policy agenda affects timing of normalization • Brzezinski bolsters position by linking normalization to domestic SALT discussion • Decision not to consult Congress until after normalization agreement made with PRC • Opportunity taken before electoral politics becomes a factor	• Pan-Asian group stresses need to focus on relationship with Taiwan and Japan as cornerstone of political, economic, and military policy in East Asia • Shultz prioritizes economic relations • Haig sought PRC acquiescence to avoid domestic politicization and argued Reagan could not be the president who disrupted relationship with PRC • White House advisers saw usefulness of China summit as election approached • President's Cold War credentials help to mitigate criticism from the Taiwan lobby
Supporting conditions/ tactics	• Back-channel negotiations essential to "spring" the surprise • Incremental change to prepare domestic ground	• Bureaucratic infighting until Brzezinski gains control of policymaking agenda and discussions • Brzezinski involves broad group of cabinet-level actors to broaden the coalition of support	• Bureaucratic infighting led to confusing signals in East Asian priorities • Incremental commitment of president to strategic association position was possible once Taiwan question was resolved

Congress gained a greater degree of direct influence over Sino-American relations. Coalitions of unlikely allies from the political left and right took advantage of the situation to challenge presidential prerogative in China policymaking. The first President Bush was forced to acquiesce to sanctions legislation in June 1989, and by the 1992 election Clinton's campaign accusation that George H.W. Bush had kowtowed to the Chinese leadership still resonated with the public. Ironically, the same kind of opposition Clinton had helped energize constrained his own China policy as well. Republicans added the accusation that Clinton was a poor steward of U.S. policy and betrayed old friends like Taiwan. Even in the post–September 11 context, George W. Bush faced a growing domestic backlash on his China policy. In 2004, he was accused by liberals of allowing the trade imbalance to grow to record levels and failing to prevent outsourcing of U.S. jobs to China.

Although their initial positions were quite different, ultimately George H.W. Bush, Clinton, and George W. Bush shared some of the same assumptions about the nature of the Sino-American relationship. Clinton was much more confrontational toward China tactically in comparison to the senior Bush, but his approach rested on some of the same neoliberal assumptions, for example, that economic liberalization would eventually lead to political liberalization. The first Bush administration and Clinton's, however, had different reference points. For example, Bush's rationale emphasized the great accomplishment of China's liberalization in such a short period of time and the tremendous changes that Deng Xiaoping had wrought in China in the 1980s at great personal risk to himself. Clinton, in contrast, emphasized what Deng had not done, focusing on his lack of receptiveness to political reform. However, when Clinton saw his policies undermine his economic goals, he shifted tactics and pushed to involve China in a web of interdependence that would reshape its behavior. For his part, George W. Bush came to endorse a position close to both these presidents, emphasizing areas of strategic cooperation while downplaying contentious ones. Colin Powell's claim that the relationship was the best it had been in thirty years is an example of the simplified framing for public consumption that puts a positive spin on the relationship despite recurring problems.

Comparing the two Bushes and Clinton shows how presidents have had to struggle against energized opponents to sustain stable relations with China. Table 9.2 compares policy framing in these three administrations.

Comparing Cold War and
Post–Cold War Policy Contexts

What do the previous discussions tell us about strategic framing during the Cold War and post–Cold War periods? First, the framing game was a decisive part of internal political dynamics and the choices leaders made. Across these administrations, engagement advocates presented their policy priorities in symbolic and practical win-win terms to influence the president, others in the inner circle, and domestic actors. Because policy symbols could be manipulated more than one way, strategic framing efforts were accompanied by hard lobbying efforts at multiple policy levels. During the Cold War, defining the policy in terms of China as a friend in a larger conflict against the Soviets made opposition difficult to sustain. Since the end of the Cold War, however, no single event or interest has emerged to provide the same kind of stability in the Sino-American relationship. Clinton tried to do this with a strategic economic frame and George W. Bush with his focus on the global war on terror. Today, multiple interests still challenge the president's prerogative in this area.

Second, the potential for economic opportunity in China added another positive strategic theme that solidified the win-win nature of the relationship during the Cold War, and it has helped define the relationship after the Cold War. As the argument for the potential for economic reform and political progress in China gained prominence, this increasingly resonated with U.S. neoliberal notions. China was seen differently than the Soviet Union precisely because it was undergoing dramatic economic reform. The shock of Tiananmen Square, however, directly challenged these assumptions and because these themes resonate with the U.S. public, domestic politics has been a greater factor in U.S. China policy ever since. The problem is that as the nature of the economic relationship has become more complex, it no longer fits well within a simple win-win equation. Complex interdependence has had both positive and negative results. For many years, historically high trade deficits with China and accusations that Chinese companies have an unfair trade advantage, among other issues, have complicated the picture.

To maintain the positive frame of U.S. policy toward China, a pattern developed on a whole series of issues such as human rights, arms proliferation, and market access, in which U.S. administrations deliberately have downplayed differences in public references—thus adding a sense of optimism to the relationship and simplifying disagreements. In

Table 9.2 Strategic Engagement Frames in the Post–Cold War Context

	George H.W. Bush	Clinton	George W. Bush
Problem diagnosis	• Challenge to maintain stable relationship and not isolate PRC; need to overcome domestic pressure	• Challenge to push China on human rights and to expand commercial relations; eventually to establish a strategic partnership	• Fundamental disagreement about the degree to which China could be trusted, and how to balance the need for China's cooperation in areas of strategic common interest such as North Korea without undermining the long-term commitment to Taiwan • EP-3 crisis reinforces need to engage PRC to promote peace and stability in East Asia
Themes that resonated with president and public *Presidential beliefs*	• PRC strategically important vis-à-vis the USSR and given its position in East Asia; remarkable economic reform	• Domestic economic lens for foreign policy • 1st term—PRC of peripheral importance but assumes can gain PRC acquiescence; reform should be the priority • 2nd term—marriage of economic and strategic goals emphasized	• Predisposition to see China as potential threat and give priority to Taiwan as an old friend; September 11 triggers new, broader threat perceptions that put China into pragmatic context
Policy themes	• Scowcroft reinforces strategic view that the Soviet threat is viable and given PRC's status as a growing power, its cooperation is needed in areas like arms proliferation • Baker reinforces link between	• Human rights position advocates sanctions and punishment as means to reform PRC • Commercial position sees threat in linkage and works to highlight threat to president's economic policy goals	• Hawks and hard-liners focus on the need to recognize China as a potential hostile power (i.e., reorient policy away from China to long-term allies such as Japan and Taiwan)

	economic reform and political reform; East European model of inevitability of reform	• Strategic military position advocates dialogue • Strategic economic position evolves in 2nd term	• Pragmatic engagers see need to avoid confrontation with China and to manage China in pragmatic ways within a multilateral framework • Pragmatic position is reinforced by post–September 11 strategic context • Anti-Chinese rhetoric muted in post–September 11 environment; hostile rhetoric increases domestically as 2004 election approaches
Political considerations	• United in presenting presidential prerogative arguments and to refer to Bush's experience in foreign policy and remain unresponsive to public calls for greater sanctions • Compromise only when they can maintain presidential flexibility on exceptions to sanctions • Baker argues for careful handling of Congress; placate Taiwan interests in context of 1992 election	• MFN struggle neutralized at first because of agreement with Democratic leadership for linkage; 1994 interim election puts Republicans in charge of both houses of Congress • Scandal environment after 1996 makes it difficult to form a strategic partnership and affects timing of PNTR	
Supporting conditions/ tactics	• Centralized advisory system from the first; back-channel contacts had only limited utility	• Decentralized advisory system exacerbated internal disagreements in 1st term. Initial coalition building with congressional Democrats is short-lived; administration centralizes decisionmeking within the NSC in 2nd term	• Highly centralized administration values consensus-driven policies but ineffectively manages bureaucratic conflict; this conflict hinders coherent foreign policy development

terms of a hierarchy of values, the anti-Soviet theme trumped the other arguments and led Nixon, Carter, Reagan, and George H.W. Bush before June 1989 to acquiesce to Chinese behavior that otherwise might have raised a red flag. By emphasizing China's strategic importance, the United States undercut some of its traditional values and compromised on issues like human rights in ways it was unwilling to do with the Soviet Union. For example, on December 7, 1978, a Chinese Great Wall poster endorsing U.S. human rights policy called on President Carter to pay attention to human rights in China, but the NSC concluded it was too early for the president or senior officials to respond to this appeal because it would jeopardize other U.S. interests.[1] Ronald Reagan's human rights rhetoric on the Soviet Union also never targeted the PRC. In fact, following Reagan's visit to China in 1984, the president was convinced that Chinese leaders were not "typical" Communists. He admired their economic reform efforts and believed those would logically lead to political reform as well. George H.W. Bush from the start emphasized the strategic importance of China and resisted pressure for sanctions from the left and right. Once positive relations with China became priorities for Clinton and George W. Bush, each softened his rhetoric and emphasized areas of agreement to mitigate domestic opposition.

Since Tiananmen Square, it has been important for policymakers to proceed carefully so that they do not oversell a policy to the extent it becomes vulnerable to political backlash and failure. As we have seen, extreme euphoria is just as dangerous as overselling the Chinese threat. The concrete consequences of the backlash to the U.S. "love affair" with China are plain to see in the struggle to maintain a pragmatic relationship with China today.

The Advisory System and Shaping Policy Choices

The study of the advisory systems in these administrations illustrates many similarities but also differences about how policy was formulated. For example, George H.W. Bush and Richard Nixon, two knowledgeable foreign policy actors, fostered advisory systems that allowed for a relatively stable and coherent policy message in Sino-American relations but in very different ways. Bush developed a coherent message in his foreign policy because he was committed to a particular path and stayed involved, because he delegated primary authority to his national security adviser, and because there were no major differences in orientation among his advisers. Nixon's hierarchical structure and the predominance of Henry Kissinger accomplished the same task. It fostered a coherent message and allowed the administration to make the China policy change. Similarly, George W. Bush's hierarchical system was set up to centrally control the policy agenda, but ideological differences among central advisers and the resulting infighting made that impossible.

Although the centralized Nixon and George H.W. Bush systems had a more unified and predictable message, their systems also raised the possibility of premature closure on options considered. These circumstances potentially lead to suboptimal decisions because options are eliminated too quickly as conformity patterns are established in the group. While Nixon's rapprochement with China was a great success, it also was handled in a manner that delayed much of the political opposition. In his haste to keep control of the terms of debate, he left normalization unfinished and Taiwan became a constant part of the policy equation that lingers today. George H.W. Bush was resistant to congressional concerns, which in turn generated greater congressional opposition that made him vulnerable in the 1992 election.

In contrast, Carter, Reagan, and Clinton's open advisory systems fostered their own problems. They allowed the kind of access to the inner circle that almost guaranteed bureaucratic conflict. The high degree of bureaucratic infighting led to a fragmented policy in each administration that persisted until the president or his direct agent got involved.

Presidential priorities and level of involvement also proved to be key factors in a successful policy process and outcome in these administrations. As noted above, George H.W. Bush was able to maintain a level of internal discipline that Carter, Reagan, Clinton, and George W. Bush did not have. However, on the occasions when each of those presidents or his NSC became involved, East Asia policy did become more focused and was handled more effectively.

The cognitive predispositions of these leaders shaped their advisory systems and responses to policy challenges. George H.W. Bush's priorities and beliefs remained remarkably stable despite the end of the Cold War producing a natural opportunity for leaders to rethink the basis of U.S. foreign policy; his sense of efficacy and expertise made him less flexible and more resistant to change. Similarly, Nixon stuck to his guns despite considerable domestic pressure and reinforced his efforts to push for change. George H.W. Bush and Nixon were similar to expert advisers who, in John Steinbrunner's terms, are more set in their perspectives because they are influenced by the "theoretical thinking" particular to a community of experts in their area of specialization. Coherent images that are more resistant to change are likely to form if individuals have considerable expertise in the relevant area.

On the other side of the coin, high-level decisionmakers can be more flexible precisely because they have greater freedom to pursue their own purposes and to act as "uncommitted thinkers."[2] This line of reasoning assumes that individuals with little experience or knowledge in an area are novices who are more likely to exhibit fragmented and contradictory beliefs.[3] Carter, for example, was generally known as a diligent student in foreign policy, but China policy was not an early priority. His indecision and the mixed messages on China policy continued until the president decided to move forward with normalization on Brzezinski's terms. Carter shifted to a harder stance, making China a new priority once he had abandoned his arms control agenda. As a political pragmatist, Clinton recognized when it was politically expedient to change.[4] For example, he came to realize that his economic foreign policy and domestic policy goals were endangered by his confrontational approach toward China. In these circumstances, he shifted tactics and emphasized cooperation with China as the means to reach mutual goals.

While Reagan and George W. Bush were true foreign policy novices, they differed from Carter and Clinton in that they also held deep-seated ideological beliefs about the way the world worked. Reagan and George W. Bush saw the world in black-and-white terms, with a clear "us" and "them" defined. For Reagan, when his anti-Soviet beliefs were primed and Taiwan became a nonissue, China could be plugged in to his preexisting schema. George W. Bush's early schema for China was not well developed and contained contradictory elements such as a high threat perception along with a general commitment to commercial relations. Once September 11 occurred, however, the identification of a new strategic threat placed China in the "friend" category.

For different reasons, Carter, Reagan, Clinton, and George W. Bush proved changeable in their approach toward the PRC in the face of the constant barrage from their advisers. They shifted away from their initial priorities vis-à-vis the Chinese to adopt positions that reflected those of influential advisers. These shifts in policy seemed to reflect a change in schemas and their primary reference points rather than a change in overall foreign policy beliefs (with the possible exception of Jimmy Carter).

A broader look at the foreign policy game shows that the strategic framing game also takes place outside the inner circle and at multiple levels, as policymakers rhetorically play one level of analysis off of another. Repeatedly, the international-level game was manipulated to undercut the role of Congress or other bureaucratic actors. Various presidents' dramatic announcements of forthcoming trips to China are good examples of external tactics used to create a positive domestic climate for their policies. However, when President Carter did not reveal the nature of normalization negotiations, then sprung it on the Congress as a fait accompli, he galvanized his domestic opposition rather than created a climate conducive for his policy. He had to fight to keep the Taiwan Relations Act from undercutting the agreement he had made with the Chinese. Particularly after the Cold War, securing the domestic ground became a necessary strategy for issues such as PNTR.

On the other hand, presidents have also used the domestic context as a bargaining tool vis-à-vis the Chinese. On more than one occasion, an administration sought concessions from the Chinese by arguing that Congress had tied its hands unless certain concessions were made. For example, when George H.W. Bush faced great domestic pressure to impose sanctions after Tiananmen Square, he tried to convince the Chinese to make small concessions so that domestic sanctions pressures could be subverted. President Clinton also sought concessions from the Chinese with the argument that he needed to show Congress progress if MFN in 1994 was to be renewed. Thus the domestic context could be manipulated to influence negotiations with the Chinese, and such negotiations could be used to pressure domestic opponents but with mixed results.[5]

The previous discussion points out that by identifying pertinent factors in the advisory process (and how they interrelate) and the policy context, we can begin to explain why policy choices evolved as they did. By understanding how and why specific themes resonate with important members of the decision group, we can anticipate what policy choices will result.

Lessons for the Second George W. Bush Term and Future Presidents

The discussion of policymaking in the past six presidential administrations highlights the bureaucratic, congressional, and domestic pressure each president faces regarding policy toward China. Two major policy lessons emerge. The first is that the policy consensus on engagement, which has survived despite presidents with very different political pedigrees, exists for a very good reason—it is the only reasonable policy alternative. At a pragmatic level, China as a rising power cannot be contained or ignored. Even those who initially emphasized Taiwan relations or the need to take a harder line with China eventually recognized that stable U.S.-China relations were integral to promoting U.S. interests in East Asia. It is not an easy relationship, but our integrated economies, shared interests, and even disagreements make it essential to maintain a cordial working relationship.

Second, maintaining stable relations has been no easy task. Periodic crises and the potential for future crises over issues such as Taiwan make the relationship volatile and unpredictable. The greatest danger comes from policies based on single-issue agendas that emphasize differences rather than shared interests. As long as Taiwan remains a flashpoint, the U.S.-China relationship remains on slippery ground. The stable status quo is vulnerable to decisions by leaders in Taiwan and hard-line factions within both the U.S. and Chinese governments whose policy choices risk inflaming passions on both sides of the Taiwan Strait. Recent events such as the EP-3 incident demonstrate how certain U.S. policy circles and the public, as well as the Chinese public, are primed to react harshly despite costly long-term damage to shared interests.

Part of the problem is that U.S. policy still rests on hopes for regime change in China. The difference now is that rather than pressuring for immediate change through military means, the policy seeks to place China in a web of interdependence that policymakers anticipate will eventually lead to liberal reforms. Regardless of the regime in power, engagement, although imperfect, provides the only means to influence China's future. As Madeleine Albright notes, engagement with China is not an endorsement of its system but an opportunity to appeal to the pragmatism of the new generation of Chinese leaders to find areas where our interests coincide.[6]

In managing the relationship with the PRC, we need to focus on long-term opportunities rather than short-term problems. The U.S. government and public must recognize the only pragmatic position remains engagement with China—an engagement that acknowledges shared interests as well as areas of disagreement. We need to avoid the dangers of symbolic politics and not be quick to paint China in the role of an enemy or a friend. In this context, China is neither an "us" nor a "them" but embodies a complex relationship made up of daily contacts between multiple agencies and departments at various levels of importance, from the most mundane tasks to the occasional high politics.

Notes

1. Memo from Michel Oksenberg to Brzezinski, "Chinese Wall Poster Endorsing U.S. Human Rights Policy," no date, National Security Affairs, Brzezinski Material Country File, Box 9, File: China (PRC), December 1978, Carter Presidential Library.

2. Steinbrunner, *The Cybernetic Theory of Decision.*

3. Jerel Rosati, "A Cognitive Approach to the Study of Foreign Policy."

4. It was Clinton's style to defer choice until the last minute and to vacillate among policy options. Because he had elevated both human rights and economic priorities on his China agenda, he eventually had to choose between these. As noted, multiple advisers tried to gain the president's ear and fought for control of the policy agenda. Because the administration was unable to sort out domestic from foreign priorities, the president's desire for conflict avoidance and harmony postponed decisions so that no firm strategy was ever established. See David Lampton, *Same Bed, Different Dreams: Managing U.S.-China Relations 1989–2000.*

5. It is also important to recognize China's manipulation of the U.S. political process. Repeatedly, China has recognized and cultivated its advocates and worked to better its position in the fights within these administrations. In many circumstances, it seems that the U.S. card has been played by the Chinese, rather than vice versa.

6. Albright, *Madam Secretary.*

Appendix A:
Research Strategy

The research strategy underpinning this study has been influenced by scholarship on the comparative case-study method that explains the need to systematically approach and define the nature of a comparative project.[1] The tasks include defining the purpose of the analysis, explaining the focus of each case analysis and how it will be compared, explaining how the analysis proceeded (i.e., the steps in the comparative process), and the strategy to address challenges to the comparative method.

The purpose of this analysis is twofold: (1) to explore and refine a theory of strategic framing in the context of foreign policy advisory systems and (2) to use this approach to explain continuity and change in Sino-American policy—thus exploring how process variables shape the decisions that are made. By comparing the cases, we can discuss the implications of the strategic framing literature for the study of advisory systems and the making of U.S. foreign policy. Alexander George's method of structured-focused comparison provides the appropriate criteria for focusing case analyses selectively on "certain aspects of the historical case" and in a structured way to employ "general questions to guide the data collection analysis in that historical case."[2]

Steps to the Comparative Case Method

The first step is to identify the research puzzle for focused comparison. The variable to be discussed here is strategic framing and how it impacts both the policy process and the decision outcome. In general, the structure of the advisory process, the nature of presidential involvement, and the interaction patterns among central advisers set the context for analysis of strategic framing. Following that, the research questions for this study explore how and why advisers can use strategic framing to dominate the policy process. To work out the theoretical approach to strategic framing, I conducted a pilot study focusing on the strategic framing of arms control policy and U.S.-Soviet policy in the Carter administration. This earlier study provided a dry run for the research design that fine-tuned this study's organization and guided the collection of evidence for the study of strategic framing in China policymaking.[3]

The case study approach has allowed me to apply a general theory of framing to a new context—presidential advisory processes and the making of China policy. Public sources such as newspaper articles archived through the 1970s on Lexis-Nexis and books focusing on Sino-American policy provided useful overviews of U.S. policy that helped narrow the scope of the case studies. The cases were carefully chosen to explain both the early approach of each administration toward Sino-American relations and the specific focusing events or potential turning points in the relationship. For example, President Carter's decision to normalize relations with the Chinese and President Reagan's negotiations for a communiqué of understanding on Taiwan arms sales in 1982 represented the major efforts of each administration with regard to U.S.-China policy. This focus provides the circumstances under which presidents and important advisers are most likely to be involved in the decision process.

There are important similarities and differences among each president's foreign policy experiences with China that limit the range of factors that must be considered to explain strategic framing of China policy. Each president following Nixon worked from a reactionary basis in responding to the opening of China and the positive frame established by Nixon's historic trip in 1972. Virtually all the presidential advisers worked from the premise that the relationship with China needed to be managed, although they differed on the centrality it had to overall East Asian policy, China's relationship to issues such as Taiwan, and how it intersected other security, economic, and political issues. There were differences among the presidents that reached beyond their personal styles and the organization of their advisory systems. The most significant difference coincided with the domestic and international changes at the end of the Cold War and following the Tiananmen Square massacre.

This period represented a break from a period when administrations focused on consolidating a growing positive relationship, to a point when questions were raised addressing the viability of the relationship. China policy underwent a drastic review, and a different set of domestic concerns came to the forefront after 1989. Each administration was forced to build governing coalitions in increasingly turbulent domestic and international contexts. More and more, the long-term communication of a coherent vision became difficult.

Because the object of study is the dynamic advisory process surrounding China policymaking, identifying specific independent and dependent variables can be problematic. Although strategic framing is the general explanatory variable in this study, much time is spent differentiating strategic framing and identifying the different steps to framing. The outcome variable to be explained is not only the nature of the decision process across the administrations but also the degree to which that process shaped China policy itself. The variations in the decision process across these administrations regarding its structure, level of presidential involvement, and the interaction patterns among advisers allow for possible causal inferences about the nature of the process and the potential outcome.

Through the method of structured, focused comparison these cases provide some evidence for causality, but more significantly, they highlight the similarities and differences in how the strategic framing process and China policy decisions unfolded in each administration.[4] The focus on China policy across thirty years is of particular interest because it provides a sufficient length of time to explore continuity and change in the relationship as well as common themes used by policymakers. The major advantage of case study research is that it allows one to trace a decision process over time. My hope is that studies such as this begin to bridge the gap between process-oriented studies and those that focus on policy outcomes.[5]

Overcoming Challenges to the Comparative Case Method

The greatest challenge to in-depth studies of this kind is finding appropriate, uniform, and comparable sources of primary data. One way to address this concern is to rely upon multiple sources of evidence with the goal of finding "convergence" around a specific interpretation of facts. Using multiple sources of data enhances the construct validity of a study's conclusions.[6]

For the Nixon and Carter administrations a great source of information proved to be the wealth of archival data available in the Nixon Presidential Project at the National Archives in College Park, Maryland, and the Carter Presidential Library in Atlanta, respectively. The archival record for later administrations is less complete. For example, only selective files have been opened at the Reagan Presidential Library in Simi Valley, California, and the George H.W. Bush Library in College Station, Texas. At the time of completing this project, no papers were available from the new Clinton Presidential Library in Little Rock, Arkansas. The most comprehensive archival source proved to be the memorandums and documents available from the National Security Archives Collection on China and the United States entitled "China and the United States from Hostility to Engagement, 1960–1998."

Personal, oral history, and exit interviews provided a second data source to complement the document record on these administrations. The U.S. Foreign Affairs Oral History Collection, produced by the Association for Diplomatic Studies and Training, provides nearly one thousand interviews with former members of the Foreign Service and State Department. The oral history interviews with Robert Barnett, William Clark, Charles Freeman, Marshall Green, Herbert Hansell, John Holdridge, Art Hummel, Paul Kriesberg, Peter Rodman, Paul Russo, Gaston Sigur, Harry Thayer, and Robert Wade were particularly useful for information for the Nixon, Carter, Reagan, and George H.W. Bush administrations. In addition, I conducted more than three dozen interviews with former NSC, State Department, Defense Department, and White House officials, among others, to ask specific questions related to my interests in U.S.-China relations. Interviewees on the record included Morton Abramowitz, James Baker, Charlene Barshefsky, Frank Carlucci, Mickey Kantor, Winston Lord, Leon Panetta, William Rope, Brent Scowcroft, John Shattuck, and Caspar Weinberger; numerous other persons who served in various capacities within these administrations provided background information and remain unnamed at their request. Interviews from publications such as *Newsweek,* the *New York Times,* and the *Washington Post,* as well as congressional testimony, proved helpful as sources of timely, rather than retrospective, analyses of policy events.

A third source of information included available memoirs that helped reconstruct the policymaking record. The memoirs of James Baker, Zbigniew Brzezinski, George H.W. Bush and Brent Scowcroft,

Jimmy Carter, William Christopher, Richard Clarke, Robert Gates, Alexander Haig, H. R. Haldeman, John Holdridge, Henry Kissinger, James Lilley, Richard Nixon, Paul O'Neil (through Richard Suskind's book), Ronald Reagan, George Shultz, Gaston Sigur, Cyrus Vance, and Caspar Weinberger were particularly useful. These sources provided an important, if somewhat self-serving, recollection of notable political events over the last thirty years. Combining these sources provided the means to reconstruct how the decision process proceeded.

Notes

1. Juliet Kaarbo and Ryan Beasley, "A Practical Guide to the Comparative Case Study Method in Political Psychology."
2. Alexander George, "Case Studies and Theory Development: The Method of Structured, Focused Comparison," 61–62.
3. See Jean A. Garrison, "Framing Foreign Policy Alternatives in the Inner Circle: The President, His Advisors, and the Struggle for the Arms Control Agenda." Kaarbo and Beasley in "A Practical Guide to the Comparative Case Study Method" (p. 383) convincingly argue that the key is to specify ahead of time what is necessary for the case analysis in order to code a variable in a particular way. In this study, seeing a shift in a target's orientation toward China or a related issue would provide evidence of framing effects.
4. See Alexander George, "Case Studies and Theory Development."
5. As noted, the question of aggregation is one of the greatest challenges in foreign policy advisory studies that acknowledge advisory groups as shaping ultimate decisions. Studies in cognition, belief systems, and operational code, among others, give us testable hypotheses about how belief systems influence individual decisionmaking. A strategic framing approach within a case study approach seems to provide a means to overcome the aggregation question, that is, to see how policy positions are defined and then selected within the group decision process.
6. Robert Yin, *Case Study Research: Design and Methods,* 37–40, 92.

Appendix B:
U.S. Opinion of U.S.-China Relations

Table B.1   Public Opinion of China, 1972–2004

	Favorable	Neutral/No Answer	Unfavorable
1972	23		71
1973	49		43
1974	42	6	53
1975	28		58
1976	20	7	74
1977	27	22	52
1978	21		67
1979 February	30	7	64
1979 September	64	10	25
1980	42	4	54
1981[a]	36	14	50
1982[b]	37	43	20
1983	43	7	52
1985	38	11	51
1986	34	7	57
1987 April	65	7	28
1987 November	34	11	55
1988[a]	58	6	36
1989 February	72	15	13
1989 August	31	11	58
1990	31	8	61
1991	35	12	53
1993	41	8	51
1994	41	7	53
1996 January	49	6	45
1996 March	39	10	51
1997	33	17	50
1998 June	39	10	51
1998 July	44	9	47
1999 March	34	7	59
1999 May	38	6	56
2000 January	33	16	51
2000 March	35	9	56
2000 November	36	7	57
2001 February	44	5	51
2001 February	45	7	48
2002 February	44	7	49
2003 February	45	9	46
2004 February	41	5	54

Sources: Unless otherwise noted, poll data is taken from Gallup or Roper and was last accessed via LexisNexis Academic Universe on February 23, 2005. Poll questions are one of the following types:

Question Type 1: What is your general attitude toward China: very favorable, somewhat favorable, somewhat unfavorable, or very unfavorable?

Question Type 2: You will notice that the boxes on this card go from the highest position of "plus 5" for a country which you like very much, to the lowest position of "minus 5" for a country you dislike very much. How far up the scale or how far down the scale would you rate the following countries? . . . China. Type 2 questions were interpreted as follows: Answers between +5 and +1 were considered a "favorable" opinion of China. Answers between –1 and –5 were considered an "unfavorable" opinion.

Notes: a. Yankelovich, Shelly, and White Poll. Accessed October 31, 2002, via LexisNexis Academic Universe. Question reads as follows: Have your impressions of the People's Republic of China become more favorable recently, stayed the same or gotten worse, or aren't you that familiar with that country?

b. Los Angeles Times Poll. Accessed October 31, 2002, via LexisNexis Academic Universe. Question reads as follows: What is your impression of the government of China? As of today, is your impression very favorable, somewhat favorable, somewhat unfavorable, or very unfavorable—or haven't you heard enough about that yet to say?

Table B.2   Public Perception of China, 1979–2003: Friend or Foe?

	Ally/Friend	Neutral/Neither	Enemy/Unfriendly
1979	51	23	9
1980	44		46
1981[a]	33	18	49
1982 June	24	39	23
1982 November	49	31	12
1983 May[b]	52	25	21
1983 June 4	21	37	29
1983 June 7	31	38	24
1984 May	29	33	25
1984 November	50	29	16
1985	31	34	19
1987	26	41	19
1988[c]	59	27	6
1990[d]	20	50	21
1994	35		59
1995	28	45	24
1996	29		59
1997	25	27	9
1998 June	31	25	8
1998 August	35	33	24
1999 March	29	26	10
1999 June[e]	32	19	46
2000 March	28	32	21
2000 August	24	37	27
2001 April 4[f]	49		44
2001 April 20	27		69
2001 April 23[g]	49		45
2001 October	40	33	16
2003 August	31	36	33
2003 September	53	5	42
2004 August	32	38	16

Sources: Unless otherwise noted, polls are from Gallup, Roper, or Harris and were last accessed February 23, 2005, via LexisNexis Academic Universe. Questions generally followed one of the following formats:

Type 1: As far as you are concerned, do you feel that the People's Republic of China is a close ally of the U.S., is friendly but not a close ally, is not friendly but not an enemy, or is an enemy of the U.S.?

Type 2: I'd like to have your impressions about the overall position that some countries have taken toward the U.S. (Card shown respondent—list of countries.) Would you read down that list, and for each country, tell me if you believe the country has acted as a close ally of the U.S., has acted as a friend but not a close ally, has been more or less neutral toward the U.S., has been mainly unfriendly toward the U.S. but not an enemy, or has acted as an enemy of the U.S.? . . . Mainland China.

Notes: a. ABC News/Washington Post Poll. Question: I'm going to mention the names of some foreign countries. For each, I'd like you to tell me whether you think that country is a reliable ally of the United States—one that can be trusted to cooperate with the United States in almost any circumstances—or not. Would you say that . . . Mainland China . . . is a reliable ally of the United States or not?

b. Los Angeles Times Poll. Question: How would you describe the relationship between the People's Republic of China and the United States? Would you say the People's Republic of China is an ally . . . or friendly, but not an ally . . . or unfriendly, but not an enemy . . . or an enemy of the United States—or haven't you heard enough about that yet to say?

c. Marttila and Kiley Poll. Question: I'm going to read you a list of countries. For each one please tell me if you think it's a close ally of the U.S., is friendly but not a close ally, is not friendly but not an enemy, or is unfriendly and an enemy of the U.S. . . . China?

d. Hart and Teeter Research Companies. Question: Let me read you a list of some countries around the world. For each, please tell me whether you think that country is a strong ally and friend of the United States, a basically friendly nation, a neutral country which is neither an ally nor an enemy of the U.S., or an enemy of the United States. . . . China?

e. Potomac Associates and Opinion Dynamics Poll. Question: I'd like to have your impressions about the overall position that some countries have taken toward the United States. As I read down a list of countries, do you believe that country has acted as a close ally of the US, has acted as a friend but not a close ally, has been more or less neutral toward the US, has been mainly unfriendly toward the US but not an enemy, or has acted as an enemy of the US? . . . China?

f. CBS News Poll. Question: Do you consider China an ally of the United States, friendly but not an ally, unfriendly, or an enemy of the United States?

g. CBS News Poll. Question: Do you consider China an ally of the United States, friendly but not an ally, unfriendly, or an enemy of the United States?

Table B.3   Public Approval of Presidential Policy Toward China, 1975–2002

	Approve	Neutral/No Answer	Not Approve
Gerald Ford			
1975 April	34	16	50
1975 May	41	14	45
1975 August	37	16	47
1975 October	37	19	44
1976 January	39	11	50
Jimmy Carter			
1977 May	38	26	36
1977 September	31	25	44
1978 December	52	7	41
1979 February	56	5	39
1979 March	49	10	41
1979 May	51	7	42
1980 November	49	4	47
Ronald Reagan			
1982 September 11	38	41	21
1983 September 24	40	41	19
1984 May	61	6	33
(presidential trip)			
1985 July	53	5	42
George H.W. Bush			
1989 June 8	67	14	19
1989 June 15	92	2	6
(cut off arms sales after Tiananmen Square)[a]			
1989 June 15[b]	60	5	35
1990 May[c]	44	27	29
Bill Clinton			
1993 June	41	17	42
(MFN renewal)[d]			
1994 April[e]	63	12	25
1995 February	58	23	19
(trade sanctions)[f]			
1996 March	54	10	35
(Taiwan)[g]			
1997 September[h]	37	26	37
1998 June 22	40	37	24
1999 April[i]	44	24	32
1999 May 13[j]	38	19	43

(continues)

Table B.3   continued

	Approve	Neutral/No Answer	Not Approve
George W. Bush			
2001 April 5[k]	49	23	28
2001 April 6 (EP-3 situation)[l]	61	8	31
2001 April 20	54	11	35
2001 April 20 (EP-3)[m]	71	4	25
2002 June[n]	39	9	52

Sources: Unless otherwise noted polls are from Gallup, Roper, or Harris and were accessed via LexisNexis Academic Universe on October 28, 2002. Questions generally followed one of the following formats:

Type 1: How would you rate (President X) on his handling of relations with China—excellent, pretty good, only fair, or poor?

Type 2: How would you rate (President X) on his handling of relations with China—positive, negative, or not sure?

Type 3: Do you generally approve or generally disapprove of (President X's) handling of relations with China?

Notes: a. ABC News/Washington Post Poll. Question: (President) Bush has cut off the sale of all U.S. military equipment to the Chinese government. Do you approve or disapprove of Bush's decision?

b. ABC News/Washington Post Poll. Question: Do you approve or disapprove of the way (President George) Bush is handling relations with China?

c. Princeton Survey Research Associates. Question: Now let me ask you about some specific foreign and domestic problems. As I read off each problem, would you tell me whether you approve or disapprove of the way President Bush is handling that problem. . . . Relations with China?

d. Hart and Teeter Research Companies. Question: Recently, President (Bill) Clinton approved a one-year renewal of Most Favored Nation status for China, which is the standard protection against trade restrictions that the U.S. (United States) gives to most of its trading partners. Do you favor or oppose the decision to give this status to our trade relations with China?

e. Hart and Teeter Research Companies. Question: For each of the following, please tell me how well you think (President) Bill Clinton has handled the situation—very well, somewhat well, not very well, or not at all well. . . . Relations with China. Has Bill Clinton handled the situation very well, somewhat well, not very well, or not at all well?

f Princeton Research Associates. Question: Now I am going to read you a list of policy decisions made by the Clinton administration. Please tell me if you approve or disapprove of each of the following. If you are unaware of the decision please tell me that. Do you approve or disapprove of President Clinton's . . . decision to impose trade sanctions on China?

g. ABC News/Washington Post Poll. Question: As you may know, China has been making threatening moves toward Taiwan, which it sees as a breakaway province, and the United States has increased its naval presence in that part of the world. Do you approve or disapprove of the way (Bill) Clinton is handling the situation involving China and Taiwan?

h. Princeton Survey Research Associates. Question: Do you approve or disapprove of the way Bill Clinton is dealing with China?

i. Princeton Survey Research Associates. Question: Do you approve or disapprove of President Clinton's . . . decision to impose trade sanctions on China?

j. Princeton Survey Research Associates. Question: Do you approve or disapprove of President Clinton's . . . decision to impose trade sanctions on China?

k. CBS News poll asking "Do you approve or disapprove of the way George W. Bush is handling relations with China?" conducted on April 4–5, 2001. An ABC *Washington Post* poll from April 5 reported that 36 percent approved strongly, 28 percent approved somewhat, 11 percent disapproved strongly, 13 percent disapproved somewhat, and 12 percent had no opinion. Both polls were last accessed December 6, 2003.

l. Gallup. Question: As you may know, a US Navy plane was involved in a mid-air collision with a Chinese plane and had to land in Chinese territory. The plane and its 24 crew members are currently being held by China. . . . Do you approve or disapprove of the way George W. Bush is handling this situation?

m. Gallup. Question: Thinking about the recent situation involving China, the US Navy reconnaissance plane and the 24 crew members that were recently released (Wednesday, April 11, 2001) by China . . . do you approve or disapprove of the way President (George W.) Bush handled the situation?

n. Harris Interactive. Question: How do you rate the (President's) administration's handling of the following problems? Would you say the administration's handling of . . . relations with China has been excellent, good, fair, or poor? Specifically 4 percent answered excellent, 35 percent good, 41 percent fair, 11 percent poor, and 9 percent were not sure or did not respond. The not-approve category represents the addition of fair at 41 percent with poor at 11 percent.

Table B.4   U.S. Ratings of China, Russia, and Taiwan, 1976–2003

	Favorable Opinion of China (%)	Favorable Opinion of Russia (%)	Favorable Opinion of Taiwan (%)
1976	20	21	56
1977	27	39	56
1978	21	37	
1979	30	34	60
1980	42	14	59
1981	36	21	
1982	37	21	
1983	43	8	
1985	38	4	44
1986	34	10	32
1987	34	13	
1988	58		
1989 February	72	62	
1989 August	31	51	
1990	31	60	
1991	35	66	
1992		57	
1993	41		
1994	41	56	
1995		49	
1996	43	59	64
1997	33	56	
1998	44	37	
1999	38	46	
2000 March	35	40	47
2000 November	36	40	
2001	45	52	70
2002 February	44	66	62
2002 June	31	46	37
2003 February	45	63	
2004 February	41	59	

Sources: This poll data has been taken from Gallup or Roper and was accessed via LexisNexis Academic Universe on October 31, 2002, and February 23, 2005. Poll questions are one of the following types.

Question Type 1: What is your general attitude toward China: very favorable, somewhat favorable, somewhat unfavorable, or very unfavorable?

Question Type 2: You will notice that the boxes on this card go from the highest position of "plus 5" for a country which you like very much, to the lowest position of "minus 5" for a country you dislike very much. How far up the scale or how far down the scale would you rate the following countries? . . . China. Type 2 questions were interpreted as follows: Answers between +5 and +1 were considered a "favorable" opinion of China. Answers between –1 and –5 were considered an "unfavorable" opinion.

Acronyms and Abbreviations

APEC	Asian Pacific Economic Cooperation
ASEAN	Association of Southeast Asian Nations
CIA	Central Intelligence Agency
COCOM	Coordination Committee for Multilateral Export Controls
CVID	Complete Verifiable and Irreversible Dismantlement
DIA	Defense Intelligence Agency
EAP	Bureau of East Asian and Pacific Affairs (Department of State)
EXIM	Export Import Bank
GATT	General Agreement on Tariffs and Trade
INR	Bureau of Intelligence and Research (Department of State)
JCCT	Joint Commission on Commerce and Trade
JCS	Joint Chiefs of Staff
MOFTEC	Ministry of Foreign Trade and Economic Cooperation (China)
MFN	Most Favored Nation
MTCR	Missile Technology Control Regime
NDU	National Defense University
NEC	National Economic Council
NIE	National Intelligence Estimate
NPT	Non-Proliferation Treaty
NSA	National Security Affairs
NSC	National Security Council
NSD	National Security Directive

NSDD	National Security Decision Directive
NSDM	National Security Decision Memorandum
NSPD	National Security Presidential Directive
NSSD	National Security Study Directive
NSSM	National Security Study Memorandum
NTR	Normal Trade Relations
OECD	Organization for Economic Cooperation and Development
OMB	Office of Management and Budget
OPIC	Overseas Private Investment Corporation
PDD	Presidential Decision Directives
PLA	People's Liberation Army
PNTR	Permanent Normal Trade Relations
PRC	People's Republic of China
PRM	Presidential Review Memorandum
RG	Record Group
SALT	Strategic Arms Limitation Talks
S/PC	Policy Planning Council (Department of State)
TRA	Taiwan Relations Act
UN	United Nations
USSR	Union of Soviet Socialist Republics
USTR	United States Trade Representative
WHORM	White House Office of Record Management
WTO	World Trade Organization

Bibliography

Abramowitz, Morton. Interview by the author. Washington, D.C., June 14, 2002.

"Address to Accompany the 1971 A Year of Breakthrough Toward Peace in the World (Third Annual Foreign Policy Report)." *Department of State Bulletin* (March 1972): 289–291.

Aitken, Jonathan. *Nixon: A Life.* Washington, D.C.: Regnery, 1993.

Albright, Madeleine. Files. Carter Presidential Library, Atlanta, Georgia.

———. *Madam Secretary: A Memoir.* New York: Miramax Books, 2003.

Allison, Graham. *Essence of Decision: Explaining the Cuban Missile Crisis.* Boston: Little, Brown, 1971.

Allison, Graham, and Philip Zelikow. *Essence of Decision: Explaining the Cuban Missile Crisis,* 2nd ed. New York: Longman, 1999.

"American Optimistic in Beijing." *Washington Post,* November 18, 1995, A24.

Apple, R.W. Jr. "Bush Hails Seoul for Building Ties with North Korea." *New York Times,* February 27, 1989, A1.

———. "New World: Is Bush Prepared to Imagine the Future?" *New York Times,* January 15, 1989, Section 4, p. 1.

Armitage, Richard. "A Republican View: Managing Relations with Russia, China, India." Interview by online journal *U.S. Foreign Policy Agenda,* September 2000. Available at http://usinfo.state.gov/journals, last accessed October 1, 2004.

Bachman, David. "The United States and China: Rhetoric and Reality." *Current History* 100, no. 647 (September 2001): 257–262.

Baker, James A. Files. Reagan Presidential Library, Simi Valley, California.

———. Telephone interview by the author, November 7, 2002.

———. Hearings before the Senate Foreign Relations Committee, June 20,

1989. Federal News Service, available at http://web.lexis-nexis.com, last accessed June 1, 2002.

———. Testimony in hearings before the House Foreign Affairs Committee, June 22, 1989. Federal News Service, available at http://web.lexis-nexis.com, last accessed June 1, 2002.

Baker, James A. III, with Thomas M. DeFrank. *The Politics of Diplomacy: Revolution, War, and Peace, 1989–1992*. New York: G. P. Putnam's Sons, 1996.

Barnes, James, Margaret Kriz, Christopher Madison, W. John Moore, David C. Morrison, Jonathan Rauch, Rochelle Stanfield, and Kirk Victor. "A Familiar Look." *National Journal*, January 1, 1993, 24–29.

Barnett, Robert W. Oral history interview, March 2, 1990. Foreign Affairs Oral History Collection (CD-ROM, 2000), Association for Diplomatic Studies and Training, Arlington, Virginia.

Barrett, James Reston. "Carter, Panama, and China." *New York Times*, August 24, 1977, 19.

Barshefsky, Charlene. Telephone interview by the author, September 18, 2002.

Behr, Peter. "Offering China a Carrot on Trade." *Washington Post*, January 29, 1994, C1.

———. "U.S. Sidesteps Piracy Trade Issue with China Until After Rights Deadline." *Washington Post*, May 1, 1994, A25.

Beisner, Robert. "History and Henry Kissinger." *Diplomatic History* (Fall 1990): 511–527.

Bennett, W. L. "Toward a Theory of Press-State Relations in the United States." *Journal of Communications* 40, no. 2 (1990): 103–125.

Berger, Samuel. "Building a New Consensus on China." Remarks before the Council on Foreign Relations, New York, June 6, 1997. Released by the White House Office of the Press Secretary.

Bernstein, Richard, and Russ Munro. "China I: The Coming Conflict with America." *Foreign Affairs* 76, no. 2 (March–April 1997): 18–32.

Bishop, James K. Oral history interview, November 15, 1995. Foreign Affairs Oral History Collection (CD-ROM, 2000), Association for Diplomatic Studies and Training, Arlington, Virginia.

Blustein, Paul. "U.S. Pushes China Hard on Trade." *Washington Post*, April 15, 2004, E1.

Blustein, Paul, and R. Jeffrey Smith. "Economic, Political Concerns Put Clinton on the Spot in China Policy." *Washington Post*, February 11, 1996, A26.

Broder, David S., and Bill Peterson. "U.S. to Normalize Ties with Peking, End Its Defense Treaty with Taiwan." *Washington Post*, December 16, 1978, A1.

Bruni, Frank. "The 2000 Campaign: The Syntax." *New York Times*, January 23, 2000, Section 1, p. 19.

Brzezinski, Zbigniew, National Security Adviser. Collection. White House Central Files–Geographic and Subject File. Carter Presidential Library, Atlanta, Georgia.

————. *Power and Principle: Memoirs of a National Security Advisor.* New York: Farrar, Straus, and Giroux, 1983.

Burke, John, and Fred Greenstein. *How Presidents Test Reality: Decisions on Vietnam in 1954 and 1965.* New York: Russell Sage Foundation, 1989.

Burr, William. *The Kissinger Transcripts: The Top Secret Talks with Beijing and Moscow.* New York: New Press, 1999.

Bush, George H.W., and Brent Scowcroft. *A World Transformed.* New York: Alfred A. Knopf, 1998.

Busmiller, Elisabeth. "Bush's Tutor and Disciple, Condoleezza Rice." *New York Times,* November 17, 2004, A1, A19.

Butterfield, Fox. "Brzezinski in China; The Stress Was on Common Concerns." *New York Times,* May 24, 1978, A2.

————. "China's Communists End Party Meeting, Pick New Politburo." *New York Times,* August 21, 1977, A1.

————. "Mr. Vance Will Find the Main Topic in China Is Still Taiwan." *New York Times,* August 21, 1977, Section 4, p. 3.

————. "Vance Finishes Visit with Peking Leader." *New York Times,* August 27, 1977, A1.

————. "Vance, in China, Calls for Efforts to Improve Ties." *New York Times,* August 23, 1977, A1.

Cable News Network. Cold War Series Collection. Available at http://turnerlearning.com, last accessed June 1, 2002.

Callaghan, Karen, and Frauke Schnell. "Assessing the Democratic Debate: How the News Media Frame Elite Policy Discourse." *Political Communication* 18, no. 2 (2001): 183–214.

Carlucci, Frank. Interview by the author. Washington D.C., June 6, 2002.

Carothers, Thomas. "Promoting Democracy and Fighting Terror." *Foreign Affairs* 82, no. 1 (January–February 2003): 84 98.

Carter, Jimmy. *Keeping Faith: Memoirs of a President.* Toronto and New York: Bantam Books, 1982.

————. Presidential Papers. White House Central Files–Executive Files. Carter Presidential Library, Atlanta, Georgia.

Carter-Brezhnev Project. Vertical File. Carter Presidential Library, Atlanta, Georgia.

Cary, Anne O., Consul General. Oral history interview, November 30, 1995, Foreign Affairs Oral History Collection (CD-ROM, 2000), Association for Diplomatic Studies and Training, Arlington, Virginia.

Chandler, Clay, and Daniel Williams. "Bentsen to Push China on Economic Reforms." *Washington Post,* January 6, 1994, D10.

Change, Jaw-ling Joane. "How Clinton Bashed Taiwan—and Why." *Orbis* 39, no. 4 (Fall 1995): 567–582.

Chief of Staff [Hamilton] Jordan Files. Carter Presidential Library, Atlanta, Georgia.

Christopher, Warren. "American Interests and the U.S.-China Relationship." Speech before the Asia Society, the Council on Foreign Relations, and the National Committee on U.S.-China Relations. New York City, May 17, 1996.

————. *In the Stream of History: Shaping Foreign Policy for a New Era.* Stanford, Calif.: Stanford University Press, 1998.

————. Transcript of interview by Elizabeth Farnsworth of PBS, May 17, 1996. Available at http://www.pbs.org, last accessed June 1, 2002.

Clark, William. Files. Reagan Presidential Library, Simi Valley, California.

————. Oral history interview, January 11, 1994. Foreign Affairs Oral History Collection (CD-ROM, 2000), Association for Diplomatic Studies and Training, Arlington, Virginia.

Clarke, Richard. *Against All Enemies: Inside America's War on Terror.* New York: Free Press, 2004.

Clinton, William J. *My Life.* New York: Alfred A. Knopf, 2004.

————. "Remarks by the President on China." Paul Nitze School of Advanced International Studies, March 8, 2000. Office of the Press Secretary, www.sais.jhu.edu/events/clinton.html, last accessed February 2004.

————. "Speech on U.S. Policy Toward China." Washington, D.C., April 7, 1999. White House Press Office, http://usinfo.state.gov/regional/ea/uschina/clint407.htm, last accessed February 28, 2004.

Cobb, Roger, and Charles Elder. *Participation in American Politics: The Dynamics of Agenda Building.* Baltimore, Md.: Johns Hopkins University Press, 1983.

Cody, Edward. "Chen's Inaugural Address Skirts Independence Vow." *Washington Post,* May 21, 2004, A15.

"A Conversation with William Rogers, with Eric Severaid." *Department of State Bulletin* (January 19, 1970): 53–58.

Cooper, Kenneth. "Bush to Veto Bill Prolonging Students' Stays; Instead, Thornburgh Instructed to Grant Extensions for Chinese." *Washington Post,* December 1, 1989, A45.

Cossa, Ralph A. "The Bush Administration's 'Alliance-based' East Asian Policy." *Asian-Pacific Review* 8, no. 2 (2001): 66–80.

Council of Economic Advisers, Paul Wonnacott TPRG Files. Bush Presidential Library, College Station, Texas.

Crabb, Cecil V. Jr., and Kevin Mulcahy. *Presidents and Foreign Policy Making: From FDR to Reagan.* Baton Rouge: Louisiana State University Press, 1986.

Daalder, Ivo H., and James M. Lindsay. *America Unbound: The Bush Revolution in Foreign Policy.* Washington, D.C.: Brookings Institution, 2003.

Department of Defense. *Quadrennial Defense Review Report.* Washington, D.C., September 30, 2001. Available at http://www.defenselink.mil/pubs/qdr2001.pdf, last accessed September 1, 2004.

————. *United States Security Strategy for the East Asia–Pacific Region.* Washington, D.C., February 1995.

Dewar, Helen. "Senate Narrowly Votes to Sustain Veto of Chinese Students Bill." *Washington Post,* January 26, 1990, A1.

Dewar, Helen, and Richard L. Lyons. "Congress Begins Weighing China Trade Favors." *Washington Post,* January 23, 1980, A2.

Dickson, Bruce J. "New Presidents Adjust Old Policies: U.S.-Taiwan Relations Under Chen and Bush." *Journal of Contemporary China* 11, no. 33 (November 2002): 645–656.

Dione, E. J. Jr. "Goodbye to Human Rights?" *Washington Post,* May 31, 1994, A17.

Dobbs, Lou. "Our New Diplomatic Partner." *U.S. News and World Report,* December 22, 2003, 42.

Dobbs, Michael, and R. Jeffrey Smith. "Second Carrier Group Sends a Clear Signal." *Washington Post,* March 12, 1996, A10.

Dowd, Maureen. "Two U.S. Officials Went to Beijing Secretly in July." *New York Times,* December 19, 1989, A1.

Drew, Elizabeth. *On the Edge: The Clinton Presidency.* New York: Simon and Schuster, 1994.

Duffy, Michael, and Dan Goodgame. *Marching in Place: The Status Quo Presidency of George Bush.* New York: Simon and Schuster, 1992.

Dumbrell, John. "Unilateralism and 'America First'? President George W. Bush's Foreign Policy." *Political Quarterly* 73, no. 3 (July 2002): 379–387.

Eagleburger, Lawrence, Deputy Secretary of State. Testimony before the hearings of the Senate Foreign Relations Committee, February 8, 1990. Federal News Service, available at http://web.lexis-nexis.com, last accessed June 2002.

Erlanger, Steven. "U.S. Set to Impose Limited Sanctions on China." *New York Times,* February 21, 1996, A9.

———. "U.S. Studying Limited Penalties for Chinese Sales." *New York Times,* March 29, 1996, A6.

Erlanger, Steven, and David Sanger. "On World Stage, Many Lessons for Clinton." *New York Times,* August 29, 1996, A1.

Faison, Seth. "Clinton Likely to Visit China in 1997 If He Is Re-elected." *New York Times,* July 10, 1996, A3.

Farnham, Barbara. "Perceiving the End of Threat: Ronald Reagan and the Gorbachev Revolution." In *Good Judgment in Foreign Policy: Theory and Application,* edited by S. Renshon and D. Welch Larson, 153–190. Lanham, Md.: Rowman and Littlefield, 2003.

Farnsworth, Clyde. "Trade Shift on China Seen Near." *New York Times,* June 17, 1983, D1.

Festinger, Leon. "Informal Social Communication." *Psychological Review* 57 (1950): 271–282.

Fewsmith, Joseph. "America and China: Back from the Brink." *Current History* 93, no. 584 (September 1994): 250–255.

Finney, John W. "Congress Chiefs Pleased." *New York Times,* July 16, 1971, A1, A3.

Fitzwater, Marlin. "Statement by Press Secretary Fitzwater on United States Sanctions Against the Chinese Government," June 20, 1989. Bush Presidential Library online research resources, available at: http://bush library.tamu.edu/papers/1989/89062007.html, last accessed June 1, 2002.

"Forum on the Role of the National Security Adviser." Cosponsored by the

Woodrow Wilson International Center for Scholars and the James A. Baker III Institute for Public Policy of Rice University. Available at http://www. rice.edu/webcast/speeches/text/20010412secadv.pdf, last accessed February 22, 2004.

Freeman, Charles (Chas) Jr. Oral history interview, April 14, 1995. Foreign Affairs Oral History Collection (CD-ROM, 2000), Association for Diplomatic Studies and Training, Arlington, Virginia.

Friedman, Thomas L. "Bush Is Set Back by House Override of Veto on China." *New York Times,* January 25, 1990, A1.

———. "Clinton's Foreign Policy: Top Adviser Speaks Up." *New York Times,* October 31, 1993, A8.

———. "Congress, Angry at China, Moves to Impose Sanctions." *New York Times,* June 23, 1989, A5.

———. "Crackdown in Beijing; Administration Ponders Steps on China." *New York Times,* June 5, 1989, A12.

———. "Crackdown in China; Foley Says U.S. Should Consider Further Sanctions Against China." *New York Times,* June 19, 1989, A10.

———. "Deal with China Urged by Bentsen." *New York Times,* March 20, 1994, A20.

———. "Trade vs. Human Rights." *New York Times,* February 6, 1994, Section 1, p. 1.

———. "Turmoil in China; A Rocky Period Lies Ahead for Washington and Beijing." *New York Times,* June 10, 1989, Section 1, p. 5.

———. "Turmoil in China; U.S. and Chinese Seek to Resolve Rift on Dissident." *New York Times,* June 13, 1989, A1.

———. "U.S. May Ease Rights Goals with Beijing." *New York Times,* March 24, 1994, A1.

———. "White House Asks an Irate Congress for China Support." *New York Times,* January 24, 1990, A1.

Friedman, Thomas, and Elaine Sciolino. "Clinton and China: How Promise Self-Destructed." *New York Times,* May 29, 1994, Section 1, p. 1.

Friedman, Thomas L., Elaine Sciolino, and Patrick Tyler. "How President Clinton Agonized Over His Crucial China Policy." *Chinatown News* 41, no. 18 (1994): 5–8.

The Gallup Poll: Public Opinion 1935–1971, Vol. I. American Institute of Public Opinion. New York: Random House, 1972.

The Gallup Poll: Public Opinion 1972–1977, Vol. II. American Institute of Public Opinion. Washington, D.C.: S. R. Scholarly Resources, 1978.

Gamson, William. *Talking Politics.* New York: Cambridge University Press, 1992.

Gamson, William, and Andre Modigliani. "The Changing Culture of Affirmative Action." In *Research in Political Sociology,* Vol. 3, edited by R. Braungart, 137–177. Greenwich, Conn.: JAI Press, 1987.

Garrison, Jean A. "Explaining Change in the Carter Administration's China Policy: Foreign Policy Advisor Manipulation of the Policy Agenda." *Asian Affairs: An American Review* 29, no. 2 (Summer 2002): 83–98.

———. "Foreign Policy Decisionmaking and Group Dynamics: Where We've Been and Where We're Going." *International Studies Review* 5, no. 2 (2003): 177–183.

———. "Framing Foreign Policy Alternatives in the Inner Circle: The President, His Advisors, and the Struggle for the Arms Control Agenda." *Political Psychology* 22, no. 4 (2001): 775–808.

———. "Framing the National Interest in U.S.-China Relations: Building Consensus Around Rapprochement." *Asian Perspective* 24, no. 3 (2000): 103–134.

———. *Games Advisors Play: Foreign Policy in the Nixon and Carter Administrations.* College Station: Texas A&M University Press, 1999.

Garrison, Jean A., ed. "Foreign Policy Analysis in 20/20: A Symposium." *International Studies Review* 5, no. 2 (2003): 155–202.

Garson, Robert. *The United States and China Since 1949: A Troubled Affair.* Madison, N.J.: Fairleigh Dickinson University Press, 1994.

Garthoff, Raymond. *Détente and Confrontation: American-Soviet Relations from Nixon to Reagan.* Washington, D.C.: Brookings Institution, 1994.

———. *The Great Transition: American-Soviet Relations and the End of the Cold War.* Washington, D.C.: Brookings Institution, 1994.

Gates, Robert. *From the Shadows.* New York: Simon and Schuster, 1996.

Gelb, Leslie. "Foreign Policy System Criticized by U.S. Aides." *New York Times* (City Final Edition), October 19, 1981, A1.

———. "How Haig Is Recasting His Image." *New York Times,* May 31, 1981, Section 6, p. 23.

———. "U.S.-China Ties: Lower Expectations." *New York Times,* February 2, 1983, A3.

Gelman, Barton. "Reappraisal Led to New China Policy, Skeptics Abroad Bet U.S. Strategic Partnership Yielding Results." *Washington Post,* June 2, 1998, A1.

George, Alexander. "Case Studies and Theory Development: The Method of Structured, Focused Comparison." In *Diplomacy: New Approaches in History, Theory and Policy,* edited by A. L. George, 43–68. New York: Free Press, 1979.

———. *Presidential Decision Making in Foreign Policy: The Effective Use of Information and Advice.* Boulder: Westview, 1980.

"George W.'s World View." *New Perspectives Quarterly* 18, no. 1 (Winter 2001): 35–37.

Gertz, Bill. "Rumsfeld Confers at Pentagon with His Chinese Counterpart." *Washington Times,* October 29, 2003, A8.

———. "State Confirms N. Korea Light-Water Reactor Talk." *Washington Times,* May 20, 2004, A3.

———. "Taiwan Shoring Up Defenses with U.S. Assistance." *Washington Times,* February 29, 2004, A3.

———. "U.S. to Continue Sale of Defensive Arms to Taiwan." *Washington Times,* April 22, 2004, A12.

Gertz, Bill, and Rowan Scarborough. "Nation, Inside the Ring." *Washington Times*, May 28, 2004, A5.

———. "Nation, Inside the Ring," *Washington Times*, December 5, 2003, A6.

Getler, Michael. "Pentagon Willing to Sell Chinese Some Equipment." *Washington Post*, January 25, 1980, A1.

Geyelin, Philip. "Reagan: The Best of Both 'Chinas.'" *Washington Post*, January 13, 1984, A23.

Glad, Betty. "Black and White Thinking: Ronald Reagan's Approach to Foreign Policy." *Political Psychology* 4, no. 1 (Spring 1983): 33–75.

Goffman, Erving. *Frame Analysis*. Cambridge, Mass.: Harvard University Press, 1974.

Gordon, Michael. "Rumsfeld Limiting Military Contact with the Chinese." *New York Times*, June 4, 2001, A1.

———. "U.S. Aide Admits North Korea Nuclear Policy May Not Work." *New York Times*, May 6, 1994, A6.

Graber, Doris. *Media Power in Politics*. Washington, D.C.: CQ Press, 1994.

Graham, Bradley. "Pentagon Announces Plans to Sell Radars to Taiwan." *Washington Post*, April 1, 2004, A27.

Green, Marshall. Oral history interview, 1998. Foreign Affairs Oral History Collection (CD-ROM, 2000), Association for Diplomatic Studies and Training, Arlington, Virginia.

Greenhouse, Steven. "New Tally of World's Economies Catapults China into Third Place." *New York Times*, May 20, 1993, A1.

———. "Renewal Backed for China Trade." *New York Times*, May 28, 1993, A5.

Greenstein, Fred I. "The Contemporary Presidency: The Changing Leadership of George W. Bush: A Pre– and Post–9/11 Comparison." *Presidential Studies Quarterly* 32, no. 2 (2002): 387–396.

Haig, Alexander Jr. *Caveat: Realism, Reagan and Foreign Policy*. New York: Macmillian, 1984.

Haldeman, H. R. *The Haldeman Diaries: Inside the Nixon White House*. New York: G. P. Putnam Sons, 1994.

Halloran, Richard. "New Jets for Taiwan: An Issue Surrounded by Nettles." *New York Times*, January 27, 1981, A2.

Hansell, Herbert J. Oral history interview, March 29, 1995. Foreign Affairs Oral History Collection (CD-ROM, 2000), Association for Diplomatic Studies and Training, Arlington, Virginia.

Hanson, Elizabeth. "Framing the World News: The *Times of India* in Changing Times." *Political Communication* 12, no. 4 (October–December 1995): 371–393.

Harding, Harry. *A Fragile Relationship: The United States and China Since 1972*. Washington, D.C.: Brookings Institution, 1992.

———. "Asia Policy to the Brink." *Foreign Affairs* 73, no. 2 (Fall 1994): 61–73.

Heilbrunn, Jacob. "Condoleezza Rice: George W.'s Realist." *World Policy Journal* (Winter 1999–2000): 49–54.

Hermann, Margaret, and Thomas Preston. "Presidents, Leadership Style, and the Advisory Process." In *Domestic Sources of American Foreign Policy: Insights and Evidence,* edited by E. Wittkopf and J. McCormick, 351–368. Boston: Rowman and Littlefield, 1999.

Hiatt, Fred. "U.S. Used China Trip to Press Its Courtship." *Washington Post,* October 5, 1983, A19.

Hillsman, Roger. *The Politics of Policymaking in Defense and Foreign Affairs.* Englewood Cliffs, N.J.: Prentice Hall, 1987.

Hoffman, David. "Bush Never Issued Executive Order Protecting Chinese Students in U.S." *Washington Post,* April 5, 1990, A25.

———. "China Executions Push Bush to Focus on Future; President Replaces Criticism of Beijing with Strategy to Salvage Relationship over Long Run." *Washington Post,* June 25, 1989, A25.

Holbrooke, Richard. "A Crisis with China Must Be Avoided." *New York Times,* January 10, 1982, Section 4, p. 23.

Holdridge, John. *Crossing the Divide.* Lanham, Md.: Rowman and Littlefield, 1994.

———. Oral history interview, December 14, 1989. Foreign Affairs Oral History Collection (CD-ROM, 2000), Association for Diplomatic Studies and Training, Arlington, Virginia.

———. Oral history interview, July 20, 1995, Foreign Affairs Oral History Collection (CD-ROM, 2000), Association for Diplomatic Studies and Training, Arlington, Virginia.

Hummel, Arthur. Oral history interview, April 4, 1994. Foreign Affairs Oral History Collection (CD-ROM, 2000), Association for Diplomatic Studies and Training, Arlington, Virginia.

Hurst, Steven. *The Foreign Policy of the Bush Administration.* London: Cassel, 1999.

Iyengar, Shanto. *Is Anyone Responsible? How Television Frames Political Issues.* Chicago: University of Chicago Press, 1991.

Jacoby, William. G. "Issue Framing and Public Opinion on Government Spending." *American Journal of Political Science* 44, no. 4 (2000): 750–767.

Janis, Irving. *Groupthink: Psychological Studies of Policy Decisions and Fiascoes.* Boston: Houghton Mifflin, 1971.

Jehl, Douglas. "Clinton Makes No Progress with Beijing." *New York Times,* May 3, 1994, A8.

———. "U.S. Agrees to Discuss Arms Directly with North Korea." *New York Times,* April 23, 1993, A10.

Jervis, Robert. *Perceptions and Misperceptions in International Politics.* Princeton, N.J.: Princeton University Press, 1976.

Johnson, Haynes. "China and Double Standards." *Washington Post,* December 15, 1989, A2.

Johnson, Richard Tanner. *Managing the White House.* New York: Harper and Row, 1974.

Kaarbo, Juliet, and Ryan Beasley. "A Practical Guide to the Comparative Case

Study Method in Political Psychology." *Political Psychology* 20, no. 2 (1999): 369–391.

Kagan, Robert, and William Kristol. "The 'Adults' Make a Mess." *Weekly Standard,* May 14, 2001, 11.

Kahneman, Daniel, and Amos Tversky. "Prospect Theory: An Analysis of Decision Under Risk." *Econometrica* 47 (1979): 263–292.

Kaiser, Robert G. "House and Senate Adopt Taiwan Bills; Similar Measures Establish New Basis for Washington's Relations with Taipei." *Washington Post,* March 14, 1979, A1, A10.

Kantor, Mickey. Interview by the author. Washington, D.C., June 13, 2002.

Kelly, James. Assistant Secretary of State for East Asian and Pacific Affairs, Testimony in Hearings Before the Senate Foreign Relations Committee on latest round of six-way talks on nuclear weapons in North Korea, July 15, 2004. Available at LexisNexis Congressional, http://web.lexis-nexis. com/congcomp, last accessed October 1, 2004.

Kenworthy, Tom, and Ann Devroy. "House Votes to Reject Chinese-Student Veto; Senate Vote Today Expected to Be Close." *Washington Post,* January 25, 1990, A1.

Kenworthy, Tom, and Helen Dewar. "As Congress Returns to Work, Democrats Seek Advantage Over Bush." *Washington Post,* January 24, 1990, A4.

Kessler, Glenn. "Cheney to Reassert U.S. Position on Taiwan's Status." *Washington Post,* April 14, 2004, A20.

———. "Cheney Urges Increase in Freedoms for Chinese." *Washington Post,* April 16, 2004, A14.

Kessler, Glenn, and Edward Cody. "Cheney Warns China About Hong Kong." *Washington Post,* April 14, 2004, A14.

Khong, Yuen Foong. *Analogies at War.* Princeton, N.J.: Princeton University Press, 1992.

Kingdon, John. *Agendas, Alternatives, and Public Policies,* 2nd ed. Boston: Little, Brown, 1994.

Kissinger, Henry. *White House Years.* Boston: Little, Brown, 1979.

Kniazkov, Maxim. "China Developing 'Credible Military Options' to Confront Taiwan, US Warns." Agence France-Presse, May 30, 2004. Available at http//web.lexis-nexis.com, last accessed October 1, 2004.

Korfonta, Paul. Files. White House Office of Cabinet Affairs Collection. Bush Presidential Library, College Station, Texas.

Kreisberg, Paul. Oral history interview, April 8, 1989. Foreign Affairs Oral History Collection (CD-ROM, 2000), Association for Diplomatic Studies and Training, Arlington, Virginia.

Kurlantzick, Joshua. "Look Away, A Do-nothing Korea Policy." *New Republic,* December 15, 2003, 14–16.

Kusnitz, Leonard. *Public Opinion and Foreign Policy: America's China Policy, 1949–1979.* Westport, Conn.: Greenwood Press, 1984.

Lake, Anthony. "From Containment to Enlargement." Address presented at the Johns Hopkins School of Advanced International Studies, Washington, D.C., September 21, 1993. Available at http://www.fas.org/news/usa/1993/usa–930921.htm, last accessed Octoer 25, 2002.

————. Remarks Before the Japan-America Society, Washington, D.C., October 23, 1996. Available at http://clinton3.nara.gov/WH/EOP/NSC/html/speeches/19961023.html, last accessed October 5, 2002.

Lampton, David. *Same Bed, Different Dreams: Managing U.S.-China Relations 1989–2000.* Berkeley: University of California Press, 2001.

————. "The Stealth Normalization of U.S.-China Relations." *National Interest,* no. 73 (Fall 2003): 37–49.

Lebow, Richard Ned. *Between Peace and War: The Nature of International Crisis.* Baltimore, Md.: Johns Hopkins University Press, 1981.

"Letter to the Speaker of the House of Representatives and the President of the Senate on Trade with China," December 19, 1989. Bush Presidential Library online research resources. Available at http://bushlibrary.tamu.edu, last accessed December 9, 2004.

Levy, Jack. "Political Psychology and Foreign Poicy." In *Oxford Handbook of Political Psychology,* edited by David O. Sears, Leonie Huddy, and Robert Jervis, 253–284. New York: Oxford University Press, 2003.

Lewis, Anthony. "The Clinton Doctrine." *New York Times,* January 22, 1993, A17.

Lewis, Paul. "Is the U.S. Souring on Free Trade?" *New York Times,* June 25, 1996, D1.

Lilley, James, with Jeffrey Lilley. *China Hands: Nine Decades of Adventure, Espionage, and Diplomacy in Asia.* New York: Public Affairs, 2004.

Lippman, Thomas. "U.S. Sees Engagement in Current Policy, But China Feels Containment." *Washington Post,* July 9, 1995, A23.

Lord, Winston. Files. Policy Planning Council (S/PC) Director's Files. General Records of the Department of State. National Archives, College Park, Maryland.

————. Files. Record Group 59 (RG59), General Records of the Department of State. National Archives, College Park, Maryland.

————. "Misguided Mission." *New York Times* editorial, December 19, 1989, A23.

————. Telephone interview by the author, March 21, 2003.

————. Testimony on Taiwan. Hearing of the East Asian and Pacific Subcommittee of the Senate Foreign Relations Committee, February 7, 1996. Available at http//web.lexis-nexis.com, last accessed December 10, 2002.

————. "The Nixon Doctrine: A Foreign Policy for the 1970's (Draft Presidential Statement)." Planning Staff Folder. National Archives, College Park, Maryland.

Mann, James. *About Face: A History of America's Curious Relationship with China, from Nixon to Clinton.* New York: Alfred A. Knopf, 1999.

————. "How Taipei Outwitted U.S. Policy." *Los Angeles Times,* June 8, 1995, A1.

————. *Rise of the Vulcans: The History of Bush's War Cabinet.* New York: Viking, 2004.

Mann, James, and Doyle McManus. "Official Says U.S. Taking Softer Approach to China." *Los Angeles Times,* July 18, 1996, A18.

Maoz, Zeev. "Framing the National Interest: The Manipulation of Foreign Policy Decisions in Group Settings." *World Politics* 43, no. 1 (October 1990): 77–110.

Marder, Murrey. "The China Policy That Isn't, Beyond Curbing the Soviets, Haig and Deng Have Little to Agree On." *Washington Post,* June 14, 1981, C1.

Mathews, Jay. "China Warns Factions Against Change So Rapid That Stability Is Threatened." *Washington Post,* March 13, 1979, A8.

———. "Sudden Shift Stuns Taiwan; Leaders Embittered: Chiang Says U.S. Broke Assurances." *Washington Post,* December 16, 1978, A1, A13.

McAllister, Bill. "Lawmakers Ask Strong U.S. Action; Punish Authorities, White House Told." *Washington Post,* June 5, 1989, A24.

McDermott, Rose. "Prospect Theory in International Relations: The Iranian Hostage Rescue Mission." In *Avoiding Losses/Taking Risks: Prospect Theory and International Conflict,* edited by B. Farnham, 73–100. Ann Arbor: University of Michigan Press, 1994.

———. *Risk-Taking in International Politics: Prospect Theory in American Foreign Policy.* Ann Arbor: University of Michigan Press, 1998.

Meyer, David. "Framing National Security: Elite Public Discourse on Nuclear Weapons During the Cold War." *Political Communication* 12, no. 3 (April–June 1995): 173–192.

Milbank, Dana, and Mike Allen. "Bush to Drop Annual Review of Weapons Sales to Taiwan." *Washington Post,* April 25, 2001, A1.

Mitchell, Alison. "Despite Tensions, Clinton Urges Renewal of China's Trade Status." *New York Times,* May 28, 1996, A1.

———. "The Clinton Record: Foreign Policy; Clinton's Three Big Objectives Include Peace Through Trade." *New York Times,* July 29, 1996, A15.

Mohr, Charles. "Carter Orders Steps to Increase Ability to Meet War Threats." *New York Times,* August 26, 1977, A7.

Mosher, Steven. *China Misperceived: American Illusions and Chinese Reality.* New York: Basic Books, 1990.

Mulcahy, Kevin. "The Bush Administration and National Security Policy-making: A Preliminary Assessment." *Governance* 4, no. 2 (April 1991): 207–220.

Murphy, Sean Patrick. "A Sweet and Sour Relationship: Interview with Winston Lord." *Current History* (September 1995): 248–251.

"National Foreign Policy Conference for Editors and Broadcasters with Secretary Richardson." *Department of State Bulletin* (February 2, 1970): 113–124.

National Intelligence Council. *Foreign Missile Developments and the Ballistic Missile Threat Through 2015* (unclassified summary). Central Intelligence Agency online. Available at http://www.cia.gov, last accessed October 1, 2004.

National Security Affairs, Brzezinski Material, Country File. Carter Presidential Library, Atlanta, Georgia.

National Security Affairs, Staff Materials. Armacost Chronological File. Carter Presidential Library, Atlanta, Georgia.

National Security Affairs, Staff Materials. Carter Presidential Library, Atlanta, Georgia.

National Security Archives Collection. China and the United States from Hostility to Engagement, 1960–1998 (published and postpublication collections). National Security Archives, Washington, D.C.

National Security Archives Collection. National Security Memorandum Collection from Truman to Clinton. National Security Archives, Washington, D.C.

National Security Council, Douglas Paal Files. Bush Presidential Library, College Station, Texas.

National Security Council, Roman Popandiule [OA/ID CF 0067] Files. Bush Presidential Library, College Station, Texas.

National Security Council, Staff Materials. Carter Presidential Library, Atlanta, Georgia.

National Security Decision Documents. National Security Archives, Washington, D.C.

National Security Directive (NSD) 1. "Organization of the National Security Council System," January 30, 1989. Bush Presidential Library online research resources. Available at http://bushlibrary.tamu.edu, last accessed December 9, 2004.

National Security Directive 23. "United States Relations with the Soviet Union," September 22, 1989. Bush Presidential Library online research resources, http://bushlibrary.tamu.edu, last accessed June 3, 2003.

National Security Presidential Directive-1 (NSPD-1), February 13, 2001. Subject: Organization of the National Security Council System. Available at http://www.fas.org/irp/offdocs/nspd/nspd-1.htm, last accessed February 22, 2004.

The National Security Strategy of the United States of America. September 2002, White House, Washington, D.C., available at http://www. whitehouse.gov, last accessed February 28, 2004.

Nations, Richard. "A Tilt Towards Tokyo." *Far Eastern Economic Review,* April 21, 1983, 36–37.

———. "Why the Pentagon Pumps for Japan." *Far Eastern Economic Review,* April 21, 1993, 37.

Nelson, Thomas, Rosalee Clawson, and Zoe Oxley. "Media Framing of a Civil Liberties Conflict and Its Effect on Tolerance." *American Political Science Review* 91, no. 3 (September 1997): 567–584.

New York Times, Editorial Desk. "One China for Mr. Reagan Too." May 13, 1982, A26.

———. "The Opened Door." July 17, 1971, 22.

———. "Quit Over That?" March 27, 1981, A26.

New York Times, Foreign Desk. "Excerpts from the President's News Conference on China and Other Matters." January 26, 1990, A8.

———. "Turmoil in China; Poll Says Two-Thirds Back Bush on Beijing." June 14, 1989, A17.

———. "U.S. Is Going Ahead with Taiwan Sale." April 14, 1982, A1.

New York Times, National Desk. "The Clinton Record: Foreign Policy; Clinton's Three Big Objectives Include Peace Through Trade." July 29, 1996, A15.

————. "Special to the Times: Excerpts from Interview with President on Foreign and Domestic Issues." June 27, 1989, A21.

Nichols, Robert. Oral history interview, August 30, 1998. Foreign Affairs Oral History Collection (CD-ROM, 2000), Association for Diplomatic Studies and Training, Arlington, Virginia.

Nixon, Richard. "American Role in the World." *Department of State Bulletin* (June 23, 1969): 525–526.

————. "Asia After Vietnam." *Foreign Affairs* 46, no. 2 (October 1967): 111–125.

————. "Presidential Address: Strengthening the Total Fabric of Peace." *Department of State Bulletin* (October 6, 1969): 297–302.

————. *RN, the Memoirs of Richard Nixon.* New York: Grosset and Dunlap, 1978.

————. "State of the Union." *Department of State Bulletin* (February 9, 1970): 145–147.

Oberdorfer, Don. "Teng Hints Use of Force Along Vietnam Border." *Washington Post,* February 1, 1979, A1.

————. "U.S. Optimistic Dissident Fang Will Be Freed; Subject Taken Up in Recent Talks." *Washington Post,* December 16, 1989, A28.

Oberdorfer, Don, and David Hoffman. "Scowcroft Warned China of New Hill Sanctions; U.S. Emissaries Stressed Need for Action by Beijing, Sources Say." *Washington Post,* December 15, 1989, A1.

Office of the Press Secretary. "Remarks by the President . . . at Signing of China Permanent Normal Trade Relations." October 10, 2000. Available at www.unconsulate.org.hk/uscn/wh/2000/101001.htm, last accessed December 1, 2001.

————. . "Remarks by the President on China." Paul Nitze School of Advanced International Studies, March 8, 2000. Available at www.sais.jhu.edu/evals/clinton/html among other sites, last accessed February 28, 2004.

Osgood, Robert. Planning Staff Folder. November 19, 1969. National Archives, College Park, Maryland.

Paal, Douglas. Files. Reagan Presidential Library, Simi Valley, California.

Pan, Philip. "Taiwan's President Unfazed by U.S. Warning." *Washington Post,* December 11, 2003, A47.

Panetta, Leon. Telephone interview by the author, October 11, 2002.

Pear, Robert. "Crackdown in Beijing; President Assails Shootings in China." *New York Times,* June 4, 1989, 21.

Pomfret, John. "China Lauds Bush for Comments on Taiwan." *Washington Post,* December 12, 2003, A44.

Pomfret, John, and Philip Pan. "U.S. Hits Obstacles in Helping Taiwan Guard Against China." *Washington Post,* October 30, 2003, A1.

Powell, Colin. Confirmation hearing before the Senate Foreign Relations Committee, 107th Congress, 1st session, January 17, 2001. Available at http://www.state.gov/secretary/rm/2001/index.cfm?docid=443, last accessed July 29, 2003.

"President Nixon Announces Acceptance of Invitation to Visit PRC." *Department of State Bulletin* (August 2, 1971): 121.

"President Nixon Briefs Media Executives from 13 Midwest States." *Department of State Bulletin* (July 26, 1971): 93–97.

"President Nixon's News Conference of January 27, 1969." *Department of State Bulletin* (February 17, 1969): 141.

Presidential Decision Directives (Various). NSDM Folder. National Security Archives, Washington, D.C.

Presidential Press Office, Subject Files. Bush Presidential Library, College Station, Texas.

"The President's News Conference," June 5, 1989. Bush Presidential Library online research resources. Available at http://bushlibrary.tamu.edu, last accessed December 9, 2004.

"The President's News Conference." June 27, 1989. Bush Presidential Library online research resources. Available at http://bushlibrary.tamu.edu, last accessed December 9, 2004.

Preston, Thomas. *The President and His Inner Circle: Leadership Style and the Advisory Process in Foreign Affairs.* New York: Columbia University Press, 2001.

Putnam, Robert. "Diplomacy and Domestic Politics: The Logic of Two-Level Games." In *Double-Edged Diplomacy: International Bargaining and Domestic Politics*, edited by P. Evans, H. Jacobson, and R. Putnam, 431–468. Berkeley: University of California Press, 1992.

Rasky, Susan F. "House Toughening China Curbs." *New York Times,* June 29, 1989, A10.

Reagan, Ronald. *An American Life.* New York: Pocket Books, 1990.

"Remarks and a Question-and-Answer Session with Newspaper Editors," December 11, 1989. Bush Presidential Library online research resources. Available at http://bushlibrary.tamu.edu, last accessed December 9, 2004.

Renshon, Stanley. "The World According to George W. Bush." In *Good Judgment in Foreign Policy: Theory and Application,* edited by S. Renshon and D. Welch Larson, 271–308. Lanham, Md.: Rowman and Littlefield, 2003.

Rice, Condoleeza. "George W.'s World View." *New Perspectives Quarterly* 18, no. 1 (Winter 2001): 35–37.

———. "Promoting the National Interest." *Foreign Affairs* 79, no. 1 (2000): 45–63.

———. "Bush to Focus on Terror, Security, Economy in Asia Trip." Transcript of Condoleezza Rice Briefing to Press on eve of presidential visit to Asia, February 14, 2002. Available at http://hongkong.usconsulate.gov/ustw/wh/2002/021402.htm, last accessed February 22, 2004.

Richburg, Keith. "U.S. Withdraws Its Threat of Sanctions Against China." *Washington Post,* June 18, 1996, C1.

Rodman, Peter W. Oral history interview, May 22, 1994. Foreign Affairs Oral

History Collection (CD-ROM, 2000), Association for Diplomatic Studies and Training, Arlington, Virginia.

Rohwer, Jim. "The Titan Stirs." *Economist* 325, no. 7787 (November 28, 1992): 3.

Romberg, Alan. *Rein In at the Brink of the Precipice: American Policy Toward Taiwan and U.S.-PRC Relations.* Washington, D.C.: Henry L. Stimson Center, 2003.

Rope, William. Interview by the author, Washington, D.C., June 2002, and correspondence with author, October 2003.

Roper Center at the University of Connecticut. *Gallup Polls 1969–2002; Time, Yankelovich, Shelly, and White Poll May 12, 1981; CBS News/New York Times Poll conducted June 22–27, 1981 and April 28, 1984; Roper Report August 15–22, 1981, and September 19–26, 1981.* Public Opinion Online, LexisNexis. Available at http//web.lexis-nexis.com, last accessed February 28, 2004.

Rosati, Jerel. *The Carter Administration's Quest for Global Community: Beliefs and Their Impact on Behavior.* Columbia: University of South Carolina Press, 1987.

———. "A Cognitive Approach to the Study of Foreign Policy." In *Foreign Policy Analysis: Continuity and Change in Its Second Generation,* edited by L. Neack, J. Hey, and P. Haney, 49–70. Englewood Cliffs, N.J.: Prentice Hall, 1995.

———. "The Power of Human Cognition in the Study of World Politics." *International Studies Review* 2, no. 3 (Fall 2000): 45–76.

Rosenau, James. "Pre Theories and Theories of Foreign Policy." In *Approaches to Comparative and International Politics,* edited by R. B. Farrell, 27–92. Evanston, Ill.: Northwestern University Press, 1966.

Rosenthal, A. M. "On My Mind; The Absent Americans." *New York Times,* May 19, 1989, A35.

Ross, Robert. "China II: Beijing as a Conservative Power." *Foreign Affairs* 76, no. 2 (March–April 1997): 33–44.

———. *Negotiating Cooperation: The United States and China, 1969–1989.* Stanford, Calif.: Stanford University Press, 1995.

Rumsfeld, Donald. *Quadrennial Defense Review Report.* Washington, D.C.: Department of Defense, 2001.

Russo, Paul. Oral history interview, February 8, 1991. Foreign Affairs Oral History Collection (CD-ROM, 2000), Association for Diplomatic Studies and Training, Arlington, Virginia.

Sanger, David. "In Manila, Asians Pore Over Washington's Inner Truths." *New York Times,* November 24, 1996, A1.

———. "Jobs Figuring Large in Diplomacy." *New York Times,* November 5, 1994, A41.

———. "U.S. Would Defend Taiwan, Bush Says." *New York Times,* April 26, 2001, A1.

Sanger, David, and Steven Erlanger. "U.S. Warns China over Violations of Trade Accord." *New York Times,* February 4, 1996, A1.

Schaefer, Donald. "U.S. Foreign Policies of Presidents Bush and Clinton: The Influence of China's Most Favored Nation." *Social Science Journal* 35, no. 3 (1998): 407–422.

Schlesinger, Arthur Jr. *The Imperial Presidency.* New York: Houghton Mifflin, 1989.

Sciolino, Elaine. "Bush's Washington: Who's Who—Second Article of a Series." *New York Times,* January 17, 1989, A1, A25.

———. "Clinton Is Stern with Indonesia on Rights But Gleeful on Trade." *New York Times,* November 17, 1994, A1.

———. "U.S. to Try a Conciliatory Tact with China." *New York Times,* March 23, 1994, A12.

———. "Winston Lord: Where the Buck Stops on China and Human Rights." *New York Times,* March 27, 1994, Section 1, p. 8.

Scobell, Andrew. "Crouching Korea, Hidden China: Bush Administration Policy Toward Pyongyang and Beijing." *Asian Survey* 42, no. 2 (March–April 2002): 343–369.

Scowcroft, Brent. Telephone interview by the author, September 16, 2002.

Semple, Robert Jr. "Two Senate Leaders Will Go to China; Invited by Chou." *New York Times,* March 1, 1972, Section 1, p. 16.

Sergounin, Alexander. "An Age of Uncertainty: Building a Post–Cold War U.S. Security Strategy for East and Southeast Asia." *Journal of Northeast Asian Studies* 15, no. 2 (Summer 1996): 25–50.

Shambaugh, David. "Sino-American Relations Since September 11: Can the New Stability Last?" *Current History* 101, no. 656 (September 2002): 243–249.

Shattuck, John. Telephone interview by the author, September 26, 2002.

Shimko, Keith. *Images and Arms Control: Perceptions of the Soviet Union in the Reagan Administration.* Ann Arbor: University of Michigan Press, 1991.

———. "Metaphors and Foreign Policy Decision Making." *Political Psychology* 14 (1994): 657–673.

Shultz, George. *Turmoil and Triumph.* New York: Charles Scribner's Sons, 1993.

———. "United States and East Asia: A Partnership for the Future." Department of State, Bureau of Public Affairs, March 5, 1983.

Sigur, Gaston. Files. Ronald Reagan Presidential Library, Simi Valley, California.

———. Oral history interview, April 24, 1990. Foreign Affairs Oral History Collection (CD-ROM, 2000), Association for Diplomatic Studies and Training, Arlington, Virginia.

———. "U.S. Policy Priorities for Relations with China." Department of State, Bureau of Public Affairs. April 22, 1987.

Smith, Hedrick. "Who's in Charge of Foreign Policy? Well . . ." *New York Times,* July 12, 1981, 1.

Smith, Michael B. Oral history interview, August 25, 1993. Foreign Affairs Oral History Collection (CD-ROM, 2000), Association for Diplomatic Studies and Training, Arlington, Virginia.

Smith, R. Jeffrey, and Ann Devroy. "U.S. to Seek Closer Ties with China; More High-level Talks Contemplated Between Top Officials This Spring." *Washington Post,* February 21, 1996, A27.

Snow, David, E. B. Rochford Jr., S. Worden, and Robert Benford. "Frame Alignment Processes, Micromobilization, and Movement Participation." *American Sociological Review* 51 (August 1986): 476–477.

Snow, David, and Robert Benford. "Ideology, Frame Resonance, and Participant Mobilization." In *International Social Movement Research,* Vol. 1, edited by B. Klandermans, H. Kriiesi, and Sidney Tarrow, 197–217. Greenwich, Conn.: JAI Press, 1988.

Southerland, Daniel. "Clinton Sending First Trade Delegation to China." *Washington Post,* February 27, 1993, C1.

Speakes, Larry, with Robert Pack. *Speaking Out: The Reagan Presidency from Inside the White House.* New York: Charles Scribner's Sons, 1988.

Staff Offices, Counsel Lipshutz. Carter Presidential Library, Atlanta, Georgia.

Staff Offices, Special Assistant to the President Bourne. Carter Presidential Library, Atlanta, Georgia.

Staff Offices, Science and Technology. Adviser to the President Press. Carter Presidential Library, Atlanta, Georgia.

"State of the Union Excerpts." *Department of State Bulletin* (February 7, 1972): 141.

"Statement on the Chinese Government's Suppression of Student Demonstrations," June 3, 1989. George Bush Presidential Library online research resources. Available at http://bushlibrary.tamu.edu, last accessed December 9, 2004.

Steinbrunner, John. *The Cybernetic Theory of Decision.* Princeton, N.J.: Princeton University Press, 1974.

Stern, Eric K., and Bengt Sundelius. "Understanding Small Group Decisions in Foreign Policy: Process Diagnosis." In *Beyond Groupthink: Political Group Dynamics and Foreign Policy-making,* edited by P. t'Hart, E. K. Stern, and B. Sundelius, 123–150. Ann Arbor: University of Michigan Press, 1997.

Stoessinger, John, ed. *Nations in Darkness, Nations at Dawn: China, Russia, and America,* 6th ed. New York: McGraw-Hill, 1994.

Stokes, Henry Scott. "Brzezinski Tells Japan's Premier Peking Is Pressing for Peace Pact." *New York Times,* May 24, 1978, A2.

Suettinger, Robert. *Beyond Tiananmen: The Politics of U.S.-China Relations 1989–2000.* Washington, D.C.: Brookings Institution, 2003.

Suskind, Ron. *The Price of Loyalty: George W. Bush, the White House, and the Education of Paul O'Neil.* New York: Simon and Schuster, 2004.

Sutter, Robert. "Bush Administration Policy Toward Beijing and Taipei." *Journal of Contemporary China* 12, no. 36 (August 2003): 477–492.

———. *The China Quandary: Domestic Determinants of U.S. China Policy, 1972–1982.* Boulder: Westview, 1982.

Swift, Elizabeth Ann, Consul. Oral history interview, December 16, 1992. Foreign Affairs Oral History Collection (CD-ROM, 2000), Association for Diplomatic Studies and Training, Arlington, Virginia.

Szulc, Tad. "Move by President Seems to Outflank His Potential Foes." *New York Times,* July 17, 1971, Section 1, p. 2.

Tarnoff, Peter. "Press Conference in Kuala Lampur." March 22, 1996. U.S. Department of State, Bureau of Public Affairs, Washington, D.C.

Tarrow, Sidney. *Power in Movement.* New York: Cambridge University Press, 1994.

Terkildsen, Nadya, Frauke Schnell, and Christina Ling. "Interest Groups, the Media, and Policy Debate Formation: An Analysis of Message Structure, Rhetoric, and Source Cues." *Political Communication* 15, no. 1 (January–March 1998): 45–61.

Tetlock, Phil. "Accountability: The Neglected Social Context of Judgment and Choice." *Research in Organizational Behavior* 7 (1985): 297–332.

———. "An Alternative Metaphor in the Study of Judgment and Choice: People as Politicians." In *Research on Judgment and Decision Making,* edited by W. Goldstein and R. Hogarth, 657–680. New York: Cambridge University Press, 1997.

Thayer, Harry E.T. Oral history interview, November 19, 1990. Foreign Affairs Oral History Collection (CD-ROM, 2000), Association for Diplomatic Studies and Training, Arlington, Virginia.

Tolchin, Martin. "House, Breaking with Bush, Votes China Sanctions." *New York Times,* June 30, 1989, A1.

Tower Commission (President's Special Review Board). *The Tower Commission Report.* New York: Bantam, 1987.

Tucker, Nancy Bernkopf. "A Precarious Balance: Clinton and China." *Current History* 97, no. 620 (September 1998): 243–249.

———. "The Clinton Years: The Problem of Coherence." In *Making China Policy: Lessons from the Bush and Clinton Administrations,* edited by R. Myers, M. Oksenberg, and D. Shambaugh. Lanham, Md.: Rowman and Littlefield, 2001.

Tyler, Patrick. "China Is Insisting Clinton Reaffirm One-China Policy." *New York Times,* July 13, 1995, A8.

———. *A Great Wall: Six Presidents and China.* New York: Century Foundation Books, 1999.

———. "Rights in China Improve, Envoy Says." *New York Times,* January 1, 1994, A5.

"U.S. Foreign Policy for the 1970's: Building for Peace." *Department of State Bulletin* (February 25, 1971): 342–419.

"U.S. Foreign Policy for the 1970's: The Emerging Structure for Peace." *Department of State Bulletin* (March 13, 1972): 313–418.

"U.S. Foreign Policy for the 1970's: A New Strategy for Peace." *Department of State Bulletin* (February 18, 1970): 273–279.

"U.S. Foreign Policy: Some Major Issues—Statement by Secretary Rogers." *Department of State Bulletin* (March 31, 1969): 305–312.

USSR-U.S. Conference. Verticale File. Carter Presidential Library, Atlanta, Georgia.

Vance, Cyrus. *Hard Choices: Critical Years in America's Foreign Policy.* New York: Simon and Schuster, 1983.

Vertzberger, Yaacov. *Risk Taking and Decisionmaking: Foreign Military Intervention Decisions.* Stanford, Calif.: Stanford University Press, 1998.

Wade, Robert H. B., Ambassador. Oral history interview, January 20, 1990. Foreign Affairs Oral History Collection (CD-ROM, 2000), Association for Diplomatic Studies and Training, Arlington, Virginia.

Walters, Vernon. *Silent Missions.* New York: Doubleday, 1978.

Waltz, Kenneth. *Man, the State, and War.* New York: Columbia University Press, 1959.

Weinberger, Caspar W. *Fighting for Peace: Seven Critical Years in the Pentagon.* New York: Warner Books, 1990.

———. Telephone interview by the author, May 15, 2002.

Weisman, Steven. "Haig Remark on China Puzzles White House Aides." *New York Times,* June 27, 1981, Section 1, p. 5.

Weisskopf, Michael. "Baker Outlines Goals of Mission to Beijing; Resolving Human Rights Differences, Forestalling Isolation, Briefing on Summit Cited." *Washington Post,* December 12, 1989, A25.

———. "Decade of Sino-U.S. Détente Has Woven Complex Relationship." *Washington Post,* March 2, 1982, A13.

———. "Zhao's Nonproliferation Stand Seen as Path to U.S. Aid Pact." *Washington Post* (Final Edition), January 13, 1984, A18.

White House Central File. Carter Presidential Library, Atlanta, Georgia.

White House Office of Correspondence, Beverly Ward Files, Bush Presidential Library, College Station, Texas.

White House Office of Record Management (WHORM), Subject Files. BE, Business-Economics, and PR, Public Relations. Reagan Presidential Library, Simi Valley, California.

———. General File. Bush Presidential Library, College Station, Texas.

White House Press Office, Press Secretary File. Bush Presidential Library, College Station, Texas.

White House Press Office, Subject File. Bush Presidential Library, College Station, Texas.

White House Press Office, Marlin Fitzwater Guidance Files. Bush Presidential Library, College Station, Texas.

Wicker, Tom. "In the Nation; Darkness in China." *New York Times,* June 6, 1989, A31.

Wildavsky, Aaron. "The Two Presidencies Thesis." *Transaction* 4 (1966): 175–186.

Wildavsky, Ben. "Beyond MFN." *National Journal* 28, no. 22 (June 1, 1996): 1205–1208.

———. "Under the Gun (at the National Economic Council)." *National Journal* 28 (June 29, 1996): 1417–1421.

Williams, Daniel, and R. Jeffrey Smith. "Clinton to Extend China Trade Status." *Washington Post,* May 28, 1993, A1.

———. "U.S. to Renew Contact with Chinese Military." *Washington Post,* November 1, 1993, A1.

Williams, Daniel, and Clay Chandler. "The Hollowing of a Threat; Trade Is Squeezing Rights out of China Policy." *Washington Post,* May 12, 1994, A1.

———. "U.S. Aide Sees Relations with Asia in Peril." *Washington Post,* May 4, 1994, A38.

Wittkopf, Eugene R., and James M. McCormick, eds. *The Domestic Sources of American Foreign Policy,* 3rd ed. Lanham, Md.: Rowman and Littlefield, 1999.

Wolfowitz, Paul. "Bridging Centuries." *The National Interest,* Issue 47 (Spring 1997): 3–9.

Wonnacott, Paul. Files. Bush Presidential Library, College Station, Texas.

Wu, Sofia. "MND Mum on U.S. Crisis-Simulation Drill Reports." Taiwan Central News Agency, July 16, 2004. Available online through Lexis-Nexis.

Xiang, Lanxin. "Washington's Misguided China Policy." *Survival* 43, no. 3 (Autumn 2001): 7–25.

Yin, Robert. *Case Study Research: Design and Methods.* Thousand Oaks, Calif.: Sage Publishing, 1994.

Yost, Paula. "Sununu Defends Selling Jetliners to China; Bush Decision Called Move to Encourage Leniency to Demonstrators." *Washington Post,* July 10, 1989, A17.

Zagoria, Donald. "Clinton's Asia Policy." *Current History* 92, no. 578 (December 1993): 401–405.

Zaller, John, and Dennis Chiu. "Government's Little Helper: U.S. Press Coverage of Foreign Policy Crises, 1945–1991." *Political Communication* 13, no. 4 (October–December 1996): 385–406.

Index

About the Book

What explains the twists and turns in U.S.-China relations since Richard Nixon initiated a policy of engagement in the early 1970s? Addressing this question, Jean Garrison examines the politics behind U.S. China policy across six administrations—from Nixon to George W. Bush.

Garrison finds that a focus on the internal decisionmaking process is key to understanding both continuity and change in more than three decades of U.S.-China relations. Incorporating interactions at the levels of strategic context, presidential beliefs and leadership style, and bureaucratic politics, she constructs a comprehensive explanation of how China policy was formed in each administration. Her thorough—and engaging—account sheds new light on U.S. foreign policy making in general, as well as on Washington's China policy.

Jean A. Garrison is associate professor of political science at the University of Wyoming. She is author of *Games Advisors Play: Foreign Policy in the Nixon and Carter Administrations.*